CW00665424

WAGE POLITICS IN BRITAIN

For Jane, with love – again

Wage Politics in Britain

The Rise and Fall of Incomes Policies since 1945

PETER DOREY

BRIGHTON • PORTLAND

2 4 6 8 10 9 7 5 3 1

First published 2001 in Great Britain by
SUSSEX ACADEMIC PRESS
PO Box 2950
Brighton BN2 5SP

and in the United States of America by
SUSSEX ACADEMIC PRESS
5824 N.E. Hassalo St.
Portland, Oregon 97213-3644

British Library Cataloguing in Publication Data
A CIP catalogue record for this book is available from the British Library.

Library of Congress Cataloging-in-Publication Data
Dorey, Peter, 1959–
Wage politics in Britain : the rise and fall of income policies since 1945 / Peter Dorey.
p. cm.
Includes bibliographical references and index.
ISBN 1–902210–91–3 (alk. paper)
1. Wages—Great Britain—History. 2. Income distributes—Great Britain—History. 3. Great Britain—Economic policy—History. 4. Great Britain—Politics and government—1945– I. Title.

HD5015.D67 2001
331.2'941'09045—dc21 2001031185

Typeset and designed by G&G Editorial, Brighton
Printed by TJ International, Padstow, Cornwall
This book is printed on acid-free paper

Contents

Acknowledgements

One of the pleasures in having a book published is the opportunity publicly to thank the people who have provided advice, assistance and encouragement during its gestation. I would therefore like to express my heartfelt appreciation to the following: Dr Martin Maw, formerly Conservative Party archivist at the Bodleian Library, Oxford, and his successor, Jill Davidson, for their courtesy and efficiency in retrieving countless files and boxes of Conservative archival material for my perusal.

Similarly, I am extremely grateful to the staff of the Public Records Office, Kew, for the efficient and good-humoured manner in which they provided me with a vast array of Cabinet papers and ministerial correspondence spanning the 1940–69 period.

I would like to thank my academic colleagues in the School of European Studies at Cardiff University, for their valuable advice and encouragement whilst I was writing this book, with David Broughton, Hugh Compston, Mark Donovan, Barry Jones, Steve Marsh and Karen Owen deserving particular mention.

Finally, I would like to thank my wife, Jane, for her unwavering support and encouragement, as well as her treasured love and affection. It is to her that this book is dedicated.

PETER DOREY
Bath, Somerset
February 2001

1

Wage politics in Britain

One of the most important and problematic features of post-war British politics was the concern of successive governments to persuade the trade unions and employees to restrain pay increases, primarily to curb inflation and maintain full employment. However frequently and vociferously the Labour and Conservative parties, when in Opposition, denounced incomes policies and defended free collective bargaining (whereby trade unions and employers were left to determine matters pertaining to pay between themselves), they frequently felt obliged to seek various forms of wage restraint when in Office, often through an explicit incomes policy, either negotiated with the trade unions (and often employers too) in order to secure their acquiescence, or occasionally imposed unilaterally when union agreement was not forthcoming.

Indeed, only two British governments between 1945 and 1979 resisted recourse to an incomes policy, namely the 1951–5 and 1955–9 Conservative governments, yet even the latter of these soon deemed it necessary to pursue institutional innovations and intense "educational" campaigns in order to persuade the trade unions of the need for wage moderation, and to avail workers of the economic facts of life.

All other post-war governments, however, felt obliged to go further in their efforts at seeking or securing wage restraint, to the extent that with the exception of the 1950s, the 1945–79 period witnessed a plethora of policies and institutions concerned to limit, and occasionally "freeze", pay increases. Indeed, as table 1.1 indicates, no less than 19 incomes policies of one kind or another can be identified between 1945 and 1979.

The various incomes policies reflected governmental attempts at securing as a balance between the maintenance of full employment and the control of inflation, in an era when the former served to enhance the bargaining power of the trade unions, thereby enabling them to pursue pay claims which were widely deemed to be inflationary. Yet incomes policies were also prompted at various junctures by concern at Britain's poor balance of payments situation, whereby the increased purchasing power accrued from "excessive" pay increases was held responsible, in

Table 1.1 *Incomes policies in Britain 1945–79*

Period	Name	Details	Voluntary/ Statutory/ Imposed	TUC Stance
Feb. 1948–Oct. 1950	Wage freeze	Productivity increases only	Voluntary	Supportive
Jul. 1961–March 1962	Pay pause	Public sector	Imposed	Hostile
Apr. 1962–Oct. 1964	Guiding light	2–3.5% limit stipulated for pay increases	Voluntary	Hostile
Dec. 1964–Aug. 1965	Statement of Intent	3–3.5% norm	Voluntary	Supportive
Sep. 1965–Jun 1966	Early warning	3–3.5% norm	Voluntary but statutory powers held in reserve	Aquiescent
July 1966–Dec. 1966	Pay Freeze	No increases permitted	Statutory	Aquiescent
Jan. 1967–June 1967	Severe restraint	Productivity increases only permitted	Statutory	Aquiescent
July 1967–March 1968	Nil norm	Increases only permitted if certain criteria met	Statutory	Increasingly hostile
March 1968–Dec. 1969	No norm	Up to 3.5% increase if certain criteria met	Statutory	Hostile
Dec. 1969–June 1970	Guiding light	Increases of 2.5–4.5%, subject to criteria met	Statutory	Largely hostile, disregarded
June 1970–Feb. 1972	N-1	Public sector pay to be 1% less each year	Imposed	Hostile
Nov. 1972–March 1973	Stage 1	No increases permitted	Statutory	Hostile

Apr. 1973–Oct. 1973	Stage 2	4% + £1 p.w.	Statutory	Hostile
Nov. 1973–Feb 1974	Stage 3	7% or £2.25	Statutory	Hostile
Aug. 1975–July 1976	Phase 1	£6 p.w	Voluntary	Supportive
Aug. 1976–July 1977	Phase 2	5% norm	Voluntary	Supportive
Aug. 1977–July 1978	Phase 3	10% maximum	Voluntary	Reluctant acquies cence
Aug. 1978–Feb. 1979	Phase 4	5% norm	Imposed	Hostile
Feb. 1979–Apr 1979	Phase 4 (rev.)	9% norm	Voluntary	Supportive

Source: Adapted from Brittan and Lilley, 1977: 154–5.

large part, for the relatively high levels of imports yielding a deficit on the country's visible earnings.

At the same time, inflationary pressures in the economy, coupled with poor balance of payments figures, periodically caused acute anxiety amongst the international financial community and overseas holders of sterling, whereupon the government of the day felt further obliged to seek wage restraint from organized labour.

Furthermore, the role attributed to excessive or unwarranted wage increases in causing such economic problems as inflation, trade deficits and an overall lack of confidence on the part of Capital (during the 1960s especially) meant also that the trade unions became the "scapegoats of national decline" (Taylor, 1993: 1–14, 341). Indeed, not only were the trade unions deemed to render incomes policies necessary as a consequence of their alleged irresponsibility over pay bargaining, they were then frequently blamed for the subsequent breakdown of these policies.

Yet throughout most of the 1945–79 era, there existed a *de facto* consensus between the Labour and Conservative parties over the need for "a national wages policy", due to the widespread recognition that "free collective bargaining in circumstances of full employment had potentially inflationary consequences" (Kavanagh and Morris, 1989: 58). Or, as another commentator explained: "The analysis on which the incomes policy approach is based consists essentially of the proposition that full employment, stable prices, and unfettered collective bargaining are incompatible with each other" (Stewart, 1972: 233).

Consequently, parties and governments up until 1979 tended to oscillate between advocacy of free collective bargaining and the search for a national wages policy, either in the form of education and exhortation about the need for pay restraint and "responsible" behaviour by the trade unions, or more commonly through an explicit incomes policy, be it negotiated or imposed.

As such, it was once observed that although incomes policy "has gone underground from time to time . . . it has always re-emerged", and whilst over time "the difficulties of operating an incomes policy have become more apparent . . . the need for it has become more apparent still", hence the fact that "with much hesitation and backsliding, governments increasingly came round to accepting the need for an incomes policy" (Stewart, 1972: 233, 297). Yet it has also been noted that "wage restraint has been the rock on which successive Governments have foundered in the post-war years" (Coates and Topham, 1980: 183).

Part of the explanation for the problems encountered by British governments with regard to incomes policies between 1945 and 1979 derives from, or reveals, certain paradoxes of trade unionism in Britain. The most notable, perhaps, is that whilst the trade unions were almost universally portrayed as being too powerful, and thus unwilling to cooperate with governments in the pursuit of incomes policy, part of the problem was that in one crucial respect, British trade unionism was too weak. What this means is that the trade unions were – and remain – characterized by considerable decentralization, with bargaining over terms and conditions of employment often conducted at local level, irrespective of national-level agreements entered into by senior union officials. This decentralization also ensured that the TUC was never anything more than a federal body with little authority or control over its affiliated members, and thus heavily dependent on exercising moral authority or persuasion *vis-à-vis* its affiliates.

In this context, therefore, the problems and failures of post-war incomes policies in Britain are partly attributable to the organizational and structural weakness of the trade unions, rather than their oft-alleged excessive power, for trade union leaders at the national level were frequently unable to ensure the compliance of their mass members when formulating incomes policies with government ministers. Indeed, on numerous occasions, these national-level trade union leaders were as exasperated as ministers themselves over the extent to which their membership at local or work-place level pursued pay increases in excess of those formally agreed with the government.

Furthermore, it was precisely the extent to which national-level trade union leaders were seen entering into agreements with government ministers over incomes policies intended to secure wage restraint that enabled local-level union officials and shop stewards to win the loyalty of the mass membership by securing higher pay increases at the factory level. This in turn yielded the problem of "wage drift", whereby actual earnings increased at a faster or higher rate than envisaged by national-level increases and agreements (Jones, 1987: 139–40; Taylor, 1993: 12).

Another paradox of British trade unionism engendered by incomes policies, particularly those pursued by Labour governments, concerns the political and ideological characteristics of the unions. Their critics have often denounced them for being class-based institutions with strong socialist aspirations, and thus inimical to the principles of capitalism and the market economy. Such a view of the ideology of British trade unionism largely derives from the frequent left-wing rhetoric of many union officials and leaders, coupled with their historically close organizational and financial links with the Labour party.

Yet had Britain's trade unions been as class-based or socialist as their detractors claimed, then post-war incomes policies might actually have proved more acceptable and successful, for the reality has been that the unions are primarily sectional organizations, representing workers according to the occupation or industry in which they are employed, rather than on the basis of social class. A homogeneous and solidaristic working class has only ever existed in the revolutionary fantasies of middle-class Marxists, for the sectional character of Britain's trade unions has reflected and reinforced divisions between – and within – different occupations and industries in Britain, and thus rendered even more problematic the TUC's efforts at securing the support of affiliated members for incomes policies.

Thus have skilled workers jealously guarded their differentials against any narrowing income gap *vis-à-vis* semi-skilled or unskilled workers, which in turn has had serious implications for incomes policies that incorporated larger pay increases for the low-paid in order to tackle poverty. On the other hand, the low-paid have themselves understandably evinced little enthusiasm for incomes policies, in spite of any egalitarian objectives enshrined within them, for the ultimate objective of most incomes policies has remained that of wage restraint.

As such, whatever their rhetorical denunciations of the iniquities of capitalism and the free market, trade unions have seen their first and foremost function as being to secure the best possible pay deals for their members, in accordance with the inviolate doctrine of free collective bargaining, especially as they know that few, if any, curbs would be imposed on company profits or directors' salaries. In this respect, trade unions are creatures of capitalism, and act in accordance with market rationality, much to the repeated frustration of Conservative and Labour governments alike.

Indeed, one further irony has variously manifested itself in this respect, namely that whereas Labour governments have often viewed trade union defiance of incomes policies as a betrayal of socialist principles and objectives, Conservative ministers during the 1960s and early 1970s depicted such defiance as politically-motivated, a left-inspired attempt by the unions to challenge the market and ultimately undermine capitalism by demanding pay increases which undermined profitability.

Yet until the late 1970s, the bipartisan commitment to full employment ensured that Conservative and Labour governments generally pursued incomes policies of one sort or another, in order to curb inflation and secure price stability. Until this time, politicians and policy-makers largely operated within a Keynesian paradigm, convinced that demand management and other forms of government intervention – including incomes policies – would facilitate the economic holy trinity of low inflation, full employment and steady growth. Indeed, it has been claimed that prior to the late 1970s:

> The British opinion-forming classes – civil servants, politicians, commentators, and academics – had largely stopped thinking in terms of the market mechanism. They felt much more at home with politically determined "strategies". Consequently, the market was readily assumed to have "failed" even when it was working, and when inflation did worsen this was always attributed to the inherent weaknesses of collective bargaining rather than to prior monetary excess. (Brittan and Lilley, 1977: 178)

From the late 1970s, however, there was a dramatic change in the intellectual and political climate, as the doctrine of Monetarism and ideas of Milton Friedman replaced the hitherto hegemony of Keynesian and consensus politics. A new intellectual and political paradigm established itself, termed the New Right, which aggressively promoted the free market and private enterprise, whilst simultaneously orchestrating a populist backlash against bureaucrats, trade unions, public sector professions and the state itself, all of whom were charged with fostering an anti-enterprise culture in post-war Britain.

For the New Right, the problem with the market in Britain was not that it had failed, but that it had never been permitted to function, due to a fatal combination of politico-bureaucratic interference and trade union obduracy. As such, it was not capitalism or the market which were deemed to be in crisis by the late 1970s, but social democracy and corporatism.

Thus did the British variant of the New Right, Thatcherism, assiduously pursue a range of policies throughout the 1980s which decisively dispensed with Keynesian techniques of demand management, abandoned full employment, weakened and marginalized the trade unions, and firmly rejected incomes policies in favour of an initial return to free collective bargaining, followed by increased advocacy of individual bargaining or local-level pay deals. This approach was not reversed when John Major replaced Margaret Thatcher as Conservative leader and Prime Minister in November 1990. On the contrary, his administrations fully sustained the approach, further marginalizing the trade unions and promoting even more enthusiastically the alleged virtues of individual or local-level pay determination in place of collective bargaining. Incomes policy was never remotely on the agenda, even after Thatcher's departure, although throughout the 1980s and 1990s, the public sector was subjected to rigorous cash limits, which effectively placed strict limits on the scope for pay increases.

Even the election of a Labour government in May 1997 failed to facilitate a revival of incomes policy. Indeed, ever since becoming party leader in July 1994, Tony Blair has been emphatic that "New Labour" would not seek to revive the corporatist-style arrangements which previous Labour governments sought to construct; the trade unions would not enjoy the "insider" status which they had been granted by the Attlee, Wilson and Callaghan governments. This, coupled with New Labour's own emphasis on securing economic stability and low inflation through monetary policy, adjustments of interest rates, and the continued stringent control of public expenditure, ensured that the 1997–2001 Blair government also rejected recourse to incomes policy.

If incomes policies were originally part of the post-war social democratic consensus up until the 1970s, then it is evident that rejection of incomes policy has become a significant feature of the post-Thatcher neo-liberal consensus. What follows is thus a detailed examination, from a political science perspective, of the rise and fall of incomes policy in Britain since 1945, with chapters 2 to 8 examining the pay policies of each of the administrations which governed Britain in the post-war period, up to (and including) the first Blair government, and chapter 9 delineating the main characteristics, issues and problems engendered by these various incomes policies.

2

What is to be done about wages? The Attlee governments, 1945–1951

The war-time legacy

It was during the Second World War that serious consideration was first given to the extent to which government could – or should – intervene in the realm of collective bargaining between employers and employees, with a view to regulating wage increases. The war effort had engendered unprecedented levels of government intervention in economic and industrial affairs, in order to secure the most efficient and effective allocation of manpower and resources. However, such intervention meant that government could no longer display a lack of interest as what was happening with regard to wages; ministers had now to give serious consideration to the implications of permitting the continuation of free collective bargaining. This did not actually result in a formal incomes policy, but it did mean that ministers felt obliged to display a greater interest in wage determination than they had hitherto, with increased ministerial exhortations about the need for responsibility and restraint by the trade unions when negotiating with employers over pay.

The war-time coalition government did impose some limitations on trade union activities, but what was most surprising about these was how limited they were, and how sparingly the state actually invoked its formal powers *vis-à-vis* the unions. The most obvious example was the adoption, in July 1940, of Order 1305, which outlawed strikes, and, instead, decreed that where employers and trade unions could not reach agreement in matters pertaining to terms and conditions of employment, then they would be legally obliged to submit the case to a new National Arbitration Tribunal, the decision of which would be binding on both sides. This measure did not prevent unofficial strikes during the war, nor did the government, via the Ministry of Labour, regularly invoke Order 1305. On the contrary, the Minister of Labour, Ernest Bevin (see below), was very reluctant to resort to Order 1305, preferring instead to rely, as far as possible, on exhortation when management and trade unions appeared unable to resolve their differences. This partly reflected a genuine belief in the power of reason and rational argument, but also assumed that most workers would not want to take industrial action which might jeopardize the war effort, thereby unwittingly aiding and abetting the triumph of Nazism.

In any case, the Ministry of Labour was acutely aware that at a time of serious labour shortages in certain industries, it would be extremely unwise for the government to pursue the prosecution – possibly resulting in imprisonment – of workers who defied Order 1305. As Bevin himself noted:

> The Order has a substantial deterrent effect, but is an instrument which would probably be shown to be useless if any considerable body of workpeople chose to defy it. A large number of workpeople cannot be sent to prison, and it is undesirable to make martyrs by selecting a few for prosecution. It is therefore the policy of the Ministry of Labour to continue to deal with disputes on the basis of cooperation with the organization in industry, and to take legal action only in cases in which it can rely upon the support of the constitutional elements among the workpeople. (Quoted in Middlemas, 1979: 280–1)

There was also a recognition within the Ministry of Labour that if the state intervened too frequently or too readily when industrial disputes occurred, it might actually make matters worse, by fuelling the grievances or feelings of resentment which often underpinned industrial action, particularly if such intervention routinely appeared to favour employers.

Furthermore, the adoption of Order 1305 did not mean the abandonment of free collective bargaining in favour of an incomes policy. Even though the Order outlawed strikes and provided for compulsory arbitration, it did not seek to stipulate a limit or "norm" for wage increases. Levels of pay were still left to employers and employees (usually via their trade unions) to determine through collective bargaining. Although Order 1305 formally placed curbs on trade union action once wage negotiations had broken down, it in no way constituted an incomes policy, although the Treasury had favoured a system of statutory wage control ever since the beginning of the war.

In recommending such an incomes policy, the Treasury, whose arguments in favour of statutory wage controls were invariably echoed by Lord Stamp, the Economic Adviser to the Cabinet, and William Beveridge, expressed concern that the shortages of labour in certain industries would lead to employers paying higher wages in order to retain or recruit labour, whilst at the same time, the relative lack of consumer products, due to the focus on manufacturing and production for the war (rather than the domestic market), would result in too much money chasing too few goods and commodities, thereby fuelling inflation. Indeed, at the beginning of May 1940, just days before Ernest Bevin was appointed Minister of Labour, Lord Stamp presented a paper to the Cabinet which was highly critical of the Ministry of Labour's reliance on voluntary wage restraint and exhortation, insisting instead that the degree of economic efficiency necessary for the war effort rendered statutory wage control essential.

Yet when the coalition government was formed a few days later, and Ernest Bevin became Minister of Labour, the introduction of a statutory incomes policy or wage freeze became even less likely, for Bevin was a staunch believer not only in free collective bargaining, but also in the belief that trade unions and employers were best placed to understand – and thus solve – industrial relations problems, not the state. In other words, Bevin's appointment ensured that the Treasury and its allies were faced with an implacable supporter of voluntarism. Indeed, precisely because he was a senior trade unionist, Bevin not only recognized that the trade unions would resist state interference in industrial relations and wage determination, he was able to persuade his new ministerial colleagues that this was the case, and thereby ensure that the Cabinet as a whole did not succumb to Treasury pressure for a statutory incomes policy (see, for example: PRO T 230/110, Memorandum by Minister of Labour on "Wages regulation", 16 May 1941: PRO LAB 10/160, Tribe to Robbins, 27 January 1942; PRO T 230/66, Memorandum by Fleming on "The creation of employment", 19 February 1943).

Bevin's insistence that industrial relations and wage determination should be conducted on the basis of negotiation, rather than legislative *fiat*, had apparently been borne out by the manner in which Order 1305 was agreed. At the 4 June 1940 meeting of the recently-formed Joint Consultative Committee – formed at Bevin's instigation, and comprising seven representatives from the British Employers' Federation and seven from the TUC – it was agreed that in spite of the exigencies of the war, the existing machinery and processes of bargaining between employers and employees should be retained, but with legal curbs placed on strikes and lock-outs, coupled with compulsory and legally-binding arbitration. As his biographer noted: "Nothing could have suited Bevin better. The substance of the proposal, to continue the practice of joint negotiation . . . and the procedure by which it had been arrived at, by joint consultation by the two sides of industry" (Bullock, 1967: 22), seemed to vindicate his resistance to statutory interference in collective bargaining, thereby persuading his ministerial colleagues too of the efficacy of upholding voluntarism against Treasury encroachment.

In rejecting an incomes policy, the Cabinet sought to counter the threat of inflation by various other fiscal measures, most notably by increasing income tax and reducing tax allowances (in order to dampen down consumer spending), whilst simultaneously extending the scope of rationing, pursuing price controls, and subsidizing food prices. These were precisely the type of measures which Bevin favoured as the appropriate means of controlling inflation, rather than resorting to wage controls and pay curbs. Furthermore, Bevin pointed out to Treasury advocates of a statutory wages policy that if the state assumed responsibility for determining remuneration, it would inevitability be drawn into deciding on minimum and maximum levels of pay, whilst also having to deal with differentials and subsequent anomalies. The state might then find it necessary to turn its attention to the control of prices and profits, at which point the continued viability of the system of private enterprise itself might be called into question and the case made for the full "socialization" of industry (Bullock, 1967: 87 and 91; see also *House of Commons Debates*, 4th series, Vol. 383, col. 2039). On the basis of such arguments, Bevin was once again able to persuade his Cabinet colleagues that statutory wage controls should be resisted, in favour of fiscal measures to control inflation. Indeed, "so far as the Cabinet was concerned, Bevin's argument settled the matter, and the possibility of the direct control of wages was not raised again" (Bullock, 1967: 92).

Meanwhile, the war effort engendered the extensive incorporation of the trade unions into the machinery of the state, more especially after the creation of the coalition government in May 1940. The most obvious manifestation of this incorporation was the appointment of Ernest Bevin, leader of the TGWU (then Britain's largest trade union), as Minister of Labour and National Service, whilst other examples of such incorporation include the aforementioned Joint Consultative Committee, and the National Production Advisory Committee. As one commentator observed: "There was hardly a facet of the war effort with which the trade unions were not directly associated" (MacDonald, 1960: 125), whilst a senior TGWU official proclaimed, in 1940, that: "Organized labour will henceforth be satisfied with nothing less than full partnership in the state" (Price, 1940: 173). Similarly, a leading labour historian subsequently observed that "union leaders ended the war feeling that they had earned a right to have a say in the reconstruction of British society and industry" (Pelling, 1963: 221).

Long before the end of the war, in fact, serious consideration was being given to the economic and social policies which would follow. It was in this context that the objectives of full employment and a comprehensive welfare state became established. However, more prescient minds soon recognized that the objective of full employment could not be considered in isolation from the question of wage determination. Indeed, the White Paper on Employment Policy, which formally declared the commitment to full employment, also emphasized that:

> It will be essential that employers and workers should exercise moderation in wage matters so that increased expenditure . . . may go to increase the volume of employment . . . increases in the general level of wage rates must be related to increased productivity due to increased efficiency and effort. (HMSO, 1944: 18–19)

What provided the impetus for more specific consideration of the likely relationship between free collective bargaining and the maintenance of full employment was the TUC's assertion, in 1943, that the trade unions would support full employment by exercising voluntary wage restraint. Whilst acknowledging that:

> no Government can guarantee full employment unless they can be assured that the steps they are taking, or propose to take, will not be rendered ineffective by the failure of quite legitimate interests, including the trade union movement, to make their actions conform to the achievement of that objective,

the TUC insisted that if the trade union movement was convinced of the government's commitment to full employment, then it would "be the duty of the trade union movement to give suitable guarantees about wage settlements and reasonable assurances that such guarantees should be generally observed". However, the TUC was emphatic that it would not "in any circumstances invite the state to impose a system of compulsory arbitration in wage disputes or make it a criminal offence on the part of workmen to refuse to accept the terms and conditions of a wage settlement" (TUC Annual Report 1944: 195).

This declaration did not allay William Beveridge's doubts that the TUC's insistence upon free collective bargaining and voluntary wage restraint would be sufficient to sustain a policy of full employment without causing inflation. As he explained in his *Full Employment in a Free Society*:

> Particular wage demands which exceed what employers are able to pay with their existing prices, and which force a raising of prices, may bring gains to the workers of the industry concerned, but they will do so at the expense of all other workers, whose real wages will fall owing to the rise in prices. The other workers will naturally try to restore their position by putting forward demands of their own. There is a real danger that sectional wage bargaining, pursued without regard to its effect on prices, may lead to a vicious spiral of inflation, with money wages chasing prices, and without any gain in real wages for the working class as a whole. (Beveridge, 1944: 199–201)

Beveridge therefore urged the TUC to develop a "unified wage policy", whereby the pay claims of individual trade unions would be considered in the context of the general economic situation. He also recommended a system of arbitration which would ensure that wages would be "determined according to reason and in the light of all the facts and with some regard to general equities and not simply to the bargaining power of certain groups". Such a system, Beveridge believed, in conjunction with price stability and higher productivity, would facilitate a steady increase in "real" earnings (Beveridge, 1944: 202–3).

For their part, the trade unions were by no means dismissive of Beveridge's recommendations, declaring that:

> if the government can convince the [trade union] Movement that in general pursuit of a policy of full employment it is determined to take all other steps that are necessary to control prices, and can convince the Trade Union Movement of the need to secure equivalent guarantees that wage movements will not be such as to upset the system of price control . . . ,

then such guarantees would be forthcoming (TUC Annual Report, 1944: 197), although the precise nature of these guarantees was not made clear.

Towards the end of the war, therefore, it was becoming apparent that an informal and implicit "social contract" was emerging between ministers and the TUC, whereby political leaders would pursue policies for full employment and a more comprehensive welfare state, in return for voluntary wage-restraint and "responsible" collective bargaining by the trade unions (for more on this, see Beer, 1965: 212–16).

Yet within Whitehall, there were contrasting expectations about the impact that full employment and welfare provision would have on trade union behaviour concerning wage determination. There was apprehension in some quarters that once the fear of unemployment and poverty had been banished, many trade unions would feel less inclined to exercise wage restraint. If this proved to be the case, and inflation became uncontrollable, then government would either "have to give up the employment policy" (PRO T 230/68, Meade to Robbins, 19 April 1944), or resort to the "imposition of centrally defined maximum wage norms or . . . some form of collectivist solution" (PRO T 230/66, Marcus Fleming, "The Creation of Employment", 19 February 1943).

For his part, John Maynard Keynes commented, in June 1945, that: "One is also, because one knows no solution, inclined to turn a blind eye to the wages problem in a full employment economy" (quoted in Kahn, 1974: 387). Keynes' ambivalence on this issue seemed to be widely shared, for the dominant political perspective during the final year of the war was the hope that, having proved their moderation, responsibility and patriotism during the previous five years, the trade unions could be persuaded to display the same characteristics in peacetime, particularly if the post-war government did deliver full employment and a welfare state as pledged. Whilst there were thus doubts about the compatibility of full employment and free collective bargaining, there was also a widespread recognition that either a return to high unemployment, or the imposition of statutory wage controls, would be deeply unpopular and unacceptable.

The need to consider a policy for wages

Yet with the benefit of hindsight, we can now see that the economic and social policies pursued by the 1954–51 Labour governments rendered it inevitable that ministers would have to give consideration to the issue of wage determination, in spite of – or, perhaps, because of – the trade unions' commitment to the principle of free collective bargaining. Quite apart from the increased trade union bargaining power, and hence inflationary pressures, engendered by full employment, the Attlee governments' nationalization programme (whereby a number of industries – most notably coal, iron and steel, railways, and road haulage – were taken into public ownership) effectively ensured that, in the last instance, ministers were formally responsible for the pay of workers in this new public sector, even though it was always maintained that day-to-day control resided with the management in each industry. Even if ministers sought to insist that wage bargaining was to be conducted "freely" between the trade unions and managers in each of the nationalized industries, the government would ultimately be called upon to finance the pay increases which ensued, either through providing the industries concerned with more tax revenues and subsidies, or raising their prices. At the very least, therefore, official non-intervention in wage determination by ministers was nonetheless accompanied by constant ministerial exhortation about the need for trade unions to exercise moderation and responsibility in pay bargaining.

Similarly, the establishment of the welfare state, by greatly expanding the scope of public sector employment, also ensured that ministers could not feign disinterest with regard to pay determination. Here too, however much ministers might deny responsibility for day-to-day management and decisions within each sector of the welfare state, the fact that many welfare services were financed by government revenues (i.e., taxation) ensured that ministers would have to observe closely what was happening with regard to wage determination and levels of remuneration within this major new domain of public sector employment.

Yet it was the commitment to full employment, and the already-noted inflationary pressures that this entailed, which primarily caused many Labour ministers to look apprehensively at what was happening in the sphere of wage determination after 1945, particularly as labour shortages sometimes led employers (no longer able to recruit from a "reserve army" of unemployed), to "bid up" wages in order to attract staff from rival companies or industries. Even so, and with a couple of ministerial exceptions, the new Labour government emphasized its commitment to free collective bargaining (the retention of Order 1305 until 1951 notwithstanding), hoping that its economic and social policies, coupled with ministerial persuasion and exhortation, would encourage the trade unions to reciprocate by exercising restraint and responsibility in pay bargaining.

Limited calls for an incomes policy

To the extent that a few trade unions did evince concern at the Attlee government's stance regarding wage determination, it was precisely the refusal to pursue an incomes policy which caused unease in certain quarters of the labour movement. For example, at the TUC's annual conference in 1945, the Electrical Trades Union (ETU) argued that "there is a need for the Trade Union Movement to have an economic policy on the question of production, wages and prices"; whilst a year later, the National Union of Vehsicle Builders (NUVB) submitted a motion urging the TUC to draft a national wages policy which would include both a minimum wage and "a more satisfactory, lasting and equitable wage standard". Although the NUVB's motion was defeated by 3,522,000 votes to 2,657,000, it has been noted that "the surprisingly large size of the minority vote suggested [that] many trade union leaders were less enthusiastic about the virtues of free collective bargaining" than the TUC leadership assumed (Taylor, 1993: 49).

Calls for an incomes policy were also echoed by a couple of ministers within the Cabinet, namely Emmanuel Shinwell, the Minister for Fuel and Power, and Aneurin Bevan, the Minister of Health. Such ministers were convinced that "in order to prevent an upward spiral in wage rates, it was desirable that the government should formulate and announce a considered wages policy", one which would "establish some principles" to guide wage determination. It was even suggested that a Royal Commission be established "to investigate the wage structure as a whole" (PRO CAB 128(46) 24th conclusions, 14 March 1946; for Shinwell's support for an incomes policy, see PRO CAB 132/1, Lord President's Committee, meetings on 29 March, 26 July, and 1 November 1946). Aneurin Bevan especially was convinced that the government could only fulfil its responsibility for full employment if it also played a role in "the adjustment of wages" (PRO CAB 128(46) 33rd conclusions, 11 April 1946).

In defence of free collective bargaining

Yet during the remainder of 1945 and throughout 1946, the prevailing view on both the industrial and political wings of the labour movement was one of antipathy to incomes policy and any attempt by ministers to interfere in free collective bargaining. Within the Cabinet, the case for an incomes policy, as enunciated by Shinwell and Bevan, was consistently and emphatically rejected by the Minister of Labour, George Isaacs, and his predecessor, Ernest Bevin (now Foreign Secretary). Isaacs was a former President of the National Society of Operative Printers, Graphical & Media Personnel (NATSOPA), as well as a member of the TUC's General Council, and always retained "a deep commitment to preserving free collective bargaining" (Morgan, 1985: 133). Isaacs insisted that an incomes policy would inevitably render wages "a political issue" whilst proving "disastrous to our whole system of industrial relations". A staunch proponent of voluntarism, whereby the state did not intervene or interfere in industrial relations or wage determination (see Fishbein, 1984: 16–19: Flanders, 1974; Flanders, 1975: 288–94; Panitch, 1976: 90–1; Rogin, 1962: 521–2), Isaacs argued that "under the system of collective bargaining . . . settlements are negotiated by the accredited representatives of the men who act under the democratic constitution of their respective unions" (PRO CAB 129, LP(46) 259).

Isaacs' consistent defence of free collective bargaining, and thus opposition to incomes policies, owed much to his background in the trade union movement, for he could claim to possess a deep understanding of the principles and practices of British trade unionism. In warning his Cabinet colleagues of the dangers of interference in wage determination, he pointed out not only the practical problems concerning such criteria as exemptions, differentials and productivity deals, but also the political implications, namely that if the role of trade union leaders was undermined as a consequence of government interference in free collective bargaining, then their authority and credibility also would be weakened *vis-à-vis* their rank-and-file members. This, in turn, Isaacs warned, would enable communists within the trade unions to foment frustration amongst ordinary union members, and pursue even higher pay claims, backed readily by industrial disruption (PRO CAB 129 LP(47) 304, "Memorandum to Cabinet on Wages Policy", 11 November 1947). As one author has noted, in numerous Cabinet discussions over incomes policy prior to 1948: "The moderate views of the Ministry of

Labour held sway, not least because Isaacs was an ex-union official and could argue with the backing of personal experience" (Jones, 1987: 36; see also Lovell and Roberts, 1968: 159).

Meanwhile, Ernest Bevin – who was Isaacs' "most vocal supporter in Cabinet" (Jones, 1987: 36) – insisted that the problem of an "upward spiral of wages" was an "over-exaggeration", such that there was "no serious risk in allowing wages to continue to be settled by the traditional procedure of collective bargaining" (PRO CAB 128(46), 24th conclusions, 14 March 1946). It was also Bevin who reassured delegates attending a special conference of TUC executives in March 1946 that the Attlee government's policy was "to leave the trade unions and the state to settle wages where the state was the employer and to leave trade unions to settle wages with the employers when they were dealing with private employers". The opposition of most Cabinet ministers to incomes policy at this stage was echoed by the TUC's General Council when it declared that: "The TUC has no intention of seeking adoption of any policy which would substantially modify the present system or impose limits upon the rights of the unions to engage in collective bargaining" (TUC Annual Report 1946: 224–9).

Yet whilst eschewing formal incomes policy, ministers did become increasingly concerned during 1946 about the apparent limitations of voluntary wage restraint, especially when they learnt that earnings during the first five months of the year had increased by 11 per cent – twice the average of the last four years of the war (Taylor, 1993: 49). Indeed, when the conclusions of a ministerial committee on wages policy were presented to the Cabinet by Morrison in April 1946, it was acknowledged that "wide differences of opinion on the subject of wages policy" were developing, "ranging from the view that the government should assume direct responsibility for controlling wages to the view that all questions of wages should be left entirely to be settled between the employers and the workers themselves" (PRO CAB 128(46) 33rd conclusions, 11 April 1946).

The need to "educate" the trade unions

One suggestion, supported by the Chancellor, Hugh Dalton, was the establishment of a National Industrial Conference to provide "a channel of communication between the government and both sides of industry" to "carry out a process of education in the basic facts of the current economic situation, which would indirectly influence wage negotiations", although it was insisted that such a body would not itself be involved in wage determination. Bevan was favourably disposed to such a conference, arguing that it was "impossible to avoid some general discussion of wages policy" with trade unions and employers' representatives, for in many cases, he lamented, "the existing machinery for joint, voluntary consultation of wages did not work satisfactorily". In similar vein, Shinwell was concerned that existing methods of wage determination were unsustainable, due both to the consequences of full employment, and the loss of the discipline which war conditions had engendered. As such, he too was sympathetic to the idea of an institutional forum which would facilitate close and regular contact between the government, trade unions and employers' representatives, "with a view to working out . . . general principles which would be consistent with the pursuit of a policy of full employment" (PRO CAB 128(46) 33rd conclusions, 11 April 1946).

The main opposition to the idea of establishing a National Industrial Conference emanated, as ever, from Bevin and Isaacs, the former reiterating his "opposition to the establishment of any central authority to discuss problems of wages", for these "should . . . be left entirely to the recognized organizations of employers and workers". This perspective was faithfully echoed by Isaacs when he insisted that nothing should be done which might "undermine the well-established machinery for the voluntary negotiation of wages by organizations of employers and workers" (PRO CAB 128(46) 33rd conclusions, 11 April 1946). Bevin and Isaacs were adamant that: "Direct fixing of wages by the state is out of the question", for in addition to the "extreme administrative difficulties" of implementing such a measure, it would "destroy the whole fabric of harmonious industrial relations". Furthermore, "the government would become the focus for workers' claims and strike action", as pay bargaining became highly politicized and aroused "dangerous sectional passions" (PRO CAB 129/8, CP(46)130, 3 April 1946).

Yet Attlee reflected the view of most ministers when he declared that "in the new conditions created by the pursuit of full employment and the socialization of important industries, the government could not leave the matter entirely to the organizations of workers and employers" (PRO CAB 128(46) 33rd conclusions, 11 April 1946). Consequently, the Cabinet approved a revised proposal by Isaacs and Morrison for the establishment of a National Industrial Court, although this approval was on the condition that the body would not seek to interfere in wage determination. Shinwell instantly prophesied that the Court would prove inadequate and reiterated his view that if his colleagues were serious about pursuing full employment, they "would have to face more directly the problems of wage policy" (PRO CAB 128(46), 42nd conclusions, 6 May 1946).

Most of Shinwell's colleagues, however, were seeking to square the circle between a growing recognition of the apparent need for greater moderation concerning pay increases on the one hand, and the insistence that they had no intention of interfering in free collective bargaining on the other. Consequently, little more was heard about the National Industrial Court, the idea being quietly abandoned. The Attlee government's official policy remained that of non-interference in wage bargaining between employers and their employees, with George Isaacs seeking to convince the trade unions that ministers would "continue to rely on the existing system of negotiation in industry to settle all wage problems . . . There will be no change in the present system unless the TUC came along and asked for it" (TUC Annual Report 1946: 170).

For their part, the majority of trade unions were equally reluctant to compromise their commitment to free collective bargaining. Indeed, during a series of meetings between ministers and TUC representatives towards the end of 1946:

> It was made clear to . . . the Government that . . . the Unions would continue to be free to submit wages applications as formerly . . . Nothing was to be taken as restricting the rights of Unions to make claims through normal collective bargaining arrangements. Such claims should be considered on their merits. (TUC Annual Report 1947: 219)

By the beginning of 1947, though, the government's adherence to free collective bargaining and reliance on voluntary wage restraint by the trade unions was coming under increasing pressure, due to growing ministerial concern at the rate at which wages were continuing to increase, apparently unrelated to any corresponding increase in industrial productivity or economic growth, although a fuel crisis at this time also added to the Cabinet's anxiety. This concern prompted the Attlee government's publication of a *Statement on the Economic Considerations Affecting Relations Between Employers and Workers* in January 1947, a document which simultaneously acknowledged that the TUC had "remained throughout firmly convinced that it is impracticable and would in any case be undesirable to impose specific limits and restrictions on wage increases", whilst urging the trade unions "to exercise even greater moderation and restraint than hitherto in the formulation and pursuit of claims for wage increases" (Cairncross, 1985: 404).

Promoting productivity-related pay

In fact, the government had already established a committee specifically to examine the scope for securing "restraint against a further general increase of wage rates or other labour costs without an appropriate increase in productivity" (Cairncross, 1985: 403), whilst in Cabinet, Morrison was reiterating the need for trade union leaders to be persuaded that wage increases should be linked much more closely to productivity" (PRO CAB 128(47) 41st conclusions, 29 April 1947). Publicly, though, the government was maintaining that "despite the difficulties created by full employment, employers and employees should remain free to settle the conditions of work or wages in industry" (Stafford Cripps, *House of Commons Debates*, 4th series, Vol. 434, col. 193).

Morrison repeated his insistence on the need to link pay more closely to productivity at Labour's 1947 annual conference, when he argued that "there is little or no more to be got toward a better standard of living by squeezing the incomes of the rich . . . From now on what we get in social benefits and higher wages we shall . . . have to earn by higher production" (Labour Party Conference Report 1947: 137), whilst at the following year's annual conference, Cripps warned delegates that "there is only a certain sized cake to be divided up and if a lot of people want a larger slice they can only get it by taking it from others". As such, Cripps explained: "There is only one way by which we can, with a given volume of employment, increase our real standard of living, and that is by each of us producing more" (Labour Party Conference Report 1948: 861–2).

For their part, most trade unions remained implacable in their opposition to anything which might be construed as ministerial interference in free collective bargaining, with the TUC adamant that wage claims should continue "to be considered on their merits" (TUC Annual Report 1947: 152). Indeed, in a speech at the 1947 annual convention of the American Federation of Labor, Arthur Deakin, leader of the Transport & General Workers Union (TGWU), declared that Britain's trade unions would resist any attempt by the government "even to offer an opinion as to whether a particular wage claim should be conceded or turned down" (American Federation of Labor Report 1947: 236).

Calls for wage restraint become more urgent

Ministerial pleas for wage restraint became more urgent during July 1947, when the convertability of sterling (which had been a precondition of obtaining an American loan at Bretton Woods to fund post-war reconstruction) finally came into effect, whereupon it was immediately accompanied by heavy selling on the foreign exchanges as currency dealers purchased US dollars instead. Faced with a rapidly deteriorating economic situation, involving the near depletion of financial "credits" previously extended to Britain by the United States, Shinwell once again sought to convince his Cabinet colleagues of the necessity for an incomes policy, although his pleas continued to fall on deaf ears (PRO CAB 128(47) 57th conclusions, 30 June 1947), with Isaacs forced to reiterate his opposition to a formal incomes policy (PRO CAB 128(47) 60th conclusions), and Bevin warning the Prime Minister of the "insuperable difficulties" of adopting Shinwell's approach, which would inevitably result in the government having to fix wages (PRO PREM 8/1568, Bevin to Attlee, 16 July 1947). Meanwhile, in mid-August, the government was obliged to suspend convertibility, thereby providing a limited respite. (For detailed accounts of the events surrounding the convertibility crisis, see Cairncross, 1985: 121–64; Morgan 1985: 339–47.)

By October 1947, Hugh Dalton (as Chancellor) and Stafford Cripps (the Minister for Economic Affairs) were – separately – meeting the TUC's General Council to explain why Britain's deteriorating economic situation rendered a period of wage restraint essential. The trade union leaders were told that because of the "convertibility crisis" it was imperative that Britain embark upon an export drive, particularly as imports in 1947 were 50 per cent higher than in 1946, thereby contributing to an increase in the balance of payments deficit from £230 million in 1946 to £381 million in 1947. This, however, would not be successful if higher labour costs (caused by unjustified wage increases) undermined the competitiveness of British commodities. Although the union leaders acknowledged the logic of Dalton's and Cripps' exposition, they felt unable to offer firm assurances about wage restraint. It was only after the General Council had met Attlee too that the TUC pledged to "give very serious consideration to the possibilities of securing greater stability in wages" when conducting pay negotiations (TUC Annual Report 1948: 289).

Trade union leaders, though, remained wary about the implications of intensified ministerial demands for wage restraint, particularly as Morrison had previously announced, at a meeting with TUC leaders on 2 August 1947, that the Ministry of Labour was to establish an internal department specifically to compile information and statistics about wages. Vincent Tewson, the TUC's General Secretary, felt compelled "to issue a word of warning", namely that:

> it should not be regarded that the agreement to the setting up of this department in any way involves a recognition that this is to be the thin end of the wedge in the dislodging of the attitude of the Cabinet on this matter . . . But first you have supply of information, then the word "guidance" is brought in and down the slippery slope you may go until you get from "information" and "guidance" to "instruction". (TUC Annual Report 1947: 366)

Such anxiety led Isaacs to insist, at a meeting with the TUC's Economic Committee in November 1947, that the Ministry of Labour had not established a department "that is going to give instructions [but] . . . a department from which information can be collected as to what are the relative wages of one industry to another". It was, in other words, "purely an informative department", for it remained the government's policy "to leave industry to negotiate its own wages" (PRO PREM 8/1568).

The TUC's own pledges concerning consideration of self-administered wage restraint fell far short of an incomes policy, even a voluntary one, and trade union leaders such as Deakin remained insistent that "under no circumstances at all" would he accept that "the responsibility for the fixation of wages and the regulation of conditions of employment was one for the government". On the contrary, he declared that these were "questions for the trade unions, and the sooner some of our people on the political side appreciate that and leave the job to the unions the better" (Labour Party Annual Conference Report 1947: 32). The TUC itself, meanwhile, was adamant that: "If there was to be greater restraint on wage movements it could only come from within the trade union movement" (Labour Party Annual Conference Report 1947: 290–1).

Cabinet divisions deepen

By the end of 1947, the Cabinet was hearing Cripps insist that the government needed to take the exceptional step of establishing a set of guidelines to be taken into account by those involved in wage determination, for the annual rate of inflation in 1947 was 5.8 per cent (having been just 1.3 per cent in 1946). Cripps was now convinced that wage increases should henceforth be linked directly to increased productivity, or reflect the need to attract labour to understaffed industries. Unless either of these two criteria were met, he insisted, then "there is no reason or justification for any general increase of individual money incomes". To this end, Cripps proposed the establishment of a Central Arbitration Tribunal, to which the Minister of Labour, after consultation with the National Joint Advisory Committee, could refer those pay awards which were the outcome of arbitration, "in cases where it is considered that the national interest has not been taken into full account" (PRO CAB 129(47) 303, 11 November 1947).

These recommendations were roundly rejected by George Isaacs when he responded with an alternative paper on wages policy, listing several criticisms of Cripps' proposals, not the least of these being that the role and authority of trade union leaders would be undermined, thereby effectively enabling extremists to seize the initiative within the unions. Isaacs was also deeply concerned that a Central Arbitration Tribunal would have the effect of undermining the existing machinery for determining wages and resolving disputes.

Isaacs also questioned the logic of permitting higher pay increases in order to attract workers to industries experiencing labour shortages.

Such payments would still prove inflationary, he observed, before suggesting that, logically, it would surely be more appropriate to *cut* pay in overmanned industries, thereby rendering understaffed industries more attractive to workers. He quickly added, though, that he was not personally advocating this "hardly feasible" course of action, merely pointing out the inconsistencies of the case for wage control.

Consequently, Isaacs used Cripps' proposals as an opportunity to reiterate his own opposition to any statutory control of wages, insisting that "there is . . . no effective way of enforcing a limitation of wage payments to individual workers . . . Statutory regulations prohibiting payment above specified amounts cannot be effectively enforced". In any case, he added, there was too much emphasis on wage restraint, rather than on restraint of prices, profits and dividends. Ultimately, Isaacs warned, "it will be useless for the government to make proposals that would not be acceptable to the general membership of the Trade Unions" (PRO CAB 129(47) 304, 11 November 1947).

The competing perspectives enunciated by Cripps and Isaacs neatly reflected divisions of opinion within the Cabinet over the issue of wages policy. Those ministers endorsing Cripps' approach insisted that merely continuing with the hitherto approach to wage determination would increasingly damage to Britain's economic competitiveness, particularly with regard to international trade and the country's balance of payments.

Furthermore, it was pointed out that the government was now effectively the employer of those working in the newly "socialized" industries and local government (whose role had been greatly increased by virtue of the welfare state), with their wages being determined, ultimately, by the Treasury. As such, the government could hardly maintain formal disinterest in wage determination. It was even suggested that if the government set an example by adopting a firm stance with regard to public sector pay, then employers and employees in the private sector were also likely to pursue wage restraint.

Against these arguments, Isaacs' approach was supported by those in the Cabinet who feared that ministerial determination of wages was not only wrong in principle, but unfeasible in practice, because it "would, in the end, lead to a clash between the workers and the government". Such was the difference of opinion within the Cabinet over wages policy at this time, therefore, that no decision was taken over whether to adopt Cripps' or Isaacs' approach. Instead, the matter was deferred for future discussion, pending imminent consultations with the TUC (PRO CAB 128(47) 87th conclusions, 13 November 1947).

Introducing a "wage freeze"

By the beginning of 1948, however, the government deemed the economic situation to be sufficiently serious to warrant immediate action to secure wage restraint without obtaining the prior consent of the trade unions. Cabinet approval was therefore obtained – in Bevin's absence – for "an authoritative statement on the general economic factors which should be taken into account for wage negotiations" (PRO CAB 128(48) 8th conclusions, 29 January 1948); whereupon, in February 1948 (two months after Hugh Dalton had been replaced as Chancellor by Stafford Cripps) the government published *Personal Incomes, Costs and Prices*, a White Paper in which it was asserted that: "There is no justification for any general increase of individual money incomes without at least a corresponding increase in the volume of production." The government therefore resolved that: "Each claim for an increase in wages or salaries must be considered on its national merits and not on the basis of maintaining a former relativity between different occupations and industries" (Cairncross, 1985: 404).

In effect, the Cabinet had swung, largely in response to the urgency of economic circumstances, towards Cripps' perspective, for he had argued consistently that: "Over the last century, particular economic considerations have developed traditional or customary relationships between individual incomes in different occupations which have no relevance whatever to present day conditions and necessities." As such, Cripps insisted that: "The relation which different individual incomes bear to one another must no longer be determined by some historical development of the past, but by the urgent needs of the present" (PRO CAB 129(47) 303, 11 November 1947).

By the beginning of 1948, this viewpoint had gained much wider currency within a Cabinet now convinced that "the situation was too grave for the government to maintain a purely passive role" for "there was a grave risk that a state of uncontrollable inflation would develop", although ministerial endorsement had been further aided by Morrison's abandonment of the proposed Central Arbitration Tribunal" (PRO CAB 128(48) 9th conclusions, 2 February 1948).

Explaining trade union acquiescence

Although the trade unions were unhappy about the lack of consultation, they proved remarkably acquiescent in their immediate response to the government's announcement of what effectively purported to be "wage freeze". This was partly because they were persuaded that prices and dividends would also be subject to similar restraint, but also because the trade unions were convinced that the wage "freeze" was merely a short-term measure rendered necessary by particularly serious economic circumstances, the amelioration of which would result in a swift return to "normal" wage determination based on free collective bargaining. However, the trade unions also added, via a special conference of union executives called by the TUC in March 1948, two further "exemptions" from the conditions stipulated in the government's White Paper, namely that pay rises would also be justifiable either in the context of maintaining differentials derived from skills, training or experience, or in order to raise wages which were below a "reasonable standard of subsistence". As one commentator has noted, in adding these two criteria to the government's own conditions for pay increases in the White Paper, the TUC "clearly left considerable scope for the ambitious negotiator" (Hyman, 1993: 174); whilst a recent history of the TUC notes that these two additional conditions "could have been loopholes that might have led to the early collapse of the policy", had it not been for the remarkable restraint evinced by most trade unions at this time (Taylor, 2000: 115).

Indeed, a further reason for the readiness of the trade unions to acquiesce in the Attlee government's "wage freeze" was precisely because they convinced themselves that it did not constitute an incomes policy *per se*, nor did it, in effect, amount to a proper wages standstill, for earnings continued to increase throughout 1948, albeit at a slightly lower rate than during the previous year. As Arthur Deakin, leader of the TGWU, candidly acknowledged at the Labour party's annual conference in 1948: "We welcome the policy for the reason that it does leave us freedom for negotiation." Certainly, the so-called wage freeze was not accompanied by any ministerial sanctions in order to ensure trade union compliance, or penalize those workers who obtained unwarranted pay increases regardless. Adherence was entirely voluntary, the government relying heavily on a combination of ministerial exhortation and trade union loyalty.

Indeed, such loyalty was a further factor in explaining why most trade unions were willing to offer at least tacit support for the government's "wage freeze", this loyalty being both political and personal. Politically, this was a government which had implemented, or was in the process of implementing, a number of policies which had long-been advocated by the trade unions, particularly full employment and a more comprehensive welfare state. The Attlee government had also, within months of entering Office, repealed the despised 1927 Trade Union and Trade Disputes Act, originally passed by Stanley Baldwin's Conservative administration in the wake of the general strike of 1926. The unions had seen this Act as a vengeful and vindictive piece of legislation (even though it actually fell somewhat short of what many Conservatives and industrialists were demanding at the time), and hence were supremely grateful to Attlee and his ministerial colleagues for the speed with which they repealed it.

Certainly, Arthur Deakin, General Secretary of the TGWU from February 1946, readily acknowledged the extent to which "we have achieved solid results during the years when Labour has been governing this country", achievements which were rendered even more impressive when contrasted with "the want, the suffering and privation that came our way following the depression of 1922, bringing with it those vast tracts of depressed areas and a great army of unemployed" (quoted in Taylor, 2000: 118–19). Deakin reiterated this perspective at Labour's 1951 conference, noting that in spite of the tensions engendered by the pursuit of wage restraint, "at the bottom of the hearts of our people is the recognition that never before in the history of government in this country have we had a better deal than we have had from the Labour government during the last six years" (Labour Party Conference Report 1951: 92).

Meanwhile, the trade unions continued to be represented on a plethora of governmental committees, partly as a legacy of their incorporation into the highest echelons of the state during the war, but also because this representation was extended after the Labour party's 1945 election victory. Thus, whereas the trade unions had been formally represented on twelve governmental committees in 1939, trade union representatives sat on no less than sixty such committees by 1949 (Allen, 1960: 34).

Such proximity to the corridors of power was in addition to the other direct organizational links that the trade unions enjoyed with the Labour party, namely their significant representation on the party's National Executive Committee, and their block vote at Labour's annual conference. Meanwhile, 120 of the 393 Labour MPs elected in 1945 were sponsored by a trade union, and 29 of these were subsequently appointed to ministerial posts, of which six were in the Cabinet (Panitch, 1976: 10; Middlemas, 1979: 394; Morgan, 1985: 79–80). Such was the loyalty of many trade unions and their leaders to what they saw as "their" government that Sam Watson, leader of the NUM, at one stage declared that: "If I were confronted with the defeat of the government or the reduction of wages, then I would advocate a reduction of wages to save the Labour Government" (*Daily Herald*, 24 February 1948).

At a personal level, trade union loyalty and tacit support for the Attlee government's "wage freeze" has been attributed to the presence of Ernest Bevin in the Cabinet, for although he was now serving as Foreign Secretary, Bevin continued to take a close interest in industrial relations and wage-related issues, regularly endorsing, in the Cabinet, the arguments of his successsor at the Ministry of Labour, George Isaacs. Indeed,

Bevin maintained regular contact with other union leaders on the General Council of the TUC, particularly Arthur Deakin, the leader of his own union, the TGWU (whose membership of one million ensured that it constituted up to 15 per cent of the vote at the TUC's annual conferences). Bevin therefore provided a vital conduit between the trade unions and the Cabinet, ensuring that each was aware of the views of the other. As Bevin's biographer noted, the trade union leaders on the TUC's General Council:

> were prepared to listen to Bevin not only on foreign affairs, but on economic, industrial and political issues, as they would have done to no other Minister because they regarded him still as one of themselves. In return, Bevin's position in the government gave them access to the Cabinet, inside knowledge of what was happening and a guarantee that their point of view would never go unrepresented. Only a man as completely trusted by the Prime Minister and the Cabinet on the one hand and by the union leaders on the other could have maintained such a link . . . (Bullock, 1967: 58–9; see also, Morgan, 1985: 50)

As such, there was a view that "it should be possible for members of a Labour Government to exercise informally, through their personal contacts with the trade union movement" a restraining influence on wage questions" (PRO PREM 8/1568, Brook [Cabinet Secretary] to Attlee, 18 February 1948).

It has also been noted that many of the trade union leaders during this period had also led their unions during the war, and had thus already established a close bond of trust and a good working relationship with many of Labour ministers. Furthermore, according to Addison, "the trade union movement, and the Labour party, were controlled on the eve of the war by a generation of leaders who were essentially moderate social patriots" (Addison, 1977: 276), with Barnes and Reid similarly noting that "many of the personalities involved on the cooperation of the war years – on the one side Arthur Deakin, Thomas Williamson and William Lawther, on the other Bevin and Attlee – was a crucial factor" for the "effective working partnership between the Government and the [TUC] General Council, established during the war, continued" (Barnes and Reid, 1982: 165).

Some commentators have suggested that a further source of trade union support for the Attlee government at this time was derived from the latter's increasingly hardline stance against communism (Allen, 1960: 174; Hyman, 1993: 174). In a rapidly emerging climate of Cold War, communism was seen as a major threat not only in an international context, with regard to the Soviet Union, but also domestically, within sections of the trade union movement. Many trade union leaders were delighted at the Attlee government's hostility to communism, given that they themselves were battling against communist elements within their ranks.

Furthermore, communists tended to be strongly opposed to incomes policies and wage restraint – on the grounds that such measures constituted attempts at holding down the wages and living standards of the industrial working class in order to tackle economic problems and contradictions deemed inherent in capitalism itself – and so "moderate" trade union leaders felt inclined to support the government's "wage freeze" partly as a means of opposing communists in their unions (PRO PREM 8/1082, Isaacs to Attlee, 28 February 1949).

Yet these trade union leaders were also acutely aware that communists would probably seek to persuade ordinary trade unionists that their union leaders were "colluding" with the government to hold down their wages. Hence the TUC's General Council simultaneously pledged support for the government's "wage freeze" whilst also insisting that it did not constitute any abandonment of free collective bargaining, nor did it represent ministerial interference in pay bargaining. The General Council reasoned that the "wage freeze" did not entail "a law imposing rigid and specific restrictions upon wage claims and negotiations", but was merely "a request to unions to restrain wage claims". It was further emphasized that such restraint would be exercised by individual trade unions under the guidance of the TUC itself (TUC Annual Report 1948: 184).

It was in this context that the TUC's General Council endeavoured "to give more precise and more practical definitions of the limited and exceptional circumstances in which . . . it might still be in the national interest for trade unions to proceed with claims". Four such "definitions" were delineated, namely: wage claims based on "the fact of increased output"; the adjustment of wages "of workers whose incomes are below a reasonable standard of subsistence"; provision of wages commensurate with the need to attract workers to essential industries experiencing shortages of labour; and ensuring the maintenance of wage differentials in key industries. There was also an insistence that existing food subsidies should be maintained. Furthermore, there was a reiteration that free collective bargaining should not be impinged upon (TUC, 1948: 51). It was on this basis that a special conference of executives from trade unions affiliated to the TUC voted, in March 1948, to accept the "wage freeze" by 5,421,000 votes to 2,032,000, with the AUEW, ETU (which was communist-dominated), and USDAW providing the main opposition.

However, in a manner which presaged trends characterising subsequent incomes policies during the next thirty years or so, the "wage freeze" was largely undermined by the response of employees at plant level. Concentrating as it did on wage agreements at national or industry level, the "wage freeze" proved highly susceptible to unwarranted pay awards at plant level, thereby drawing attention to the phenomenon of "wage drift". This problem was exacerbated during the 1948 "wage freeze" by numerous pay awards which purported to reflect improved productivity at local level.

Yet during early months of 1949, what most concerned many ministers was not so much the movement of wages during the previous year, but the prospect of an imminent wages explosion in the year ahead. In a paper prepared for the Cabinet in mid-February, Isaacs argued that whilst he had been broadly satisfied with the degree of wage moderation evinced during the previous year – the wage index increasing by four points in 1948 compared to eight points in 1946 – he was concerned that neither the government nor the trade unions should become complacent (PRO CAB 129(49) 28, "Wage Movements in 1948", 15 February 1949). Indeed, Isaacs felt obliged to issue his Cabinet colleagues with an almost immediate supplementary memorandum, on the grounds that since the drafting of the original paper, there had been a number of developments "of major importance" which would have "widespread consequences", to the extent that "no period of wages stability can now be anticipated". Instead, he warned, "a further general upward movement of wages during the next six to twelve months should be expected".

In particular, Isaacs was concerned that a significant pay award just granted by the Agricultural Wages Board to farm labourers would "increase the pressure generally for higher wages in other industries", particularly where workers sought to maintain traditional differentials *vis-à-vis* agricultural workers (PRO CAB 129(49) 42, "Wage Movements in 1948 (revised)", 25 February 1949).

Although his ministerial colleagues shared Isaacs' concern at the possibility of a significant upward movement in wage levels, the Cabinet was also agreed upon the need to continue respecting "the extent to which the settlement of wages was determined by voluntary agreements between employers and employed". As such, it was acknowledged that any attempt at securing continued wage restraint should entail ministerial discussions with the General Council of the TUC, and possibly the executive bodies of individual trade unions as well (PRO CAB 128(49) 16th conclusions, 28 February 1949).

Devaluation and the implications for wage restraint

The tensions between the Labour government's incomes policy and the stance of trade union members at plant level was further fuelled in the aftermath of devaluation on 18 September 1949, when sterling's value *vis-à-vis* the US dollar was reduced by 40 per cent, from $4.02 to $2.80. The government's response to devaluation was to urge an even more stringent policy of wage restraint, one which would no longer accept "cost-of-living" as a criterion for pay increases. Ministers argued that the advantages to be accrued from devaluation, most notably ensuring that Britain benefitted from cheaper exports (which in turn would improve the country's balance of payments position and thereby restore confidence amongst the international financial community) would be undermined if unwarranted pay increases rendered British commodities uncompetitive overseas, or if increased earnings merely sucked in more imports. Indeed, some ministers believed that there should be a six-month freeze on *all* incomes, it being argued that if any exceptions were stipulated – such as to the low-paid – "a general movement in favour of wage increases might begin and get out of control".

By contrast, others in the Cabinet argued that no incomes policy was likely to be credible unless some concessions were permitted for the low-paid. The difference of opinion within the Cabinet was such that a decision was deferred, pending the presentation of a position paper from the Chancellor and the Minister of Labour (PRO CAB 128(49) 56th conclusions, 22 September 1949).

At the next Cabinet meeting, Cripps and Isaacs' paper emphasized that any competitive advantage accrued to British exports as a consequence of devaluation would be undermined if wage costs increased. As such, they urged that the government should appeal to workers and employers "in the strongest and most urgent terms" to adhere to the terms of the White Paper on *Personal Incomes, Costs and Prices* for a further nine months. Additionally, they sought the suspension of automatic "cost-of-living" increases which pertained to wages in certain industries.

With regard to the low-paid, Cripps and Isaacs were favourably disposed to the idea of permitting them certain exemptions, but were concerned about the practicalities involved. If a solution could be agreed with the TUC itself, they suggested, it might be worthwhile establishing a special national tribunal "which would consider all claims for increased wages in respect of poorly-paid workers". This last proposal reflected a deeper concern to attain the voluntary support of the trade union movement, with Cripps and Isaacs acutely aware that the incomes policy "can only be secured by consent. It cannot be enforced" (PRO 129(49) 193, "Memorandum on Wages Policy", 23 September 1949).

There was widespread ministerial support for the proposals put forward by Cripps and Isaacs, although there was some concern about the wisdom of stipulating a specific time-span for the duration of the incomes policy, lest it inadvertently paved the way for a wages explosion at the end of nine months. One suggestion was that the incomes policy should be viewed as indefinite, but subject to a six-monthly review in consultation with the TUC.

Meanwhile, whilst ministers recognized the virtues of exempting the low-paid from the strict application of a wage freeze, concern was expressed at some of the problems that this would engender, such as defining precisely who was to be defined as low paid, whether account should be taken of the differences in the cost-of-living in different parts of the country (and also between urban and rural areas), and how to deal with the inevitable demand by skilled workers for the maintenance or restoration of differentials which would be eroded by higher wages for the lowest-paid. It was also pointed out that once ministers decided on an appropriate level of remuneration for the low-paid, the government would effectively – but unwittingly – have committed itself to a national minimum wage (PRO CAB 128(49) 57th conclusions, 26 September 1949).

For its part, the TUC's General Council simultaneously proffered general support for the government's revised incomes policy, whilst continuing to insist on "the right of free collective bargaining"; meaning that "the government must not impose wages policy . . . the existing machinery of voluntary negotiation must be preserved". The TUC's General Council further declared that there was "no suggestion of a standstill on wage earnings", although it did urge affiliated trade unions to "reconsider" current pay claims, in order to secure greater stability of wages (TUC Annual Report 1950: 215).

Trade union acquiescence dissipates

The tensions which the Cabinet's wages policy subsequently engendered was not solely between the Labour government and the trade unions, crucially important though this was. Similar tensions were developing both between the TUC and its affiliated unions, and between the leaders of individual trade unions and their rank-and-file members. Loyalty to the Attlee administration (and to the Labour party generally) enabled the General Council to persuade delegates at a special TUC conference in January 1950 to endorse the government's revised (post-devaluation) incomes policy by 4,260,000 votes to 3,606,000. However, the relatively narrow margin of victory clearly indicated that trade union opposition to wage restraint was growing, with prominent unions such as the AEU, ETU, NUM and NUR opposing continued wage restraint. Indeed, later that year, at the TUC's annual conference in September, the government's incomes policy was rejected by 3,898,000 votes to 3,521,000, even though the General Council was still in favour – albeit calling for greater flexibility – and in spite of a plea by Attlee himself.

One of the reasons why some trade union leaders were opposed to continuation of the "wage freeze" was precisely because they recognized the detrimental impact that an extended incomes policy would have on the relationship between themselves and their members. Some of these union leaders were experiencing divided loyalties, wishing to maintain their support for the Labour Government, but recognizing that their primary role was to act in accordance with the interests and wishes of their members. As Bryn Roberts, leader of the National Union of Public Employees had observed, "an indefinitely prolonged policy of restraint" was liable "to create conflict within the unions and between the unions". It would also "transform the old class struggle from one between the worker and the employer into one between the trade unionist and his own executive council", leading Roberts to declare that he knew of "no policy better calculated to create dissension within the unions, to undermine the position of the leaders, and to provide glorious opportunities for disruptive elements to exploit" (TUC Report 1949: 234).

Investigating institutional innovations

By the second half of 1950, it was evident that the Labour Government and the trade unions were moving ever further apart over the issue of wage determination. An increasing number of trade unions were rejecting continued wage restraint whilst an increasing number of ministers were becoming convinced of the need for some kind of permanent incomes policy. Consequently, a July meeting of the Cabinet called upon the Minister of Labour to prepare a paper outlining the various systems deployed in Scandinavia and other parts of Europe "by which some measure of central control was established over the fixing of wage-levels" (PRO CAB 128(50) 41st conclusions, 3rd July 1950).

At about the same time, the Cambridge economist Nicholas Kaldor was also urging the government to adopt a more systematic incomes policy, what he termed "a positive policy for wages and dividends" (PRO T 171/403, 21 June 1950), whilst the Director of the Cabinet Office's Economic Section, Robert Hall, was insisting that: "we cannot maintain a full employment policy without *either* the full cooperation of employers and workers, or continued inflation, or the imposition of some system of regulation by the state" (PRO PREM 8/1568, Part 3, 1 July 1950).

By the end of the year, the Chancellor, Hugh Gaitskell, was recommending to the Cabinet's economic policy committee that a Wages

Advisory Council be established, which would be comprised of trade union leaders, employers' representatives and an assortment of "individual" figures, although it would not be empowered to *impose* wage settlements. Instead, he suggested, publication of its findings would have an "educational value and moral influence" (PRO CAB 129, ECP(50) 124, 1 December 1950). The TUC were rather less than enthusiastic about the proposed Wages Advisory Service, however, even though ministers emphasized its voluntary character, and the proposal eventually joined the National Industrial Conference and Central Arbitration Tribunal in being quietly abandoned due to lack of support.

Meanwhile, the Minister of Labour's paper on wage determination in other European countries focused on the alleged deficiencies of the various systems deployed on the Continent, thereby enabling George Issacs to reiterate his view that: "Centralized control [of wage determination] . . . is contrary to our tradition and alien to the temperament of our people". Furthermore, he emphasized, any attempt at introducing some form of centralized or statutory control over pay "will be bitterly opposed by the general body of trade unionists". He therefore argued that instead of seeking to exercise control over wage determination, the government should "foster and encourage the utmost self-government in industry" (PRO CAB 129, CP(50) 291, 30 November 1950).

None of this deterred Hugh Gaitskell from announcing, in his April 1951 Budget speech, that he and the Treasury were considering a number of initiatives concerning the creation of a "central independent authority" whose task would be to secure greater control over pay, although the subsequent general election defeat in October ensured that like others before them, these intitiatives never materialized. An important reason for the failure to pursue such institutional initiatives was a widespread recognition amongst Labour politicians that seeking to determine wages through a central government-appointed body would almost inevitably prove "administratively impracticable and politically unacceptable" (Labour Party Archives, R.46/May 1951).

The apparent need for action over wages was underlined during the summer of 1951, when an unprecedented trade deficit of £150m in June was followed by a deficit of £127m in July, which in turn fuelled a crisis of confidence in sterling amongst international financiers. Such problems, of course, were in addition to those already engendered by the economic consequences of the Korean War and the programme of rearmament, along with the upward trend in wage settlements following the dissipation of the wage freeze the previous year. Meanwhile, the rate of inflation in 1951 rose to 8.2 per cent, having been less than 3 per cent during each of the previous two years. Yet this does imply that the "wage freeze" had proved a considerable success from 1948 to 1950, having "undoubtedly slowed down the rise in wages and prices", to the extent that whereas hourly wage rates were increasing by 8–9 per cent annually from 1945 to early 1948, they thereafter fell to 2.8 per cent during the first eighteen months of the "wage freeze" (Cairncross, 1987: 405). Or as Morgan expresses it: "The general effect of the wage freeze policy was remarkably successful in the fragmented, adversarial world of British labour relations" (Morgan, 1987: 378).

By the time the TUC met for its annual conference in September 1951, Gaitskell was calling for a new period of wage restraint, whilst sugaring this bitter pill with proposals on industrial partnership. Yet Gaitskell's plea and pledge were in vain, for the TUC remained implacable in its opposition to any initiative or institution which might impinge upon free collective bargaining between trade unions and employers. The TUC was adamant that:

> In a period like the present it is all-important to maintain the health and status of the trade union movement and of the voluntary negotiating machinery which trade unions have fought so hard and long to establish. Our system of collective bargaining is the envy of the world and it has served – and is serving under present conditions – the interests of working people in a way which no alternative system could approach. (TUC Annual Report 1951: 284)

Labour ministers, however, were acutely aware that whilst free collective bargaining might well be serving the "interests of working people" (although this itself is a matter of considerable conjecture), it did not appear to be serving the wider interests of the British economy, upon whose success "the interests of working people" ultimately depended. However, with election defeat in October 1951 heralding thirteen years in Opposition, it was not until almost a decade later that the Labour party leadership once again gave serious consideration to the need for some form of incomes policy, coupled with the inevitable difficulties this engendered in securing trade union acquiescence.

During much of the 1945–51 years of government, however, the Attlee government had benefited from considerable goodwill on the part of the trade unions, in spite of their commitment to free collective bargaining, and their concomitant antipathy to what they perceived to be ministerial interference in wage determination. During this period, a pattern emerged which was to manifest itself under the next two Labour administrations, whereby the party entered Office eschewing the adoption of an incomes policy as a means of securing wage restraint, with ministers then finding themselves obliged to invoke increasingly stringent incomes policies in the context of deepening economic problems and the need to assuage the City and the international financial community as to Labour's ability to manage the economy.

For their part, the vast majority of trade unions would simultaneously welcome the return of a Labour government whilst insisting on the sanctity of free collective bargaining, before being persuaded by ministers that the economic situation was serious enough to warrant a temporary incomes policy to secure wage restraint. Voluntary acquiescence or agreement by the trade unions would then be forthcoming for two or three years (aided by a sense of political and personal loyalty and trust on the part of many trade unions leaders towards "their" government), after which growing rank-and-file resistance or defiance would herald the breakdown of the incomes policy, thereupon placing a strain on the relationship between Labour ministers and the trade unions.

The subsequent period in Opposition would then entail the Labour party and the trade unions seeking to resolve their differences and disagreements, with reconciliation assisted by their having a common "enemy" to attack in the form of a Conservative government. Yet during such periods in Opposition, senior Labour politicians would find themselves grappling with the dilemma of what the party's policy towards wages should be when next in Office, given the trade unions' unwavering commitment to free collective bargaining.

3

Seeking conciliation and consensus: The Conservatives, 1951–1964

"One nation" Conservatism in the ascendant

Following the Labour party's remarkable election victory in 1945, the Conservative party was obliged to reconsider its stance towards the working class and organized labour in Britain. Many Conservatives recognized that their party was widely perceived to be indifferent, if not hostile, towards the interests and aspirations of ordinary workers and trade unions, and as such, their future electoral prospects would remain bleak unless and until they could successfully challenge this perception.

These electoral considerations, vitally important though they were, were not the only factors explaining the conciliatory approach to organized labour which the Conservative party adopted after 1945. Also of immense significance was the prominence in the Conservative party during the 1940s and 1950s of "one nation" Conservatism, a paternalistic strand which sought a more positive approach to the working classes and trade unions, not least because of the belief that such a conciliatory stance would greatly reduce class conflict and thereby enhance social stability. This, in turn, was likely to imbue both capitalism and liberal democracy with greater legitimacy amongst the working classes (a philosophy which can clearly be traced back to the leadership of Benjamin Disraeli during the late 1860s and 1870s, and then promoted by Lord Randolph Churchill during the 1890s).

At a general level, the combined impact of electoral politics and "one nation" hegemony within the post-1945 Conservative party manifested itself in the broad acceptance of the mixed economy, welfare state, and the maintenance of full employment. During the latter half of the 1940s, whilst their party was in Opposition, a number of senior Conservatives explicitly denounced *laissez-faire* capitalism and unfettered market forces, with Anthony Eden, for example, informing delegates at the Conservative's 1947 annual conference that: "We are not a party of unbridled, brutal capitalism, and never have been . . . we are not the political children of the *laissez-faire* school". A few years earlier, Lord Hinchingbrooke had declared that:

> True Conservative opinion is horrified at the damage done to this country since the last [1914–18] war by individualist business-men, financiers, and speculators ranging freely in a *laissez-faire* economy and creeping unnoticed into the fold of Conservatism to insult the party with their votes at elections . . . and to injure the character of our people. It would wish nothing better than that these men should collect their baggage and depart. True Conservatism has nothing whatever to do with them and their obnoxious policies. (Hinchingbrooke, 1944: 21).

According to Lord Alport, meanwhile, the Conservative party "has never been frightened of using the power of the state to improve social conditions, to organize economic effort and to provide collective services such as defence, education and health" (Alport, 1946: 14).

In this context, and with specific regard to economic affairs and industrial relations, a Conservative committee on industrial policy was established in 1946, partly in response to the demands of delegates at the Conservative's annual conference that the party should clarify its principles and policies, the objective being to establish a contemporary alternative to nineteenth-century *laissez-faire* liberalism and twentieth-century state socialism.

In May 1947 this committee published *The Industrial Charter*, a policy document which simultaneously endorsed the party's commitment to private enterprise and individual liberty, whilst acknowledging the efficacy of much of the state intervention which had characterized the war-time coalition government, and which was being extended by the Labour government of Clement Attlee. In recognizing that it was "impossible for us to revert to a policy of 'go-as-you-please'", *The Industrial Charter* insisted that "there must be a partnership between the government, Industry, and the Individual" (Conservative Central Office, 1947: 10). This was something which Harold Macmillan – one of the five Shadow Cabinet members who had served on the Conservative committee on industrial policy – had already called for on more than one occasion during the inter-war years (Macmillan 1927; Macmillan 1937).

Another member of the Shadow Cabinet who served on the industrial policy committee, Rab Butler, later explained that both this body, and *The Industrial Charter*, represented an attempt by the party "to wrest from the Left much of the middle ground in the battle of ideas", and as such: "Our first purpose was to counter the charge and the fear that we were the party of industrial go-as-you-please and devil-take-the-hindmost, that full employment and the welfare state were not safe in our hands" (Butler, 1971: 135, 146).

With regard to trade unionism and industrial relations in particular, *The Industrial Charter* pledged that a Conservative government would seek to work constructively and harmoniously with the trade unions, whilst endeavouring to improve the status and security of workers. It was suggested that many industrial disputes derived ultimately from feelings of insecurity or low self-esteem on the part of employees, who were convinced that their effort and contribution were not appreciated by management in the enterprise in which they worked.

As such, the third and final section of *The Industrial Charter* – "The Workers' Charter" – recommended that workers be provided with greater security and status in the work-place, which in turn would facilitate greater trust in, and cooperation with, management. Ultimately, it was suggested, the notion of "two sides of industry"' should be replaced by the concept of a team, in which all worked together towards the same goal, albeit with management playing the role of team captain. In this sense, *The Industrial Charter* called for the "humanization", rather than nationalization, of British industry.

Seeking a rapprochement with the trade unions

In the context of the electoral and political factors noted above, coupled with the sentiments enunciated in *The Industrial Charter*, the 1950s commenced with an unprecedented degree of cordiality by the Conservatives towards the trade unions (although tensions did emerge periodically, more particularly in the latter half of the decade), for as the party's backbench parliamentary labour committee acknowledged:

> Organised labour has won its place as a full partner in the state to be consulted equally at governmental level . . . the Trade Union Movement has now firmly established itself as one of the three interests that support our industrial fabric, namely: Labour, Management and Government. The Conservative party regards the existence of strong and independent trade unions as an essential safeguard of freedom in an industrial society. It must therefore be the purpose of a Conservative government to strengthen and encourage Trade Unions. (Conservative Party Archives, ACP(51)13), 2 May 1951)

To prove the Conservative party's goodwill towards the trade unions upon winning the 1951 general election, Winston Churchill appointed the ultra-conciliatory Walter Monckton as Minister of Labour, with the instruction to "do my best to preserve industrial peace" (quoted in

Birkenhead, 1969: 276). This reflected the fact that Churchill "was determined that there should be no industrial strikes during his term as Prime Minister" (Woolton, 1959: 279–80).

The Conservative commitment to voluntarism

Although the post-1945 Conservative party was quite willing to accept a greater degree of government regulation of the economy – whilst still unequivocally committed to private enterprise in general – it was extremely reluctant to intervene in either industrial relations or the internal affairs of the trade unions; as a result, Conservative ministers refused to accede to perennial demands from a small number of backbenchers and annual conference delegates for legislative curbs on various trade union activities and practices, particularly unofficial or "wildcat" strikes.

Instead, the dominant perspective concerning industrial relations and trade unionism during the 1950s was that of voluntarism, with senior Conservatives accepting that the state should not intervene in the day-to-day working relationships between employers and employees, nor in the internal affairs and activities of the trade unions themselves.

Depicted by some commentators as a system of "collective *laissez-faire*" (McIlroy, 1995: 234–5), voluntarism appeared, during the 1950s especially, to be supported by trade unions, employers, and the state alike. Trade unions have traditionally been suspicious of what they consider to be outside interference in their affairs, particularly as such interference is likely to entail the imposition of legal restrictions on their activities, thereby weakening their bargaining position *vis-à-vis* employers.

Employers, meanwhile, were also antipathetic to state intervention in industrial relations, preferring instead to deal with employees and trade unions on their own terms, rather than on terms delineated by politicians. Some employers also recognized that legislative intervention in industrial relations, particularly if it appeared to be biased in their favour, was likely to exacerbate distrust and conflict in the work-place, and actually make management's task more difficult. For its part, the Conservative leadership was prepared to endorse voluntarism during the 1950s partly because it was a system supported by employers, and also because of the desire to avoid antagonizing organized labour. Yet there was also a recognition that if the state intervened in industrial relations, and thereby became embroiled in disputes between employers and employees, then its own legitimacy and professed liberal democratic neutrality might be called into question, particularly if organized labour perceived it to be routinely siding with employers.

Furthermore, *The Industrial Charter* had propounded a human relations perspective of industrial relations, whereby most work-place conflict was considered socio-psychological in origin and character, derived from the feelings of alienation and low self-esteem apparently experienced by many employees in an era of increasing large, bureaucratic and impersonal enterprises and industries. Such feelings, many Conservatives insisted, were unlikely to be ameliorated by industrial relations legislation: on the contrary, they were likely to be exacerbated by legislative intervention. As senior Conservatives like Robert Carr were keen to emphasize, "it is upon voluntary agreement in industry that we must depend for good industrial relations . . . good relations cannot be enforced by laws" (*House of Commons Debates*, 5th series, Vol. 568, col. 2127).

It should also be noted, in passing, that there was considerable intellectual support for voluntarism during this period amongst academic industrial relations experts, and whilst it is difficult to discern how much this itself actually influenced Conservative politicians in practice, it nonetheless provided the dominant paradigm in which debates about industrial relations took place (see, for example, Flanders, 1975).

The commitment to voluntarism reflected a number of considerations in the Conservative party during this time. First, the constructive role played by the trade unions during the war – when Ernest Bevin, the leader of the TGWU (then Britain's largest trade union) had been appointed Minister of Labour by Winston Churchill in the coalition government – encouraged a much more positive attitude towards organized labour amongst senior Conservatives. The unions had, it seemed, proven their responsibility and patriotism, and were thus entitled to greater respect in return.

Secondly, as already noted, the scale of the Labour party's election victory in 1945 was a profound shock to the Conservative party, and compelled it to acknowledge the new electoral significance of organized labour. The Conservative party would henceforth need to convince ordinary working people that it was not hostile to their interests, institutions and aspirations. Indeed, whilst some Conservatives were inclined complacently to assume that the electoral pendulum would naturally swing back in their favour, more prescient minds in the party recognized that there "can be no permanent revival of Conservativism without a positive alternative policy to the policy of the Socialist Left . . . a clear and comprehensive restatement [of Disraeli's principles] in the light of present-day conditions" (Amery, 1946: 5; see also, Hinchingbrooke, 1946; Hogg, 1945; Macmillan, 1946).

Thirdly, but inextricably linked to the previous two considerations, the Conservative party during the 1950s was determined to eradicate the legacy of distrust which had become established between

Conservatives and trade unions during the 1920s and 1930s. These two decades had witnessed the 1926 General Strike, the consequent 1927 Trade Disputes Act, and the Great Depression (entailing three million unemployed and the Jarrow March) of the 1930s. After the Second World War, the Conservative party was determined to make a fresh start with the trade unions, and win their trust. This required that Conservatives avoid the pursuit of measures or policies which would be opposed by the trade unions, thereby reviving old enmities (see, for example, Conservative Party Archives, CRD 2/7/6, Chapman-Walker to Clarke, 5 April 1950; Conservative Party Archives, CRD 2/7/6, "Sub-committee on Political Education – Report of the Working party on the Approach to the Industrial Worker", 20 July 1950; Conservative Party Archives, CRD 2/7/4, PLC(54)1, "Some background facts concerning industrial relations", 15 February 1954; Conservative Party Archives, ACP 4(54)34, "Industrial Relations", 11 June 1954).

The fourth consideration which underpinned the Conservatives' twin commitment to voluntarism and free collective bargaining throughout the 1950s was the "human relations" perspective to which most senior Conservative subscribed during this period (Dorey, forthcoming). Having originally been articulated in *The Industrial Charter*, it was consistently reiterated by Conservative ministers throughout the 1950s. It reflected the assumption that most industrial relations problems were derived from workers' feelings of alienation and low self-esteem. It was maintained that when employees did not feel that their contribution in the work-place was valued, then their commitment and loyalty would diminish accordingly, thereby yielding industrial relations problems. In such circumstances, Conservatives argued, apparently minor or insignificant grievances could flare up into industrial action. According to this perspective, therefore, the underlying cause of much industrial action owed less to the malign machinations of militants and Marxists in the trade unions than to an unappreciated and unmotivated work-force.

The remedy to ameliorate such attitudes and feelings, senior Conservatives insisted, was to foster a greater sense of partnership in the work-place, with particular emphasis being placed on clearer channels of communication and consultation between management and workers. Once workers were imbued with a greater understanding of their role and importance in their work-place, and thereby realized that they were valued members of a team in which each member had a vital role to play, Conservatives envisaged that the old "them and us" mentality would be eradicated (see, for example: Robert Carr, *House of Commons Debates*, 5th series, Vol. 568, col. 2127; David Clarke 1947: 29; Conservative Central Office 1949: 23; Anthony Eden, 1947: 421, 429–30, and 1960: 267; Walter Monckton, *The Times*, 10 December 1953; Harold

Watkinson, *The Times*, 20 October 1952 and *The Times*, 20 January 1954).

There was also a belief amongst some Conservatives that if there was a greater degree of communication between employers and employees, then the latter and their trade unions would develop a proper appreciation of the economic circumstances and problems facing their company or industry, which might in turn yield more responsible wage bargaining. According to one junior minister at the Ministry of Labour during the 1950s, if employers gave their workforce an honest account of the balance sheet of their firm, in plain, straightforward language, then they would repudiate many of the false notions about what "Communist agitators" called "the bloated profits of capitalism" (*The Times*, 20 October 1952).

The fifth reason why the Conservative party throughout the 1950s upheld a voluntarist approach with regard to industrial relations, was the concern that any legislation in this sphere would exacerbate, rather than eradicate, suspicion and conflict both between management and labour, and between a Conservative government and the trade unions. Besides, ministers frequently pointed out, the law could not compel management and employees to work more harmoniously together; partnership and cooperation on the work-place had to be based on trust. In this context, industrial relations legislation was deemed inappropriate, and likely to prove counter-productive, although Iain Macleod, who succeeded Monckton at the Ministry of Labour, believed that his department could play an important role in improving industrial relations by promoting greater cooperation between employers and employees (PRO PREM 11/3125, Macleod to Macmillan, 11 April 1957).

This reluctance to resort to legislation even extended to such matters as strike ballots, which were not only deemed impracticable, but were "not a matter upon which it would be worth incurring the inevitable opposition of the Trade Unions" (Conservative Party Archives, PLC(52)4), "Draft for Report on the Workers' Charter", 2 May 1951). Even by 1955, it was being maintained that the incidence of strikes in British industry "do not seem to provide adequate grounds for any widespread review of our policy on industrial relations" (Conservative Party Archives, ACP(55)40, "Industrial Relations: A Progress Report", 21 October 1955).

Endorsement of free collective bargaining

The voluntarist policy adopted *vis-à-vis* trade union organization and behaviour was matched by an equal commitment to free collective bargaining in the sphere of wages and salaries, whereby Conservative ministers insisted that terms and conditions of employment were for management and trade unions to determine between them, without interference by government. There was an insistence that "the principle of collective bargaining, unfettered from the outside, is the foundation of industrial relations [in Britain], questioned by neither party in industry, nor any party in state" (PRO T 227/261, "Draft White Paper on Full Employment and Price Stability", 18 June 1954).

At the time, this was widely seen as a natural reflection of the Conservative's traditional view that governments ought not to interfere in what were essentially economic decisions, yet in many other respects, as we have already noted, the Conservative party of the 1950s had effectively abandoned the *laissez-faire* model of capitalism in favour of a gently-regulated variant. Ironically, therefore, wage determination was one of the only areas of economic affairs where the Conservative party continued to insist upon a predominantly non-interventionist approach, maintaining that it was "entirely in line with Conservative policy that employers and trade unionists should be left to settle these matters through their negotiating machinery or through free bargaining" (Conservative Party Archives, PLC(54)1, "Industrial Relations", 15 February 1954).

The Conservative party's endorsement of free collective bargaining also entailed a firm rejection of compulsory arbitration in favour of "a system of voluntary arbitration . . . encouraged by the Minister of Labour". Furthermore, it was emphasized that the findings of an Arbitration Court "need not be binding" (Conservative Party Archives, ACP 1(51)13, 2 May 1951). Of course, this did not mean that the government was unconcerned with what was happening on the wages front. On the contrary, as the Attlee governments had previously discovered, an interventionist role for the state, coupled with a political and electoral commitment to full employment, ensured that any government was compelled to take an interest in what was happening with regard to pay determination. Throughout the decade, therefore, Conservative ministers found themselves simultaneously insisting that wages were not the responsibility of government, whilst exhorting trade unions and their members to exercise restraint and moderation in order to minimize inflation and maximize employment.

Indeed, from its first year in Office, the Conservative government was urging the trade unions to exercise wage restraint, although ministers fully acknowledged that it "would be impracticable to prevent claims for wage increases from being put forward" (PRO CAB 128(52), 51st conclusions, 8 May 1952). Walter Monckton, as Minister of Labour, was certainly convinced that "there is no prospect that the trade unions would accept any general wages standstill", although he was reasonably confident that "there is evidence of support from responsible trade union leaders for a policy of wage restraint" (PRO CAB 128(52), 57th conclusions, 29 May 1952).

Such confidence reflected a widespread faith amongst many senior Conservatives and departmental officials – particularly within the Ministry of Labour – during this period in the persuasive power of education and explanation concerning trade union attitudes and behaviour. It was commonly assumed that if the economic facts of life were carefully and consistently explained to the trade unions, they would respond by practising more responsible collective bargaining.

The Conservative government's triple commitment to voluntarism, full employment and free collective bargaining came under growing pressure as the decade progressed, however, due to increasing inflation (the retail price index increased from 2 per cent in 1954 to 4.9 per cent in 1956, for example), greater industrial disruption (in 1952, 1,792,000 working days had been lost due to strike action, this number increasing to 3,781,000 in 1955), and a diminution of Britain's share of the world market in manufactured exports (down from 25.5 per cent in 1950 to 16.5 per cent in 1960, whilst the same period saw West Germany increase its share from 7.3 per cent to 19.3 per cent). The concern caused by such trends was compounded by the fact that in 1960, Britain's balance of payments (excluding invisible earnings) plunged £406 million into the red.

Rejecting alternative options

With regard to inflation, and the consequent need to restrain wage increases, Conservative ministers appeared to be presented with three equally unpalatable options. One was to revert to a deliberate policy of deflation, which would generate an increase in unemployment, thereby exercising a downward pressure on the wages front. This was certainly the approach favoured by Peter Thorneycroft (PRO CAB 129/88 195, 7 September 1957), although it was totally unacceptable to most other Cabinet ministers, however, committed as they were to forging a harmonious relationship with the trade unions, and banishing the bitter memories of the 1930s. Most senior Conservative ministers at this time were determined to avoid a return to high unemployment, especially Harold Macmillan (Chancellor from December 1955 to January 1957, when he became Conservative leader and Prime Minister) who never forgot the plight of his own constituents in Stockton during the Great Depression of the 1930s. As Reginald Maudling – who served as a President of the Board of Trade and then Chancellor under Macmillan's premiership – recalled, "his [Macmillan's] experience in Stockton . . . so moulded his subsequent approach to economic affairs" (Maudling 1978: 103).

Throughout his terms as Chancellor and Prime Minister, therefore, Macmillan refused to countenance a deliberately deflationary policy which would fuel unemployment, a stance shared throughout the 1950s by most of his ministerial colleagues. As Iain Macleod's biographer notes: "The political imperative of this period, when folk memories of the 1920s and 1930s were potent and the majority of voters were working class, was to keep the numbers registered as unemployed below half a million" (Shepherd, 1994: 133).

Further endorsement of this resistance to deflation emanated from Robert Hall, Director of the Economic Section within the Cabinet Office, who noted that the level of unemployment which would be necessary "to put a really effective stop on wage increases" would be "economically wrong as well as politically disastrous", and as such he was confident that "no government in the UK would be likely to push unemployment as far as this" (PRO T 229/409, Hall to Bridges, 19 November 1951, and PRO T 229/402, Hall to Bridges, 28 November 1951).

This stance was further endorsed by the Conservative party's industrial research committee, which had been established after the 1955 election victory in order to investigate various aspects of industrial relations. The committee claimed that if unemployment were allowed to rise beyond three-quarters of a million "under a Conservative administration . . . great and lasting harm would be done to the Conservative party", for such a figure was "probably a fair estimate of the maximum unemployment the country is prepared to stand". Anything higher, and "the Conservative party is likely to get badly concussed. It might indeed sustain a shock from which it would have great difficulty in recovering" (Conservative Party Archives, ACP 4(56)41, 2 February 1956).

The second option theoretically available to the Conservative governments with regard to wages and inflation during the 1950s was recourse to an incomes policy, on the basis that reaching agreement with the trade unions and employees over permissible (i.e., lower) wage increases would yield a corresponding reduction in inflation. Yet this option was also rejected by Conservative ministers, partly on the grounds of principle, namely that in a liberal democratic society, governments had no business in seeking to determine wages and salaries. This option was further rejected on grounds of impracticability, it being assumed that an incomes policy would be unenforceable (unless the state abrogated to itself draconian powers and punitive sanctions deemed incompatible with a free society). Any incomes policy was "liable either to make radical inroads into the essential liberties of a free society or in practice to prove unfair, and in the final analysis unworkable" (Conservative Party Archives, ACP 4(56)41).

The third option ministers could have selected was the introduction of legislation to curb the activities of the trade unions – particularly unofficial or wildcat strikes – as demanded each year by a handful of Conservative MPs and conference delegates. This option was also firmly rejected during the 1950s, for not only would trade union legislation have destroyed the tireless efforts of Conservative ministers in pursuing a constructive relationship with the trade unions, it too would have faced practical problems in terms of enforceability. What could ministers really do, for example, if unofficial strikes were outlawed, but some trade unions and their members engaged in such action regardless? Would the government really want to see trade unionists sent to prison, thereby incurring the likely wrath of the whole trade union movement, and quite possibly, a shift in public opinion against the Conservative party?

In short, the assumption of most Conservative ministers was that the likely repercussions of trade union legislation were likely to prove more damaging, both to industrial relations and to the British economy, than the trade union behaviour they were seeking to eradicate in the first place. The Cabinet shared the view of the Conservative's backbench labour committee at this time, namely that: "Any suggestion of special government intervention, whether this be in the form of secret ballots or of imposed wages policy, would not only be rejected by both sides [of industry], but would itself lead to major industrial unrest" (Conservative Party Archives, PLC(54)1, "Industrial Relations", 15 February 1954).

In any case, many senior Conservatives still adhered to the view that much industrial action – such as unofficial strikes – was socio-psychological in origin, and thus legislation would be an inappropriate response. Instead, the role of ministers would remain one of encouraging the "two sides of industry" to work more closely together, thereby fostering a sense of partnership between employers and their employees, and thus eradicating "them and us" attitudes on the factory-floor.

Anthony Eden, who replaced Churchill as Conservative leader and Prime Minister in April 1955, was adamant that in spite of growing concern in some quarters over trade union attitudes and activities, the "best course to follow was to leave the two sides of industry to work out their problems and to continue to make available the machinery of the Ministry of Labour and National Service for helping to reach agreed settlements" (Eden, 1960: 354). It was also suggested that "actual stoppages due to a breakdown in relations of management and workers are not a common trouble . . . we seem to have got very near to the irreducible minimum of strikes" (Conservative Party Archives, ACP 4(55)40, 21 October 1955; see also Conservative Party Archives, CRD 2/7/6, "Notes for Mr Eden – Industrial Relations", 17 March 1954).

In rejecting the above three options – deflation, incomes policy and trade union legislation – the Churchill, Eden and Macmillan administrations of the 1950s adhered to a policy of exhortation – albeit increasingly urgent as the decade progressed – whereby trade unions were encouraged to exercise wage restraint voluntarily. For their part, ministers sought to explain the economic facts of life to trade union leaders and their members in the hope that they would then appreciate the need for moderation and responsibility when submitting pay claims. As Clem Leslie, the Head of the Treasury's Economic Information Division, explained:

> Full employment without price stability in a nation which lives by overseas trade is a long-term impossibility, but if the collective wisdom, moderation and good sense of employers and trade unionists, enlightened by a clear awareness of the issues at stake, can be brought to bear upon the problem, it will be solved . . . [It] is the duty of government to ensure that the problem in its full significance and gravity is understood throughout the country. This is the best means of ensuring that the collective wisdom and restraint of the Community will furnish in practice the remedies which no administrative formula . . . can provide. (PRO T 227/261, "Draft White Paper on Full Employment and Price Stability", 18 June 1954).

Right from the outset, therefore, in the months following the Conservative party's 1951 election victory, the Chancellor held regular meetings with the TUC's Economic Committee to explain the necessity for moderation and responsibility in wage bargaining, whilst urging also that as far as possible, pay increases should be more closely linked to increased productivity (PRO T/229/405).

Contemplating price restraint instead

Eden also believed that much of the upward pressure on wages emanated from price increases (in contrast to the orthodox view at the time that price increases were themselves largely a response to wage increases, as employers passed on their higher labour costs to the consumer). As Eden suggested to his Chancellor in April 1956: "Surely the bulk of wage demands springs from the traditional and annual reaction of the unions to the upward creep of prices . . . ?" On the basis of this prognosis, Eden suggested that the key to wage restraint lay in "doing what we can do to keep prices stable" as far as was practicably possible. Price stability would, Eden envisaged, presage wage restraint by the trade unions (Eden, 1960: 326).

Proceeding on this basis, the Eden government gave priority during the autumn of 1955 and winter of 1955–6 to securing agreement for a period of price restraint amongst the business community. The main employers' organizations of that time were approached, namely the British Employers' Confederation and the Federation of British Industries, who in turn put the case for price restraint to their affiliated members, many of whom responded favourably by pledging effectively (and entirely voluntarily) to freeze their prices until the summer of 1956.

The Eden government not only anticipated that this strategy of approaching the business community first would serve to persuade the trade unions to accept wage restraint, it was also reckoned that a Conservative government was more likely to secure a favourable response from the business community than from the trade unions, for the latter would automatically be suspicious of Conservative ministers approaching them with a request to reduce their pay claims. On the other hand, Conservatives hoped that if the business community could be persuaded of the merits of price restraint, then ministers would have more chance of success when turning their attention to the trade unions in order to seek a corresponding policy of wage restraint. Not only would Conservative ministers be able to argue that price stability rendered it unnecessary for the trade unions to seek excessive pay increases, the government would also be able to claim that it was being entirely even-handed between employers and workers.

It was on this basis that the Minister of Labour, Iain Macleod, when advising the Prime Minister, Anthony Eden, prior to a meeting on 5 March 1956 with the TUC's Economic Committee, suggested that ministers should "not try to push them much at the . . . meeting, which should be largely explanatory and exploratory". Only at the subsequent meeting, Macleod advised, might the government be able to persuade the TUC "to take a few steps along the road of restraint", and even this would be dependent upon ministers being able to provide "satisfactory assurances of help [from employers] in regard to profits and dividends" (PREM 11/1883, Macleod to Eden, 27 February 1956).

The economic implications of full employment

The trade unions failed to be persuaded by the Eden government's strategy, however, and so, increasingly concerned about the economic impact of irresponsible wage demands and pay awards, the Conservative government published, in March 1956, a White Paper entitled *The Economic Implications of Full Employment*. This explained that:

> In order to maintain full employment, the government must ensure that the level of demand for goods and services is high and rises steadily as productive capacity grows. This means a strong demand for labour and

> good opportunities to sell goods and services profitably. In these conditions, it is open to employees to insist on large wage increases and it is often possible for employers to pass on the cost to the consumer so maintaining their profit margins. This is the dilemma which confronts the country. If the prosperous economic conditions necessary to maintain full employment are exploited by trade unions and businessmen, price stability and full employment become incompatible. The solution lies in self-restraint in making wage claims and fixing profit margins and prices, so that total money incomes rise no faster than total output. (HMSO, 1956: 17)

According to the Prime Minister, Anthony Eden, the objective of *The Economic Implications of Full Employment* was to "provide the background for a new approach to stabilize prices and prevent a perpetual upward spiral in wage claims and the cost of living" (Eden, 1960: 321). This did not mean, however, recourse to an incomes policy; instead, it remained firmly in accordance with Conservative ministers' preference for education and exhortation. Senior Conservatives continued to believe that workers and trade unions could be educated as to the nature of Britain's economic situation, and thereby persuaded voluntarily to exercise restraint and responsibility when submitting pay claims. *The Economic Implications of Full Employment* was intended to provide a major means by which the trade unions would be so educated, with Eden insisting that: "The purpose of the White Paper was not to appeal for restraint in making wage claims and fixing margins of profit, but to show the need for it" (Eden, 1960: 325).

Eden himself certainly appeared confident that the trade unions would respond positively to government calls for wage restraint if they could be persuaded that the economic situation warranted it. As such, on 27 December, Eden wrote to the Chancellor, Harold Macmillan, informing him that:

> the trade unions do understand that if our costs go on rising we shall inevitably price ourselves out of world markets and they will be the first to suffer. Therefore they will always lend a sympathetic ear to any doctrine aimed at avoiding this danger. If . . . we could call for restraint in dividends and expenditure generally, and produce an attractive savings programme, we should have a fair chance of enlisting their help in trying to keep wages steady over the next few years. We have simply got to do this somehow. (Quoted in Eden, 1960: 322–3)

Frank Cousins becomes leader of the TGWU

However, by this time it was not economic circumstances alone which fuelled ministerial concern over trade unions and their wage claims.

What compounded the Cabinet's consternation was the 1956 appointment of Frank Cousins as General Secretary of the TGWU. Widely viewed as a leading left-wing figure in the trade union movement, Cousins' elevation to the leadership of the TGWU threatened a less harmonious relationship between the Conservative government and the trade unions, something which apparently dismayed many senior TUC officials just as much as Cabinet ministers.

In his first speech (as TGWU leader) to the TUC annual conference, Cousins railed against wage restraint and any hint of incomes policy, insisting instead "there is is no such thing in this country as a place where you can say 'wage levels stop here' and that we ought to be content". Accusing the government of having thrown down the gauntlet over the issue of wage restraint, Cousins declared that the trade unions ought "not refuse to pick it up if they were compelled to" (TUC Congress Report 1956: 400). Cousins was speaking in support of a motion – unanimously passed – which insisted upon:

> the right of Labour to bargain on equal terms with Capital, and to use its bargaining strength to protect workers from the dislocations caused by an unplanned economy. It rejects proposals to recover control by wage restraint, and by using the nationalized industries as a drag-anchor . . . (TUC Conference Report 1956: 528).

Many commentators have since suggested that Cousins' elevation to the leadership of the TGWU heralded the end of the constructive and relatively cordial relationship which had prevailed between the Conservative governments and the trade unions since 1951. However, one commentator has argued that:

> Even whilst Monckton was Minister of Labour, the trade union picture began to change. A new generation of union leaders clearly felt that more needed to be done by the leadership to reflect increasing shop-floor pressures which were already making themselves felt, particularly in the car industry and in the docks. Frank Cousins' appointment in 1956 as General Secretary of the Transport & General Workers Union typified this trend. (Seldon, 1981:205; see also Barnes and Reid, 1980: 27–28; Kavanagh and Morris, 1989: 57; Taylor, 1993: 102).

For example, by the time that Cousins had been elected leader of the TGWU, Jim Campbell had become leader of the National Union of Railwaymen, and Alan Birch leader of the Union of Shop, Distributive and Allied Workers, the combined impact of which was to imbue the TUC's General Council with a somewhat different political complexion. Whilst not becoming overtly militant or confrontational, the TUC's General Council nonetheless evinced greater caution over "collaboration" with the Conservative governments, particularly in the sphere of wage restraint (Dorfman, 1973: 84–5).

The Cohen Council

The Eden government's lack of success in securing trade union agreement for a period of wage restraint during the mid-1950s, even after the publication of *The Economic Implications of Full Employment*, prompted the Chancellor to establish, in August 1957, a Council on Prices, Productivity and Incomes, whose brief was:

> having regard to the desirability of full employment, and increasing standards of living, based on expanding production and reasonable stability of prices, to keep under review changes in prices, productivity, and the level of incomes (including wages, salaries and profits), and to report thereon from time to time.

Chaired by a judge, Lord Cohen (hence its more common appellation, the Cohen Council), and two economists, Sir Harold Howitt and Sir Dennis Robertson, the Council had no statutory powers, but, instead, was intended to constitute "an authoritative and impartial body to consider the wider problem of wages policy in all branches of industry". Macleod hoped that "such a body of some independent authority considering the general economic position of the country as affected by wages, profits and prices" would yield "a useful effect on public opinion" (PRO PREM 11/2878, Macleod to Macmillan, 27 April 1957).

In this respect, the Cohen Council closely corresponded to a proposal put forward at about the same time by the Conservative industrial research committee, which called for an independent body to consider the relationship between wages and inflation. The rationale for an independent body was that public opinion in general, and trade unions in particular, were more likely to accept any findings or recommendations "if they were suggested by an obviously unbiased source" (Conservative Party Archives, ACP/57/53, "Wages and Inflation 1957", 6 May 1957).

A few Cabinet ministers – including the Chancellor himself – had originally wanted the Council to stipulate a "guiding light" for pay increases, but the Cabinet had rejected this proposal for fear that such a figure would automatically be viewed by the trade unions as an automatic or minimum target for pay claims (an issue which was to re-emerge more than once in the years ahead). However, the Cohen Council had no discernible impact on wage levels and pay increases, to the extent that one commentator claims that it proved "harmless, producing a number of hand-wringing and ineffectual reports that exhorted trade unions and workers to restrain their wage demands . . . " (Taylor, 1993: 104–5).

Restating the case for voluntarism

The Cohen Council therefore failed to assuage ministerial concern over the impact of wage increases on Britain's economy. Nor did it serve to silence those voices in the Conservative party, both on the parliamentary backbenches, and amongst constituency activists in the country at large, which wanted their ministers to curb the activities and powers of the trade unions, with legislation on strikes proving a particularly popular option in these quarters of the Conservative party (see, for example, the Inns of Court Conservative & Unionist Society, 1958).

Yet the Cabinet still refused to countenance such measures at this time, such was its continued commitment to voluntarism, and determination to secure the trust of the trade unions. In any case, Macleod informed delegates at the Conservative's 1956 conference, there was no real evidence that ordinary trade union members were more moderate than their leaders, and as such, he suggested, strike ballots might actually increase the number of industrial stoppages. Macleod therefore reiterated his conviction that: "the British system of free voluntary negotiation in industry with the minimum of government interference is best . . . I believe firmly in the trade union system. These views are fundamental to my political beliefs and I have not altered in any way. Nor will I" (Conservative Party Conference Report 1956: 76).

Macmillan, meanwhile, true to his "one nation" inclinations, was also keen to dampen down demands for a tougher stance against the trade unions emanating from sections of the Conservative party. Whilst acknowledging, by the autumn of 1957, "a wide feeling among our own supporters that the thing to do is have a row with the trade unions", Macmillan insisted that there was no point in having such a row, partly because it would fatally poison the relationship between the Conservative government and the trade unions, but also because it simply would not tackle the underlying economic problems with which ministers were grappling.

Furthermore, Macmillan suggested that trade unions leaders, in spite of their professed belief in socialism, were just the same as any other merchant in a capitalist society; the commodity which they control is labour, he explained, so that if the demand for labour is greater than the supply, then like anyone in control of a commodity in such a situation, they can hardly do other than push up the price. Indeed, following this analysis, Macmillan ventured to suggest that trade union leaders had actually been very moderate and restrained in exploiting their economic opportunities, certainly more so than many other people would have been in similar circumstances. Yet this perspective also led Macmillan to conclude that whilst many trade union leaders would probably like to be able to help the government, they would be unable to do so until the government itself stopped "the flow of the inflationary tide. If we can even get slack water, or better still, a slight ebb, then their task would be much easier" (PRO CAB 129/88, C(57)194, 1 September 1957).

Macmillan was evidently enunciating a cost–push theory of inflation, implying that trade union leaders were compelled by their members to seek wage increases which kept pace with increases in the cost of living; wage increases were, it seemed, a response to inflation, rather than the cause of it. As such, an agreement with the trade unions to secure wage restraint would only become feasible once inflation had already been reduced, a perspective which contrasted starkly with the orthodox view at the time which presented wage restraint as the pre-requisite of curbing inflation.

Tensions mount

Yet at about the same time, Macmillan's successor at the Treasury, Peter Thorneycroft, was enunciating the case for a deflationary package to curb inflation, and explicitly suggesting that the unemployment rate be permitted to rise to 3 per cent "since unless we can get away from the idea that over-full employment must be supported at all costs, we have no hope of curbing inflation" (PRO CAB 129/88, 7 September 1957). Such an explicit policy of increasing unemployment in order to reduce inflation caused considerable consternation around the Cabinet table, with the Minister of Labour in particular expressing his concern about the political implications of such an increase. Furthermore, Macleod was doubtful whether the deliberate creation of unemployment would in itself weaken the bargaining power of the trade unions (PRO CAB 128(57) 31st conclusions, 10 September 1957).

Macmillan himself also remained strongly averse to adopting a deflationary policy would yield a significant increase in unemployment, so wedded was he to the principle of full employment and the need to avoid a return to the socio-economic conditions of the inter-war years. Yet he too was becoming ever more concerned at the increases in inflation and pay awards, to the extent that at a meeting of the Cabinet early in November, Macmillan presented a draft statement of the government's policy on wages, which declared that:

> while we have no intention of interfering with the established processes of collective bargaining . . . we shall refuse to create more money to finance wage awards which are not matched by increased output. This is the cardinal proposition; and on this proposition we should rest. (PRO, CAB 129/90 C(57)261, 8 November 1957)

Furthermore, by the end of the year, Macmillan himself was coming to share with the Chancellor the view that a "guiding light" might be a worthwhile initiative after all, although he recognized that such an option continued to be viewed with scepticism by many of his ministerial colleagues.

This toughening of the government's stance was most evident during the summer of 1958, when it was faced by a seven-week strike over pay by London bus drivers. The government refused to yield, preferring instead to make an example of the bus drivers which would serve as a warning to other groups of workers and trade unions, particularly those in the public sector (for a full account, see Shepherd, 1994: 134–42). The government was also responding to criticism by private sector employers during the previous two years that whilst ministers urged management to stand firm against excessive pay claims, those same ministers did not evince similar firmness towards their own employees in the public sector and nationalized industries.

In spite of this new-found willingness to stand firm in the face of strike action by public sector workers, however, Macmillan still refused to countenance a deflationary policy as a means of curbing either inflation or trade union power. Indeed, February 1958 had witnessed the resignation of the Chancellor, Peter Thorneycroft, and his two Treasury ministers, Nigel Birch and Enoch Powell, due to Macmillan's refusal to accept a deflationary budget by Thorneycroft. The Minister of Labour had also been alarmed at the proposals which the Treasury wished to include in the forthcoming Budget, not only because Macleod shared Macmillan's abhorrence of unemployment, but also because Thorneycroft wanted to include some cuts in welfare expenditure, such as abolition of child allowance in respect of a second child. Such cuts, Macleod feared, would merely be accompanied by trade union pressure for compensatory wage increases (PRO CAB 128(58) 3rd conclusions, 5 January 1957).

Later the same year, at the Conservative party's annual conference, Macleod reiterated that: "We do not believe in a national wages policy, nor do we believe in a wage freeze." He emphasized that whilst ministers had a duty to point out the consequences of excessive pay awards, the government could not compel the trade unions and their members to act more responsibly, nor should it endeavour to do so. Instead, Macleod declared that "only in a partnership independent of politics between the great partners – government, trade unions and employers – was there any real lasting hope for good, sound industrial relations".

Consequently, Macmillan and Macleod maintained their commitment to voluntarism, and continued to reject legislative measures which would undermine any trust or cooperation between the Conservative government and the trade unions. In this context, the government continued to rely mainly on exhortation in order to persuade the trade unions to behave more responsibly. Meanwhile, a Cabinet committee considering wages policy during 1959 cautioned against the setting of a "guiding light" on the grounds that any such specified figure was likely to "become the minimum from which the normal bargaining processes would begin". The option of introducing a wage freeze was also discounted, on the grounds that it "might provoke the unions to a trial of strength". This left the government with little effective choice but to continue with the policy of urging moderation and restraint concerning wage increases, with ministers using the public sector as a means of setting an example to employers and employees in the private sector. Such a policy was, however, acknowledged to be "rather negative and lacking in leadership", with the Chancellor unable to conceal his disappointment at the timidity of this approach (PRO CAB 134/2573, "Wages Policy", February 1959; PRO PREM 11/2878, Amory to Macmillan, 23 February 1959).

The 1961 "pay pause"

It was during the 1960s that incomes policies became a more permanent feature of economic management, under both Conservative and Labour governments, for it was during this decade that concern deepened considerably over the problems afflicting the British economy. By this time, some of the domestic economic problems already noted were increasingly being placed in an international or comparative context, whereupon they caused even greater concern amongst Britain's economic and political elites.

For example, the concern over inflation was intensified when it became apparent that the UK's average rate from 1950 to 1960 had been 4.1 per cent, compared to 1.9 per cent in West Germany, 2.1 per cent in the USA, and 3 per cent in Italy. During the same period, the UK's average rate of economic growth, measured in terms of GDP, increased by just 2.6 per cent, compared to 7.6 per cent in West Germany, 5.9 per cent in Italy, 4.4 per cent in France, and 3.3 per cent in the USA.

In the context of such economic indicators, Macmillan became concerned with "the next great struggle that awaits us – and the most important – the Battle of Wages" (Macmillan 1972: 376). The first salvo in this "battle" was the July 1961 announcement by the Chancellor, Selwyn Lloyd, of a "pay pause", which was intended to remain in force until April 1962, by which time the government hoped to have formulated a long-term policy for wages. Although the "pay pause" only applied to the public sector (in the form of a seven-month wage freeze), it was envisaged that it would serve as an example to the private sector, and provide employers with the resolve to resist excessive pay claims.

It was also hoped that the pay pause would alert the trade unions to the seriousness of Britain's economic problems, for Macmillan remained quietly confident that trade union leaders "knew very well in their hearts that wage claims must lead to inflation unless accompanied by an increase in productivity", even if "they dare not say so openly" (Macmillan, 1972: 379). To this extent, "the pay pause was an appeal to the common sense and patriotism of all concerned – employers, employed and the general public" (Macmillan, 1973: 44).

The wage-push theory of inflation which underpinned the "pay pause" and subsequent incomes policies, had been endorsed by a report written by six international economists and submitted, in the Spring of 1961, to the Organization of European Economic Co-ordination (Fellner *et al.*, 1961). This, in turn, "helped to convince many sceptics in the Treasury and elsewhere of the case for tackling wage inflation by intervening directly in industrial settlements, and not relying exclusively on financial policy" (Brittan, 1969: 163).

Meanwhile, shortly after his retirement as Director of the Cabinet Office's Economic Section, Robert Hall suggested that:

> With the passage of time the number of adherents of extreme positions has diminished and a large body of opinion now thinks that some form of wage policy other than leaving wages to free collective bargaining is necessary if full employment and stable prices are to be combined. (Hall, 1961: 1042)

What also facilitated the shift towards an incomes policy, which the pay pause presaged, was the appointment of a new Permanent Secretary, Sir Laurence Helsby, at the Ministry of Labour. Whereas the ministry's previous Permanent Secretaries had invariably considered the pursuit of conciliation to be their primary objective, Sir Laurence was an economist with a Treasury background, and as such "under his reign the Ministry decided as a conscious act of policy that it could no longer automatically step in to conciliate irrespective of the economic damage it produced in the process" (Brittan, 1969: 164).

One further reason why some Conservative ministers, including Macmillan himself, along with Reginald Maudling, became convinced of the need for an incomes policy during early 1960s was their concern that under free collective bargaining: "The middle classes would be outgunned by the big unions", whereas with an incomes policy, the Conservative government could offer its middle-class supporters a much greater degree of "order and control". Accordingly, it was argued, the middle classes "have everything to gain and nothing to lose by from a planned and imaginative incomes policy", whereas they "would be among the first to suffer in a free-for-all" (PRO PREM 11/4071, "Notes for talk to Cabinet on Incomes Policy", 25 May 1962).

Yet having somewhat hastily invoked the "pay pause", ministers equally swiftly became aware of the practical problems and complexities of seeking to impose a wage freeze in the public sector. Certainly, "when the Chancellor first proposed this temporary alleviation of our economic difficulties . . . neither he nor his colleagues had a clear picture of all that was implied", for:

> As the months passed, we began to realize the complexities of a policy spread over such a wide field. In many industries, there were agreements for automatic pay increases in accordance with any rise in the cost of living; in others, agreements had already been made for a rise within the near future; in others, negotiations were proceeding. In addition, arbitration agreements ruled over quite a wide field. Were these to be suspended or set aside? . . . were we to accept the inevitable leakages, hoping that the temporary dam . . . might at least stem the flood? (Macmillan, 1973: 44–5)

Such considerations further persuaded Macmillan that "there must be some permanent form of incomes policy applying both to the private and the public sector", for without such a policy, at least one of the government's four objectives – full employment, stable prices, a favourable balance of payments and the expansion of the economy – would have to be abandoned, which he deemed "unacceptable". It was in this context that Macmillan began ruminating on the need for "an impartial source of wage assessment operating over the whole field" (Macmillan, 1973: 70).

Searching for a longer-term agreement on wages

Whilst the practical problems engendered by the "pay pause" served to convince some Conservative backbenchers that it was unsustainable without recourse to some form of legislative compulsion or government sanctions, Macmillan remained adamant that coercion had to be avoided if a longer-term agreement over wage restraint was to be reached with the trade unions. Besides, compulsion and coercion were at odds with Macmillan's conception of "one nation" Conservatism, whereby social harmony and industrial peace could, by their very nature, only be secured through communication, consultation and cooperation.

Yet during this period, Macmillan and his ministers were under increasing pressure from the Treasury to pursue a deflationary policy, whilst some Conservative backbenchers were becoming convinced of the need for legislation to curb trade union power, the unions increasingly being blamed for much of Britain's relative economic decline. Neither option was acceptable to Macmillan, who "did not believe that wage inflation . . . could be cured by a general deflationary policy [as] followed, so slavishly, by successive Chancellors of the Exchequer between the wars" (Macmillan, 1973: 49). One further option was a statutory incomes policy, but as the Chancellor explained to his Cabinet colleagues in early December, there was "general agreement that it would be impracticable to establish legal control over wages, profits, dividends and prices" (PRO CAB 128(61) 68th conclusions, 7 December 1961).

Macmillan's preferred option was to develop a closer, more constructive relationship with the trade unions (and employers) in the hope that deflation could be avoided, and full employment maintained. To this end, he envisaged that the breathing space provided by the pay pause had to be used to develop "some other satisfactory and permanent system" (Macmillan, 1973: 49). What transpired were two initiatives. First, a longer-term incomes policy, and secondly, the National Economic Development Council (NEDC), officially established in 1961 (although its first meeting was not until March 1962), whose membership was drawn from the trade unions, employers organizations, and government itself. Although the impetus behind the NEDC was Selwyn Lloyd, such a tripartite body perfectly accorded with Macmillan's own brand of "one nation" Conservatism, entailing as it did a sense of partnership between the two sides of industry, Capital and Labour. This "middle way" reflected a view that: "Private enterprise as our fathers knew it, and socialism, have both failed" (PREM 11/4071, Hogg [later Lord Hailsham] to Macmillan, 8 June 1962).

Not all of Macmillan's ministerial colleagues were endeared to the NECD and the more interventionist mode of economic management which it symbolized. Indeed, Macmillan discovered that Cabinet discussions over establishing the NEDC revealed "a rather interesting and quite deep divergence of view between ministers, really corresponding to whether they had old Whig, Liberal, *laissez-faire* traditions, or Tory opinions, paternalists, and not afraid of a little *dirigisme*" (Macmillan 1973: 37). It thus took two lengthy Cabinet meetings before Macmillan was able to secure his colleagues' agreement to launch the NEDC.

The NEDC was not expressly concerned with incomes policies *per se*, its brief being to facilitate faster, sustainable economic growth via exchanges of information between its constituent members, and to identify potential or actual obstacles to such growth. At the NEDC's first official meeting, for example, in March 1962, it was agreed that an annual rate of economic growth of 4 per cent should be pursued.

Nonetheless, in spite of ministerial assurances to the TUC that the NEDC would not be involved in the formulation or administration of incomes policies, some such involvement was virtually inevitable, because any incomes policy would be based on calculations about what level of wage increases the British economy could afford, and such calculations would invariably be extrapolated from the on-going economic analyses provided via the NEDC. Indeed, whilst preparing for the creation of the NEDC, the Chancellor made clear: "My intention that all types of measures that encouraged economic growth would come within the purview of the NEDC. . . . certainly cannot be dissociated from a sensible policy for incomes" (PRO PREM 11/4069, letter to TUC's Economic Committee, 10 January 1962).

Even if the NEDC itself was not intended to be formally responsible for incomes policies, Macmillan clearly reckoned that the involvement of the trade unions in the NEDC "would at least lead them to greater understanding of the real problems with which the nation is confronted" (Macmillan 1973: 51), and thereby render them more appreciative of the need for greater wage restraint than had been evinced hitherto.

Certainly, the NEDC was established at a time when a number of senior Conservatives – including Macmillan himself, and Reginald Maudling (appointed as Chancellor in July 1962) – had become convinced of the need for a permanent incomes policy. By this time, Macmillan was emphatic that: "An incomes policy is necessary as a permanent feature of our economic life . . . an indispensable element in the foundations on which to build a policy of sound economic growth" (*House of Commons Debates*, 5th series, Vol. 663, col. 1757).

Consequently, 1962 also witnessed the creation of the National Incomes Commission (NIC), which, unlike the NEDC, was expressly concerned both to review and proffer advice on pay awards in the context of the "national interest". However, the NIC was vested with only a very modest frame of reference, to the extent that it could only "review certain pay matters where the cost was wholly or partly met from the Exchequer if the government asked it to do so, and to examine retrospectively any particular pay settlement which the government referred to it" (Blackaby, 1978: 364).

One other initiative which ministers briefly considered at the beginning of 1962 was harmonizing annual pay increases, so that wage awards would all settled at the same time each year. This, it was suggested, would eradicate the problem of pay "leap-frogging", whereby some trade unions sought pay increases which were higher than those accepted by other unions earlier in the year. No decision was taken on such a measure, however, with ministers merely leaving it as an option for the future – one which was never subsequently pursued (PRO CAB 128(62), 36th conclusions, 8 January 1962).

Back to a "guiding light"

The establishment of the National Incomes Commission followed the end of the pay pause, whereupon the government had stipulated a "guiding light" for increases in earnings of 2–2.5 per cent per annum. In establishing this guiding light, the Conservative government deemed it "essential that increases in personal incomes of all kinds should be brought into a more realistic relationship with increases in national production" (Treasury, 1962: 3). However, ministers conceded that larger increases could be permitted in certain circumstances, namely "as part of an agreement under which those concerned made a direct contribution, by accepting more exacting work, or more onerous conditions, or by a renunciation of restrictive practices, to an increase in productivity and a reduction in costs". Conversely, though, it was suggested that: "In many cases, there may indeed be no justification at present for any increases at all", whilst in others, some of the criteria previously cited to justify pay rises, such as a higher cost of living or comparability, "ought not to be given the same weight as hitherto" (Treasury, 1962: 4). The Macmillan government was nonetheless emphatic that it still sought a voluntary incomes policy, whilst also insisting that in the context of the "guiding light", it was "for employers and employees to work out the application of the considerations . . . to individual cases, in the light of the conditions and agreements existing in particular industries and areas". The government merely asked that "all negotiations affecting wages and salaries in 1962 should reflect these considerations". The success of the guiding light, it was acknowledged, "depends heavily on the willingness of workers not to press claims which go beyond the limits which this policy indicates" (Treasury, 1962: 5). This in turn reflected the view prevalent within the Cabinet at this time that "in a free society the government should not aim to coerce but to persuade", which thus meant that any incomes policy "can only be made to work if it is supported by public opinion" (PRO PREM 11/4069, Bligh to Macmillan, 23 November 1961).

Yet whilst the Cabinet explicitly avoided any compulsion against employees or trade unions in order to ensure their compliance with the incomes policy, ministers did consider whether sanctions could or should be invoked against employers who awarded pay increases in excess of the "guiding light" which did not meet relevant criteria. One option favoured by some ministers was to empower the National Incomes Commission to invoke sanctions – such as a payroll tax – against companies which granted unwarranted wage increases in excess of the guiding light. Another option mooted by some within the Cabinet was the removal of the trade unions' legal immunities, thereby rendering them liable to civil action, in the case of unlawful industrial action. From elsewhere in the Conservative party came the demand that agreements reached through collective bargaining should be rendered legally binding for one or two years at a time (Monday Club, 1963: 29–30).

Ultimately, however, the Cabinet again decided against compulsion, preferring instead to rely upon the common sense and patriotism of the two sides of industry, buttressed by the force of public opinion. It was claimed that:

> This is an adult nation and the people must accept the responsibility of being grown-up. They must be prepared to impose self-discipline. It is the government's responsibility to inform and persuade. It is no part of our way of life to try and impose an economic policy under threat of sanctions. (PRO PREM 11/4069)

Ministers also hoped that trade unions and their members would evince greater moderation and restraint if they were provided with appropriate information which placed their pay claims in a wider economic context. To this end, the "guiding light" was accompanied by a government pledge to:

> collect together and to publish in convenient form factual information on wage rates, earnings, hours of work and other conditions of employment, man-power, prices, production, profits and relevant subjects so that due weight can be given by all concerned . . . at all stages of negotiations and at arbitration. (Treasury, 1962: 6).

Ministers were also concerned that imbuing the National Incomes Commission with punitive powers would alienate the trade unions, and thereby destroy the trust and cooperation which the Conservative governments had painstakingly sought to foster during the previous ten years, and upon which future incomes policies would ultimately depend. As such, they were eager to assure the trade unions that neither the National Incomes Commission nor the guiding light signalled the end of free collective bargaining, nor was it intended as an instrument of wage restraint. Instead, they were intended to facilitate economic growth without accompanying inflation (PRO PREM 11/4073).

These assurances were not enough to prevent the trade unions from boycotting the NIC, whilst employers themselves paid it little heed. What ultimately confirmed the ineffectiveness of the NIC, however, was the fact that it only considered five cases referred to it by ministers in its three-year history. Indeed, in his *Wage Politics in Britain 1945–1967*, Dorfman does not even mention the NIC in the chapter that deals with the pay pause and the guiding light (Dorfman, 1973).

Voluntarism and conciliation under pressure

The final two years of Conservative rule up until 1964 therefore witnessed the party's proponents of conciliation, consensus and incomes policy increasingly placed on the defensive against those in the party who were becoming ever more impatient for legislative action against the trade unions, and who were more than willing to abandon both incomes policy and full employment. Those Conservatives who wished to persevere with the search for partnership with the trade unions, coupled with pursuit of a voluntary incomes policy, insisted that if their efforts had so far proved unsuccessful, then it merely obliged the government to redouble its efforts in order to secure future success.

This approach was also underpinned by continuing doubt about whether legislation would actually have the desired effect. Even by 1964, the Conservative party's backbench labour committee was arguing that:

> the law and its apparatus of injunctions, damages, fines, penal sanctions, etc., has little to contribute to the solution of the problems of industrial relations. Laws attempting to determine when strikes are illegal, under what conditions strikes may be held (i.e., after a secret ballot), what labour practices are legal, and what illegal, have been found from experience to be almost totally unenforceable and to do more harm than good. (Conservative Party Archives, PLC(64)3, "Trade Unions, Employers Associations and the Law", 19 March 1964)

However, those Conservatives who continued to subscribe to such an approach were not only becoming exasperated by the recalcitrance of certain trade unions and their members with regard to moderating wage claims and reducing unofficial strike action, they were also willing to refer explicitly to the pressure in the party for industrial relations legislation as a warning to the unions to "put their house in order", lest the case for ministerial action became unanswerable (see, for example, John Hare (Minister of Labour) *House of Commons Debates*, 5th series, Vol. 671, col. 1509, and David Renton MP, *ibid.*: col. 1539).

What was causing particular concern in the Conservative party during the first half of the 1960s was the incidence of unofficial strikes, which were deemed particularly problematic for three reasons. First, as previously noted, it was during the early 1960s that the full extent of Britain's relative economic decline (relative both to previous decades, and to the economic performance of Britain's competitors at that time) became apparent, thus resulting in increasing attention being paid to the role and activities of the trade unions, who rapidly became "scapegoats" of this decline (Taylor, 1993: 1–15).

Secondly, it was only in 1961 that the Ministry of Labour began distinguishing between official and unofficial strikes when publishing industrial relations data, whereupon it was revealed that over 90 per cent of industrial stoppages were of the unofficial variety. The third reason why unofficial strikes in particular were deemed problematic during the 1960s was precisely that such action was frequently in defiance of pay agreements reached between national level trade union officials and employers and/or ministers. In short, wage restraint and incomes policies were being undermined by the activities of shop stewards and trade union members at plant or factory level, thereby contributing to the problem of wage drift. Thus did some within the Conservative party wonder whether the rank-and-file membership of Britain's trade unions possessed the same awareness of the facts pertaining to the country's economic position as their national leaders (Conservative Industrial Department, 1963: 6). The clear implication was that they did not.

This, though, merely increased the pressure on those Conservatives who continued to favour a voluntarist industrial relations policy aligned to a voluntary incomes policy. For example, in 1963, delegates attending the annual conference of the Central Council of the National Union of Conservative & Unionist Associations only very narrowly rejected a call for legislation against unofficial strikes; whilst a few months later, at the party's annual conference, a similar call was made by delegates who complained that there had been far too much appeasement of the trade unions by the government in recent years.

Yet the most that ministers were prepared to offer at this stage was the promise of a review of trade union law *after* the next general election. Deferring such an inquiry was not only intended to provide the trade unions themselves with sufficient time and incentive to "put their house in order", it was also claimed that such an inquiry could "start in an atmosphere free from the risk of political controversy that might be engendered if it were launched with an election not far off" (Conservative Party Archives, PLC(64)3, "Trade Unions, Employers Associations and the Law", 19 March 1964).

However, the loss of the 1964 election ensured that the inquiry which many Conservatives favoured was conducted by the party itself in Opposition, although for much of the same period, a Royal Commission on trade unions (and employers' associations) was pursuing its own inquiry, having been established in 1965 by the Labour government. Only when it was freed from the constraints and responsibilities of Office did the Conservative party feel able to adopt a rather more combative approach towards the trade unions and industrial relations, whilst also moving away from its previous commitment to incomes policy. Those Conservatives urging this new approach considered themselves to have been vindicated not only by their party's own experiences in Office until 1964, but by the problems encountered by the Labour government *vis-à-vis* the trade unions, industrial relations and incomes policy during the latter half of the 1960s.

4

Through deflation and devaluation to despair: the Wilson governments, 1964–1970

Towards a "planned growth of incomes"

Following the experience of the 1948–50 "wage freeze", and having subsequently lost the 1951 general election, the Labour party gave little serious consideration to the issue of incomes policy for most of the 1950s. To a considerable extent, the electoral success of the Conservative party – winning three successive general elections during the decade – rendered the question of incomes policy an irrelevance for many within the Labour party. Furthermore, as Panitch noted, with the Conservative governments of the 1950s eschewing incomes policy, there was little political pressure on the Labour Opposition "to develop a counter-policy" (Panitch, 1976: 41).

Meanwhile, during the early 1950s especially, certain sections of the trade union movement made clear to the Labour party leadership their continued antipathy to incomes policies. As the TGWU leader Arthur Deakin explained with reference to the 1948–50 "wage freeze", "the unions have experienced difficulties and criticisms from their members by reason of the suggestion that we have been more concerned with our own party in government than in the handling of our industrial problems" (Labour Party Annual Conference Report 1952: 136).

Deakin's remarks reiterated not only the trade unions' unwavering commitment to free collective bargaining (and *inter alia* the principle of voluntarism in the sphere of industrial relations generally), but also the problems posed for union leaders when they participated in incomes policies intended to secure wage restraint, namely dissatisfaction and disillusionment amongst the rank-and-file trade union membership. In such circumstances, ordinary trade unionists were liable to enquire whether their union leaders were really pursuing or representing their material interests, or instead colluding with ministers to hold down wages. This gulf between trade union leaders at national level, and the rank-and-file union membership at work-place level – a gulf which was allegedly exploited by left-wing militants – was to become a perennial problem for all subsequent incomes policies pursued by Conservative and Labour governments alike during the 1960s and 1970s.

However, a few individual Labour MPs and left-inclined intellectuals did ponder the issue of incomes policy, with much of their contemplation focusing on the apparent tension between the trade unions' commitment to free collective bargaining, and the professed commitment to socialism. Among those grappling with this issue was Barbara Wootton, whose *Social Foundations of Wages Policy*, published in 1954, insisted that free collective bargaining both reflected and reinforced inequality of incomes and social hierarchy. Furthermore, she expressed serious concern about the likelihood of inflation arising from attempts at simultaneously upholding full employment and free collective bargaining. Recognizing that the essence of the problem derived from "the rival claims of egalitarian ideals and the sanctity of differentials", Wootton urged a "rational wages policy" which would be pursued in conjunction with progressive taxation and enlightened social policies (Wootton, 1954: 175).

Similarly, the few Labour MPs who did reflect upon the issue during their party's period in Opposition also noted the impact of free collective bargaining upon the British economy during an era of full employment, with Aneurin Bevan observing that: "Most people who have given their minds to the problem are now convinced that a national wages policy is an inevitable corollary of full employment, if we are not to be engulfed by inflation." Bevan believed that if it were possible to ensure "that real wages are not eaten into by rises in the cost of living, the way would be clearer to a national wages policy", although he readily acknowledged that much "hard thinking and perhaps harder talking will be required before we win through to something of a permanently satisfactory nature". Until such a time, however, Bevan was concerned that: "In the absence of a policy which strictly relates current adjustments of personal incomes to any surplus which may be available for distribution, mounting paper claims will continue to produce a series of crises both in industry and politics" (Bevan, 1961: 138, 139).

However, it was only the latter part of the 1950s that the Labour party began making public utterances which could be construed as hesitant steps back in the direction of an incomes policy. For example, in 1957, the Shadow Labour Chancellor, Harold Wilson, asserted that "wages are at the centre of the cost–push spiral" which meant that it was necessary to consider "the conditions in which wage restraint could once again become a reality". Wilson was emphatic that "success or failure in the battle against inflation would depend upon its [a Labour government's] ability to secure an understanding with the unions which would make wage restraint possible" (Wilson, 1957: 14).

The following year, the Labour party published an economic policy document which ventured to suggest that "the growth of money incomes must broadly keep pace with higher productivity", whilst also claiming that: "A government which is determined to restore a climate of expansion, maintain fair play between different sections of the community, promote greater equality and create a price-freeze, has the right to rely upon the goodwill and cooperation of the trade union movement." However, it was quickly emphasized that "whilst some measure of restraint on demands for higher incomes will be needed, it will be clear that no kind of wage freeze is envisaged" (Labour Party, 1958: 37).

What gradually emerged from this point up until the 1964 general election was the adoption by the Labour party, supported by the trade unions, of a "policy for incomes" explicitly linked to the wider objectives of economic growth, industrial planning and full employment. In other words, trade union support for a voluntary incomes policy was secured by presenting it as a contribution to the expansion of the economy, rather than – as had hitherto been the case – an instrument of deflation and *inter alia* a reduction in the living standards of ordinary working people. Indeed, it was suggested that the aim of any incomes policy introduced by the next Labour government should not be "to keep increases down to a minimum, but up to the maximum possible". This would ensure that "incomes policy is not wage restraint. It should allow *real* wages to rise" (Labour Party Archives, RD.433/March 1963).

By committing itself to such a strategy of economic growth, of which incomes policy would constitute a crucial component, the Labour party appeared able to offer something to all sections of society, thereby concealing some of the contradictions or tensions which might otherwise be revealed. Economic growth would apparently ensure a continued rise in incomes and living standards for the skilled working class and burgeoning middle class, whilst simultaneously improving the socio-economic position of the poorest sections of British society. This, in turn, would enable the Labour party to present its economic strategy as a means of eradicating poverty without involving the type of redistributive measures that would alienate the rapidly growing number of white-collar workers whose electoral support Labour was eager to secure.

Certainly, the purported link between an incomes policy and the eradication of poverty reflected a growing realization during the early 1960s that, contrary to the complacent assumptions of the 1950s, poverty in Britain had not been eradicated, nor had socio-economic inequalities been significantly diminished. This realization was fostered by various surveys and statistics published by social scientists during this time (for example, see: Abel-Smith and Townsend, 1965; Titmuss, 1962)

At the same time, by linking an incomes policy to the principle of economic planning, it was hoped that support could be secured from both the left and the right of the Labour party, with the right seeing greater regulation of wages as an important adjunct to their neo-Keynesian approach to the maintenance of full employment and low-inflationary economic growth, and the left persuaded that an incomes policy would be applied to all incomes – not just wages – and linked to genuine planning of the economy in order to facilitate the transition to socialism (see, for example, *Tribune*, 6 September 1963).

Labour's drift back towards support for some kind of incomes policy was underpinned, it seems, by the appointment, in November 1961, of James Callaghan as Shadow Chancellor. By his own admission, Callaghan was no economist – his appointment as Shadow Chancellor by Gaitskell was due primarily to his political stature (Morgan, 1997: 169) – and hence he immediately began appointing a team of economic advisers. This coterie contained a significant number of Oxbridge academics who had previously worked in the Treasury or the Economic Section of the Cabinet Office prior to entering academia. One of the first topics to be considered by several of them, during the Spring of 1962, was that of incomes policy, often linked to a greater emphasis on economic planning (Morgan, 1997: 173–5).

One of the Oxbridge advisers was Thomas Balogh, who subsequently became Harold Wilson's chief economic adviser. Balogh was particularly keen on a "policy for incomes" because some "general co-ordination of collective bargaining is indispensable if unemployment . . . is to be eliminated and expansion accelerated". Whilst recognizing that "it would be hopeless for a Central Board or Court to try to fix wages", Balogh ruminated about the establishment of a Council of Economic Advisers which would be able to comment on whether a particular pay award was "compatible with continued stability of prices and/or the balance of payments" (Balogh, 1963: 14–15).

By 1962, the Labour leader, Hugh Gaitskell, was able to delineate the sort of incomes policy the party had in mind. It would comprise five main elements or objectives, namely economic expansion, increased productivity, the voluntary consent of both sides of industry, apply to all forms of incomes (not just wages), and fair application to all sections of British society (*House of Commons Debates*, 5th series, Vol. 663, col. 1742). In the meantime, Gaitskell urged Callaghan and his advisers to look at the type of incomes policies being pursued in Holland and Sweden (Morgan, 1997: 179).

Eager to establish a constructive relationship with the trade unions in readiness for the next general election (due to be held in 1964 at the latest), the Labour party leadership was at pains to emphasize not only that the envisaged incomes policy would be based on a planned growth of the economy *and* of wages, but that it would be depend upon the voluntary support of the trade unions themselves. Thus did Callaghan inform delegates attending Labour's annual conference in 1962 that:

> Trade union leaders can agree with the Government to try to restrain incomes . . . but there is no union leader in this country who can in the end, override the basic wishes of those who elect him to his job. Therefore, what we have to do – and this is a gigantic essay in persuasion and co-operation – is to secure the assent of the whole nation to the idea of an incomes policy, that it is fair and that it will be equally applied, and then the trade union leaders of this country will find it possible to really represent as they will need to do, the views of their own members in cooperating with a Labour government. (Labour Party Conference Report 1962: 219)

The following year, Labour's annual conference was able to pass – by 6,090,000 votes to just 40,000 – a resolution on economic planning which called upon the Party, in partnership with the trade unions, to craft "an incomes policy to include salaries, wages, dividends and profits", in order "to promote sustained economic growth". Moved by the GMWU, the resolution was supported by all of the trade unions affiliated to the Labour party, including the TGWU, led by Frank Cousins. Indeed, Cousins actually spoke in support of the resolution, reiterating that what it represented was "a planned growth of wages, not wages restraint". Meanwhile, just months before Labour's 1964 general election victory, James Callaghan was even musing on the need, if he did become Chancellor, to persuade trade union leaders that they should observe "a wages holiday" (Callaghan, 1987: 161). Consequently, as one subsequent "insider" noted, "there is no doubt that there was a tacit agreement, or appeared to be one, between certain sections of the Trade Union movement and Labour leaders about the need for certain action – if not an incomes policy, then certainly a declaration of intent which would be meaningful in real terms" (Williams, 1972: 359).

Rejecting devaluation

When it won the general election in October 1964, therefore, after thirteen years in Opposition, the Labour party appeared to have secured trade union support for some form of voluntary incomes policy, albeit one which was geared to economic growth, rather than linked to deflation. Such support was reflected in Labour's 1964 manifesto commitment to "a planned growth of incomes broadly related to the annual rate of production" which would be applicable "in an expanding economy to all incomes: to profits, dividends and rents as well as wages and salaries". It was also emphasized that such a policy would "not be unfairly directed at lower paid workers and public employees".

Within months of being elected, the new Labour government was indeed seeking trade union support for an incomes policy, with Harold Wilson explaining to delegates at the TUC's 1964 annual conference that:

> we have the right to ask for an incomes policy because we are prepared to contribute the three necessary conditions. First, an assurance of rising production and rising incomes, so that the sacrifice, the restraint for which we ask is matched by an assurance that it will result in increased production and increased rewards. Second, an assurance of equity and social justice, in that our policies will be directed to the benefit of the nation as a whole and not to the advantage of a sectional interest. Third, an assurance that what we ask for in wages and salaries will apply equally to profits and dividends and rent. We shall not create a free-for-all for the speculator, and land profiteer and the landlord – and then ask wage and salary earners alone to show concern for the national interest that others are not required to show. (TUC 1964 Annual Conference Report: 384–5)

Immediately upon entering Office, the Cabinet had been under pressure from the City and the international financial community to prevent the economy from overheating (a partial legacy of the pre-election boost to consumer spending by the outgoing Conservative government), coupled with a balance of payments deficit (*vis-à-vis* visible earnings) in 1964 of £537 million. There was a widespread expectation that the new government would opt for devaluation (this was certainly the course of action being urged upon the Chancellor, James Callaghan, by two of his economic advisers, Nicholas Kaldor and Robert Neild), but Callaghan and his Cabinet colleagues were opposed to this policy for a number of reasons. First, ministers were aware that with the Attlee government having devalued in 1949, the impression would be given that devaluation was the instinctive option of any Labour government when faced with similar economic difficulties. This in turn would encourage speculation about the possibility of devaluation on every subsequent occasion that a Labour government encountered economic problems.

The second reason why the Labour government rejected the option of devaluation in 1964 was the concern that such a policy would make imports more expensive, which would have serious repercussions for domestic consumption, with trade unions likely to seek even higher pay increases in order to offset the increased cost of living experienced by their members.

A third consideration which informed the Labour government's eschewal of devaluation in 1964 was the fear that it would merely prompt retaliatory action by other governments, creating chaos in the international financial markets, and leaving the British economy absolutely no better off than before.

The fourth and final reason for the newly-elected Labour government's refusal to devalue the pound was that a few senior Labour figures had, prior to being elected, secretly entered into an agreement with the President of the New York Federal Reserve Bank (which was part of the Federal Reserve system in the United States) that a Labour government would not devalue sterling, in exchange for American support for sterling if economic circumstances subsequently warranted it. So secret was this agreement, in fact, that most of the new Labour Cabinet were unaware of it (Short, 1989: 37).

The "Joint Statement of Intent"

Having demurred from devaluation, however, the new government drifted instead towards deflation. Within weeks of its election victory, Labour ministers had secured trade union agreement for voluntary wage restraint, to the extent that in December a *Joint Statement of Intent on Productivity, Prices and Incomes* (hereafter the *Joint Statement of Intent*) was published. Endorsed by trade unions, employers associations (namely the Federation of British Industries, the British Employers' Confederation and the National Association of British Manufacturers, all of whom amalgamated the following year to form the Confederation of British Industry), and the government itself, the *Joint Statement of Intent* was primarily concerned with the objectives of improved productivity and increased exports. However, it also stipulated the objective of ensuring that "increases in wages, salaries and other forms of incomes" were kept in line with increased efficiency and productivity. To this end, the *Joint Statement of Intent* declared that institutional machinery would be established "to keep under review the general movement of prices and of money incomes of all kinds", and "to examine particular cases in order to advise whether or not the behaviour of prices or of wages, salaries or other money incomes is in the national interest as defined by the Government after consultation with management and unions" (Department of Economic Affairs, 1964).

The "institutional machinery" proved to be the National Board of Prices and Incomes, established in April 1965, thereupon replacing the

National Incomes Commission. As its appellation implied, the new institution was to be concerned with monitoring prices as well as incomes, although like the National Incomes Commission, it was a purely voluntary body lacking any statutory powers. With its recommendations lacking the force of law, it was obliged to rely instead on the willingness of ministers, employers and trade unions to accept them voluntarily, which in turn placed the onus on the National Board of Prices and Incomes to present a highly convincing and persuasive report. Furthermore, the National Board of Prices and Incomes was not empowered to follow up its investigations and recommendations. Even when, the following year, the Board was granted statutory powers to call witnesses and demand the submission of evidence, it declined ever to invoke them, preferring instead to rely upon voluntary cooperation with the two sides of industry (Fels, 1972: 38–9).

Another institutional innovation launched by the new Labour government was the Department of Economic Affairs (under whose auspices the National Board of Prices and Incomes operated, until it was transferred to the Department of Employment in April 1968), headed by George Brown. Wilson had envisaged that such a department would complement the work of the Treasury, being "at least as powerful", with the latter continuing to be responsible for macro-economic policy (government expenditure, monetary policy, taxation, etc.), whilst the new Department was "concerned with real resources, with economic planning, with strengthening our ability to export . . . with increasing productivity, and our competitiveness in domestic and export markets" (Wilson, 1971: 3).

Recourse to a voluntary incomes policy

Upon his appointment, Brown immediately added prices and incomes policies to the Department of Economic Affairs' remit, and whilst Wilson was happy with this at the time, he later acknowledged that "there were moments in succeeding years when I felt that the DEA had become so overborne by prices and incomes questions that it was not driving ahead sufficiently fast with industrial planning and productivity questions" (Wilson, 1971: 5).

Indeed, having secured trade union involvement with the *Joint Statement of Intent*, Brown spent much of early 1965 persuading the TUC to accept a voluntary incomes policy whereby wages and salaries would not be increased by more than 3–3.5 per cent. Although the TUC's General Secretary, George Woodcock, remained unconvinced about the viability of such a policy, Brown nonetheless succeeded in obtaining the consent of the TUC itself, via its General Council. This consent, however, was only secured in return for Brown's own agreement that the 3–3.5 per cent "norm" could be exceeded in certain cases, such as for the low paid, and where there were significant increases in productivity, this latter criterion neatly according with the government's determination to secure a faster rate of economic growth.

On this basis, the TUC endorsed the incomes policy at a special conference held in April 1965, after Woodcock had warned delegates that if voluntary pay policies failed, the government would either have to abandon full employment or abandon free collective bargaining. The voluntary 3–3.5 per cent incomes policy was subsequently supported by 4.8 million votes to 1.8 million, with most of the votes cast against coming from the TGWU, which, until his election as a Labour MP the previous year, had been led by the arch-opponent of incomes policy, Frank Cousins.

However, it was also significant that the other trade unions registering their opposition even to a voluntary incomes policy were those representing craft trades and skilled workers, precisely those whose market position meant that they benefited most from free collective bargaining. Such trade unions and the type of workers they represented were also those most concerned at the erosion of differentials which they envisaged would result from Labour's incomes policy. Britain's "labour aristocracy" was not enamoured to any incomes policy which was imbued with even the mildest of egalitarian components, or which purported to enshrine a "social dimension" intended to help the lowest-paid.

That the majority of trade unions affiliated to the TUC *were* willing to support the voluntary incomes policy was not solely due to the exceptions (*viz* the low paid and productivity) which Brown and his ministerial colleagues were willing to concede. Their support also reflected their faith in the new Labour government's commitment to faster economic growth, which, in turn, was presented as a major means by which the incomes and living standards of ordinary working people would be improved. Whereas previous incomes policies had invariably been invoked in order to secure wage restraint in the context of deflation, many trade unions were persuaded by the Wilson government's claim that its incomes policies would be linked to economic expansion. Hence the much vaunted notion of a "planned growth of wages".

Trade union acceptance of a voluntary incomes policy in 1965 doubtless reflected the unions' delight at seeing the return of a Labour government after thirteen years of Conservative rule (even though the Conservatives in Office had adopted a remarkably conciliatory and cordial stance towards the unions). The trade unions also recognized that the narrowness of Labour's parliamentary majority – just four seats – in 1964 made it virtually inevitable that another general election would be held within a year or two. Clearly, most trade unions wanted to avoid causing too much trouble for the Labour government in 1965, lest they paved the way for a return of the Conservatives in the imminent general election.

The need for something stronger

Yet even by the summer of 1965, many ministers were harbouring serious doubts about the efficacy of both free collective bargaining and voluntary incomes policies. For all its institutional innovation in establishing the Department of Economic Affairs, and the National Board of Prices and Incomes, coupled with formal trade union acceptance of a voluntary incomes policy, the Labour government was faced by continuing economic difficulties in the form of further inflation, sluggish economic growth, and a balance of payments deficit for 1965 of £272 million. As such, in July 1965, the Chancellor felt obliged to impose cuts in public expenditure and postpone planned improvements in the social wage.

Such measures, however, failed to assuage the concerns of the City and the international business community. Nor did they allay anxiety in the United States, upon whom the Labour government was relying for financial assistance in underpinning sterling. The American Secretary of the Treasury, Henry Fowler, was amongst those who:

> doubted whether the voluntary prices and incomes policy which George Brown had negotiated would be able to withstand the pressure for wage increases to which we were subject. While he did not attempt in any way to make terms or give us orders, he was apprehensive that if further central bank aid were required it would be difficult to mount if we had no better safeguard against inflation than the voluntary system. It was in these circumstances that we began first to think in terms of statutory powers. (Wilson, 1971: 131–2)

By the end of the summer, Wilson himself had come to the conclusion that "the voluntary procedures, resting on the *Joint Declaration of Intent*, were proving inadequate", to the extent that "the immediate issue facing us was the decision that had to be taken on prices and incomes policy" (Wilson, 1971: 132). At the same time, Callaghan was also becoming convinced of the need for something stronger than the existing voluntary incomes policy, having visited his counterpart in the United States, Henry Fowler, during the summer. When Fowler asked Callaghan "about the prospects for our voluntary policies", the Chancellor "found [it] increasingly hard to answer" (Callaghan, 1987: 189).

Such was the apparent urgency of the situation by the end of the summer that George Brown and Harold Wilson cut short their respective holidays in order to return to London and discuss matters with the Chancellor, with a view to developing a more concrete policy proposal which could then be presented to the TUC when it met for its annual conference starting on 3 September. This necessitated a meeting of the full Cabinet on 1 September, which meant that other ministers, such as Richard Crossman, also had to cut short their summer holidays.

At this Cabinet meeting, there ensued a "surprisingly easy passage for the prices and incomes proposals" (Castle, 1990: 31, diary entry for 1 September 1965). Ministers – or, rather, the vast majority of them – agreed that a compulsory "early warning system" should be introduced, whereby trade unions would be obliged to notify the Department of Economic Affairs of imminent pay claims (whilst employers would similarly be obliged to notify the Department of proposed price increases), whereupon the DEA could decide whether or not to refer the wage claim (or price increase) to the National Board of Prices and Incomes. Trade unions would not be permitted to take industrial action in pursuit of a pay claim whilst it was being considered by the Board. Furthermore, the National Board of Prices and Incomes would itself be vested with statutory powers, enabling it to obtain information and evidence from trade unions and employers seeking pay or price increases. Upon receiving a report from the Board, the Secretary of State for Economic Affairs would be empowered to enforce its recommendations.

This policy actually reflected a compromise between James Callaghan, who had favoured a temporary wage freeze, and George Brown, who resisted such a policy on behalf of the trade unions. Once this compromise policy was presented to the Cabinet on 1 September, "there was no real opposition. The proposals just went through . . . " (Crossman, 1975: 316, diary entry for 1 September 1965). In fact, there was *some* opposition within the Cabinet, namely that expressed by Frank Cousins, who "exploded with indignation at the proposal to turn a voluntary incomes policy, which he had always distrusted and disapproved of, into a legally controlled policy, which he utterly rejected" (Goodman, 1979: 465). Cousins was evidently not convinced by George Brown's own insistence that "I am only introducing these proposals on the strict understanding that this is *not* the first step to statutory wage control", a declaration endorsed by the Prime Minister himself (Castle, 1990: 32, diary entry for 1 September 1965).

Indeed, with the exception of Cousins, the whole Cabinet was of the view that whilst the government's prices and incomes policy should be strengthened by some statutory backing, "there could be no question of seeking to impose a statutory control on wages, since it would be unacceptable in principle, and unenforceable in practice" (PRO CAB 128/39, 46th conclusions, 1 September 1965).

Having obtained, with remarkable ease, Cabinet approval for a strengthened incomes policy, George Brown travelled down to Brighton for the more difficult task of obtaining trade union support. It took a series of meetings spanning twelve hours (the last one not ending until after midnight, on 3 September, just hours before the start of the TUC's annual conference), before Brown was able to secure the agreement of the TUC's General Council for the government's revised incomes policy. However, in order to obtain this agreement, Brown had to concede that the proposed statutory powers "could only be activated by a specific Order in Council requiring the assent of both Houses [of Parliament]" (Wilson, 1971: 133).

In return, George Woodcock, the General Secretary of the TUC, pledged that the TUC's General Council would establish its own vetting procedure, namely an "incomes policy committee" comprising nineteen members (one from each of the General Councils's "trade groups"). This TUC incomes policy committee was to call upon affiliated trade unions to submit their pay claims to the committee for consideration, along with further information and evidence if requested. It was envisaged that this vetting process would usually last for four or five weeks, by which time the incomes policy committee would make its own observations or recommendations concerning the pay claim in question.

Although TUC's incomes policy committee was not empowered to enforce its recommendations on the trade union(s) concerned – having to rely instead on persuasion and exhortation – the General Council anticipated that affiliated unions would observe the recommendations of its incomes policy committee, out of recognition that if its own vetting procedure proved ineffective, the government could, at any time, invoke the Order in Council, thereby imbuing the hitherto voluntary incomes policy with a statutory dimension.

This agreement, brokered between Brown and the TUC's General Council, was then endorsed by the TUC's annual conference later the same day, as recommended to delegates in an impassioned speech by George Woodcock himself. The TUC's General Secretary explained that:

> We want to do this . . . so that we may be able to offset legislation which otherwise is threatened . . . I would like the TUC to operate it because if we cannot, nobody can . . . If not, then the alternatives . . . become real possibilities . . . either you have a movement towards greater direction of the unions – and what do you think the Government's proposals are but greater direction of the unions? . . . or the state says the whole thing is unworkable and gives up the job of maintaining full employment and economic growth. (TUC Annual Report 1965: 472)

Yet with 5.2 million votes cast in favour, and 3.3 million against, it was clear both to the Government and the TUC's General Council that there was significant opposition within the trade union movement to the new incomes policy, an ominous portent of future developments.

As before, the TGWU were the leading opponents, but its antipathy was shared by the Electrical Trades Union. This opposition reflected not only traditional trade union hostility towards incomes policy and governmental "interference" in wage determination in general, but also distaste for the role being ascribed to the TUC's General Council via its incomes policy committee in particular. For many trade unions, interference in free collective bargaining was not rendered any more palatable by virtue of being carried out by the TUC itself.

The Labour government's recourse to incomes policy – with statutory powers now being held in reserve – clearly placed Frank Cousins in an extremely awkward situation. Whilst leader of the TGWU, Cousins had been vociferous in his condemnation of wage restraint and incomes policies when pursued by the previous Conservative governments, and he retained his staunch commitment to free collective bargaining upon becoming a Labour Cabinet Minister. Yet the doctrine of collective (ministerial) responsibility obliged Cousins to support publicly – or at least refrain from criticizing in public – the incomes policies introduced by the Wilson government in 1965. Cousins himself was driven to complain that "I myself disagree with it [the incomes policy] so utterly that I can no longer make a political speech. I can only speak on technological problems". Indeed, at one stage, Cousins declared that: "I think it's time I resigned" (Crossman, 1975: 321, diary entry for 12 September 1965), although Cousins did not resign – on this occasion.

A further attack on the government's incomes policy was launched at the Labour party's annual conference during the last week of September, via a motion moved by Clive Jenkins, leader of the Association of Supervisory Staffs, Executives and Technicians (later to become ASTMS – the Association of Scientific, Technical and Managerial Staffs). Support for the motion was provided by the acting General Secretary of the TGWU, Harry Nichols, who explained that it was not an incomes policy *per se* that he was opposed to, but "a planned incomes policy in an unplanned society".

George Brown's response on behalf of the government was three-fold. First, he insisted that the incomes policy *was* linked to a planned society, precisely because it was being pursued in tandem with the National Plan. Second, Brown attempted to link incomes policy to socialism, claiming that the alternative of free collective bargaining "puts a premium on those, and gives a bonus to those, with great bargaining power". In other words, he claimed: "We have been operating the law of the jungle ourselves while condemning it for every other purpose."

The third dimension of Brown's speech in defence of the government's pay policy was the reiteration that: "We have no intention of supplanting the voluntary system by government action if the former works" (TUC Annual Conference Report 1965: 134).

Yet the caveat "if the present system works" merely stiffened the opposition of unions such as the TGWU, who resented the fact that the Labour government would hold statutory powers "in reserve". In the eyes of those trade unions supporting Jenkins' resolution, not only were they faced with a Labour government pursuing an incomes policy *per se*, they were also being told that if the policy did not succeed on a voluntary basis, then ministers would resort to legislative means to ensure compliance. Clearly, this was totally unacceptable to many of those in the labour movement who remained most committed to free collective bargaining.

What lent the debate (and in particular, Brown's speech on behalf of the government) extra *frisson* was that Frank Cousins was sitting in the conference chamber alongside the TGWU's delegates "seething and burning like a volcano about to erupt . . . unsmiling, staring into the middle distance with [a] look of stony resolution". Meanwhile, from his position on the conference platform, "George Brown glowered down at his Cabinet colleague and the entire seated delegation of the country's largest union. Brown's *own* union" (Goodman, 1979: 468).

Although Jenkins' resolution was defeated by 3.6 million votes to 2.5 million, the vote again illustrated to the government the extent of opposition within the labour movement to incomes policy. Furthermore, the fact that the TGWU was continuing to oppose incomes policy was doubly worrying to the Labour government, for not only was it Britain's largest trade union at the time, it also had a membership which spanned many industries and sectors of the economy, thereby maximizing its potential disruptive power. Compounding ministerial concern was the fact that the AUEW also supported Jenkins' resolution, having supported the government's incomes policy less than a month before at the TUC's annual conference.

If the government had harboured few expectations that the TUC's incomes policy committee would genuinely result in lower wage claims, then its scepticism proved justified. Indeed, the incomes policy committee has been described as a "complete failure", for although it considered more than six hundred pay claims during its first nine months, "it questioned only a handful and had no real effect on the course of any of them". Furthermore, because it only met for one day each month, it sometimes considered up to fifty pay claims in one hour, thereby precluding detailed examination of them on an individual basis (Dorfman, 1973: 138; see also, Lovell and Roberts, 1968: 172–3).

The 1966 wage freeze

The Wilson government was re-elected on 31 March 1966 with its parliamentary majority increased to ninety-six. Yet any honeymoon period was very short-lived, for within weeks of its victory the government was faced with a strike by the National Union of Seamen (NUS). This served further to undermine the already limited confidence of the international financial community in the Labour government's economic programme and the condition of the British economy in general. Indeed, Labour's traditional opponents and critics in the financial community, both at home and abroad, became even more nervous once the government had been re-elected with a sizeable parliamentary majority, for this not only indicated that Labour would now govern for a whole term of Office, it was also assumed that it might be more inclined to implement a radical or redistributive programme of economic and social reform, having previously been restrained due to the narrowness of its majority and the virtual inevitability of another general election.

The strike by the NUS was called in support of a wage claim which vastly exceeded the Labour government's "pay norm". It was not merely the actual cash increase that the NUS was seeking which was deemed incompatible with the existing incomes policy, but also the fact that the NUS was seeking a reduction in the working week from fifty-six hours to forty. However, because seamen would obviously still be on board ship when at sea, the effect of such a reduction in the working week was that any work in excess of the forty hours would constitute overtime, and thus qualify for a higher hourly rate of pay. If seamen continued working fifty-six hours per week, this would mean that they would be entitled to sixteen hours per week at overtime rates, and this alone would increase their earnings greatly in excess of the government's limits.

Given Britain's island position and status as a maritime trading nation, the seamen's strike threatened a particularly serious impact on the British economy, bringing exports and imports to a virtual standstill. Such a strike would have caused concern to any government, but it was especially serious for the recently re-elected Wilson government in view of its urgent need to win the confidence and trust of the international financial community and improve Britain's balance of payments through increasing exports.

The government was therefore determined that the demands of the NUS should be resisted, not only for the sake of the incomes policy itself, but also in the hope that the business community, both at home and overseas, would be suitably impressed by the resolve of a Labour government standing firm against an excessive pay claim, backed by industrial action, by a trade union. This, in turn, ministers hoped, would stabilize the financial markets, and ease the pressure on sterling which had been increased by the seaman's strike.

These considerations also partly account for Wilson's notorious claim that the seaman's strike was, in fact, attributable to the machinations of "a tightly knit group of politically motivated men", namely a handful of communists within the NUS who were pursuing "what is at present the main political and industrial objective of the Communist Party – the destruction of the government's prices and incomes policy" (*House of Commons Debates*, 5th series, Vol. 730, cols. 1612–7).

The seaman's strike served to increase the pressure on sterling on the foreign exchanges, pressure which increased yet further in July, partly in response to the publication of another set of disappointing trade figures, but also because the French Prime Minister, Georges Pompidou, on a visit to London early in the month, intimated that Britain might need to devalue sterling as a precondition of entry into the EEC. His comments were immediately seized upon as an indication that devaluation was imminent, thereby prompting even more frenzied selling of sterling on the foreign currency exchanges. Meanwhile, the Wilson government was coming under increasing pressure from the IMF, OECD, the Treasury, and the new Governor of the Bank of England, Sir Leslie O'Brien, to reduce public expenditure and strengthen its incomes policy.

By this time, most ministers recognized that they could no longer avoid having to choose between deflation or devaluation. Certainly, a number of prominent Cabinet ministers – Tony Benn, Barbara Castle, Anthony Crosland, Richard Crossman and Roy Jenkins – were in favour of devaluation, or, at the very least, permitting sterling to float, whereupon the market, rather than the government itself, would determine the pound's true value. In this stance, they were supported by most of the government's own economic advisers. Further support for devaluation (or floating the pound) was offered by George Brown, who, having originally opposed such a policy, had gradually been "persuaded by my advisers, and by such friends outside as I dared to consult, that the case for devaluation was overwhelming and inevitable" (Brown, 1971: 114).

However, Wilson as Prime Minister, and the Chancellor, James Callaghan, were able to exercise their combined authority and rank within the Cabinet to win over other ministers in support of a deflationary package of measures, coupled with a significant strengthening of the government's incomes policy, which would hopefully obviate the need for devaluation. In rejecting devaluation in favour of deflation, Wilson and Callaghan enjoyed the support of the recently-appointed Governor of the Bank of England, who was "firm on maintaining the parity of sterling", at least, for the immediate future (Wilson, 1971: 252). Even some ministers inclined to "floating" the pound acknowledged that this ought not be carried out in the midst of an economic crisis, but should await more stable economic circumstances.

On 20 July 1966, the day after the Cabinet meeting which approved the deflationary programme, the Government announced the details of its measures, which included stricter controls on hire purchase, higher indirect taxes and postal charges, cuts in overseas expenditure, and reductions in public expenditure. Last, but certainly not least, the government announced a six-month freeze on all forms of income (wages, salaries and income from dividends), to be followed by a further six months of "severe restraint" during which time there would be a "zero norm", with pay rises only permissible if certain productivity criteria were met, or where workers were deemed to be particularly low-paid. This "freeze" was also to apply to prices, but not to profits.

The "freeze" was given statutory effect by virtue of being incorporated into the Prices and Incomes Bill which had already been presented to Parliament for its Second Reading on 14 July. Initially, the Bill was primarily concerned with vesting the Secretary of State for Economic Affairs with statutory powers to refer "excessive" or "unjustified" increases to the National Board of Prices and Incomes, whilst also granting him the power to delay implementation of certain pay or price increases. After the announcement of the government's deflationary package, however, the provisions for the wage freeze were added on to the Prices and Incomes Bill, thus constituting "Part IV" of the legislation.

Given that the trade unions and many left-wing Labour MPs had been opposed – as a matter of principle – to the Prices and Incomes Bill in its original guise, it was inevitable that they would be even more critical of the revised version enshrining the six-month wage freeze and a subsequent period of "severe restraint". Indeed, the introduction of the original Bill had already precipitated the resignation – previously threatened on more than one occasion in preceding months – from the Cabinet of Frank Cousins, who returned to his former post as leader of the TGWU and immediately spearheaded trade union opposition to the Labour government's incomes policy. In his letter of resignation, handed in person to Wilson on 3 July 1966, Cousins placed considerable emphasis on the government's incomes policy, which he insisted was "meaningless", and symptomatic of ministers' approach to wage restraint in general, which was "fundamentally wrong in its conception and approach" (quoted in Goodman, 1979: 495).

Having been invited to 10 Downing Street to discuss his resignation, Cousins continued his criticism of the government's reliance on incomes policies, accusing Wilson of not "standing-up" to his two economic ministers, Brown and Callaghan, the former being a leading exponent of incomes policy, and the latter, Cousins claimed, acting in response to international financial pressures (Goodman, 1979: 495–6). Meanwhile, when Cousins had his final audience with the Queen, to surrender his seals of Office, she asked him for the real reasons behind his resignation: "Because" he replied, "the Government no longer believe in the policies for which they were elected, Ma'am" (quoted in Goodman, 1979: 500).

Having resigned, Cousins returned both to the Government's back-benches *and* to the leadership of the TGWU (although the union's executive insisted that "at the earliest possible moment", Cousins should resign as an MP, in order that he could concentrate full-time on the TGWU's affairs). It immediately became clear that Cousins would be a leading opponent of the government's Prices and Incomes Bill (even before the addition of "Part IV"). Indeed, Cousins introduced a Commons motion, signed by six other TGWU-sponsored Labour MPs, which:

> considers that the present prices and incomes Bill containing penal legislation against the trade unions should be rejected, and that instead, measures should be introduced to improve the incomes of the lower paid workers, to launch a major drive to increase productivity linked with higher wages, to control dividends more effectively, and to set up a system of price controls . . . a system of strict import controls, a strengthening of the controls over overseas capital investment, a drastic reduction of defence expenditure . . . and the extension of public ownership in the basic industries. (*House of Commons Debates*, 5th series, 14 July 1966, col. 1792)

Yet ministers would have been mistaken had they assumed that Cousins himself was dictating the TGWU's policy with regard to the government's incomes policy. The TGWU's Acting Assistant General Secretary whilst Cousins was in the Cabinet, Jack Jones, shared his hostility to the government's resort to wage restraint, particularly when this was to be enforced by legislation. Thus did the introduction of the "wage freeze" lead Jones himself to argue that:

> The legislation will further tilt the balance in favour of . . . employers and further worsen industrial relations at a time when there is a pressing need to tackle the problem of low productivity and inefficiency. The trouble is that the authors of these policies are out of touch with day-to-day industrial life and are unfitted to solve its problems. If they had their way we would have an emasculated trade union movement with little or no influence to bring to bear on behalf of its members . . . weak or tame trade unionism is a positive danger under a Labour or any other Government . . . (Jones, 1986: 178)

Nor was it just the TGWU which was aghast at the Labour government's recourse to a statutory wage freeze. Several other trade unions were opposed to the new incomes policy, as evinced by the fact that at the TUC's annual conference in September, the government's statutory wage freeze was offered "reluctant acquiescence" by the wafer-thin margin of 4,567,000 votes to 4,223,000. Cousins' biographer interpreted such a narrow result as "a moral defeat for the Government and certainly an insufficient majority to convince ministers that they could rely on the trade unions' voluntary acceptance of the freeze" (Goodman, 1979: 518).

The TUC's reluctant acquiescence

Back in July, following the government's announcement that it was introducing, via the Prices and Incomes Bill, a six-month pay freeze, the TUC had immediately embarked upon a series of meetings with the relevant ministers (George Brown, James Callaghan and Ray Gunter). These meetings culminated in an urgent request by George Woodcock, on 25 July (two days before the next meeting of the General Council), that Harold Wilson meet the TUC's economic committee. When he did so, later the same day, it was, Wilson recalled, "a rough meeting", with many of the TUC officials present expressing their antipathy to the government's prices and incomes policy, as well as their doubts about the policy's practicability (doubts which Woodcock himself shared).

Wilson reiterated what Brown and Callaghan had told the TUC in previous days, namely that the government had been left with no alternative in the wake of the seamen's strike, increasing inflationary pressures in the economy, and the problems continuing to beset sterling on the foreign exchanges. However, he also insisted that if the government had not brought forward the new package of measures – including the prices and incomes policy – then the result might well be a rise in unemployment to two million or more (Wilson, 1971: 261). Two days later, the TUC's General Council acquiesced "reluctantly" – by 20 votes to 12 – with the government's statutory wage freeze, a decision which, according to Wilson, immediately helped to stabilize the pound on the foreign exchanges (Wilson, 1971: 262).

The TUC's reluctant acquiescence to the government's wage freeze partly reflected Wilson's success in convincing them that the likely alternative would be record post-war unemployment, but acquiescence was also derived from the expectation that supporting the government in the short-term would enhance the influence and status of the trade unions in the medium and longer-term. Ultimately, the TUC leadership felt that it had little choice but to proffer the government its support, for:

> after the most scrupulous examination of the alternative courses of action

> open to them ... the General Council reached the conclusion that the interests both of trade unionism and of the nation as a whole in the current critical situation, compelled them to acquiesce in the Government's proposal. In taking this decision the General Council understood and indeed shared the distaste with which trade unionists regard a standstill of up to twelve months in their incomes, but they did so in the belief that trade unionists will accept that, at this time, the needs of the nation must necessarily override sectional demands. (TUC Anual Report 1966: 323)

Consternation in the Cabinet

Meanwhile, the recourse to a statutory wage freeze had caused considerable consternation within the Cabinet itself, with Richard Crossman noting that: "As the discussion went on it gradually dawned on more and more of us that this would be impossible to get through Congress or through the Labour party conference" (Crossman, 1975: 591, diary entry for 28 July 1966), whilst Barbara Castle was similarly concerned that the measures would prove unacceptable (to both the TUC, and the Labour party in the country) and unenforceable, because "you could not send hundreds of trade unionists to gaol" if they defaulted on fines imposed under "Part IV" (Castle, 1990: 80, diary entry for 28 July 1966).

On the other hand, whilst supportive of the statutory wage freeze, Wilson nonetheless inclined to the view that the policy should incorporate "loopholes for productivity increases and for the lower-paid" – a view which was opposed by the Home Secretary, Roy Jenkins, partly on the grounds that "loopholes would make a nonsense of the whole thing", and partly because "on the more self-interested ground that my only hope of containing the police, who had an award due, was to have an absolute freeze for everybody" (Jenkins, 1991: 195). To the considerable surprise of several ministers, it was Jenkins' "absolutist" view which prevailed over that of the Prime Minister.

In the context of these discussions, George Brown reiterated the case for devaluation, believing that the government's emphasis on a statutory incomes policy and wage freeze, coupled with a policy of deflation, would not prove sufficient to ameliorate the problems facing the British economy, nor assuage the anxieties of the business and financial communities. Brown was emphatic that "however many times we set back the economy with another round of pointless deflation, we should come back to the need to face devaluation; that one day we should have to devalue, perhaps too late, and with a weakened economy" (Brown, 1971: 115). Indeed, Brown actually tendered his resignation, claiming that "I could not continue making a nonsense of myself and of my Department's policy by agreeing to do further harm to the economic life of the country." However, pressure from Wilson, coupled with a groundswell of support from the government backbenches (illustrated by a letter signed by about a hundred Labour MPs imploring Brown to remain in his post) persuaded Brown to withdraw his resignation, whereupon he found himself responsible for piloting the Prices and Incomes Bill through the House of Commons.

Although Brown was not persuaded of the merits of the government's recourse to a statutory incomes policy (in spite of being formally responsible for introducing the legislation), his decision to remain in the Cabinet was partly derived from concern that his resignation would serve to highlight the divisions over economic strategy within the Cabinet – particularly with regard to devaluation and a statutory incomes policy – and thereby precipitate "a most devastating run on our reserves" (Brown, 1971: 116). Ministerial concern over "Part IV" was also evident amongst many of the government's backbenchers in the House of Commons during the parliamentary debates on the Prices and Incomes Bill, when 27 Labour MPs voted against this part of the legislation.

Nor did the government's problems concerning Party management and backbench support dissipate once the Prices and Incomes Bill become law on 12 August, with "Part IV" becoming effective on 5 October. On 25 October, following a decision by the Newspaper Proprietor's Association to defy the government by awarding print workers a "cost-of-living" pay increase, the government laid before Parliament the Order in Council required to enact the penal clauses of the Prices and Incomes Act. Twenty-eight Labour MPs – including Frank Cousins – abstained, even though a three-line whip had been imposed. Less than a fortnight later, Frank Cousins resigned as an MP, in lieu of his return to the leadership of the TGWU.

Beyond "severe restraint"

Long before the expiry of the six-month wage freeze, ministers were making clear their desire that the subsequent period of "severe restraint" should be followed by reversion to some form of voluntary incomes policy, to commence in July 1967. At one stage, Wilson mooted the idea of a National Dividend, whereby ministers, TUC leaders and employers' representatives would meet to determine what the British economy could afford by way of income allocation each year. Yet pending the introduction of such an institutional innovation (which subsequently failed to materialize), the government made clear its intention of introducing a further prices and incomes policy to succeed the period of "severe restraint".

By this time, though, the Cabinet itself was evincing increasing tension over the type of incomes policy which ought to be pursued. A division emerged between those ministers who favoured the continuation of incomes policy backed by statutory powers held by the government, and those ministers who were convinced that any further incomes policy would only prove successful if it was a voluntary one, based upon self-restraint and administered by the trade unions themselves under the auspices of the TUC.

Those ministers opposed to a statutory incomes policy tended to be those with the closest links with the trade unions, such as George Brown, Ray Gunter – described by another Cabinet Minister as "a traitor within the walls . . . a kind of TUC agent" (Crossman, 1976: 252) – Richard Marsh and Fred Peart. Such ministers evidently paid the closest heed to the trade unions' voluntarist tradition and their concomitant belief in free collective bargaining. The trade unions' stance, meanwhile, was made clear to the government via a number of meetings between ministers and the TUC's Economic Committee during the early months of 1967, on which occasions senior union figures such as Frank Cousins rejected as "entirely unacceptable" the idea of further wage restraint being secured through statutory measures, whilst George Woodcock insisted that an incomes policy would only be effective if it was left to the TUC to administer, without the threat of statutory intervention by the Government (PRO PREM 13/1875, "Meetings between TUC Economic Committee and ministers", 28 February 1967 and 15 March 1967).

Meanwhile, although he did not share the same kind of personal links with the trade unions, Tony Benn also spoke out against the statutory regulation of wages, insisting that no such system initiated by the government "could possibly be practicable or effective". Instead, he suggested that the government ought to place greater emphasis on the regulation of prices than wages, whereby a levy – payable to the Treasury – would be imposed on firms which increased prices in order to underwrite wage increases. Benn suggested if such a system were introduced, then firms would have three options when presented with a wage claim: first, to grant it, but pay the levy if they consequently raised prices, whereupon the Treasury would obtain a new source of revenue to finance public expenditure; secondly, they could finance a pay claim through increased productivity, which the government should surely welcome; thirdly, they could stand firm and resist an "excessive" pay claim, whereupon any consequent strike would be between the trade unions and the employer, rather than embroiling the government itself. Ultimately, Benn argued, "if a firm can give wage increases that don't involve any price increases, there is no reason why the Government should interest itself in that settlement" (PRO PREM 13/1473, Benn to Wilson, 3 February 1967). By contrast, those within the Cabinet whom Crossman described as "middle-class intellectuals" (as opposed to "working-class trade unionists"), such as Barbara Castle, Anthony Crosland, Crossman himself and Patrick Gordon Walker, tended to be in favour of an incomes policy which entailed a statutory component (Crossman, 1976: 230).

One of the most enthusiastic advocates of a further prices and incomes policy, backed by statutory powers, to succeed the period of "severe restraint", was George Brown's successor at the Department of Economic Affairs, Michael Stewart. Indeed, early in 1967 Stewart sought to persuade the Cabinet that the government should embrace a permanent incomes policy, albeit one whereby "statutory powers to enforce it should be subject renewal by Parliament". He further suggested that such powers should only be used after consultation with the parties affected by them, and only if an independent body, possibly the Prices and Incomes Board, decided that their use was justified.

Stewart also proposed that in future, pay increases should be permissible only if they met certain criteria pertaining to productivity, manpower shortages or the amelioration of low-pay. In other words, Stewart suggested that the "underlying principle should be that that no-one was entitled automatically to an annual increase of money income". In seeking to make his proposals more palatable to his Labour colleagues, Stewart also emphasized that "an incomes policy should be part of a general plan to make the distribution of wealth more just" (Stewart, 1980: 194).

At the same time, Wilson's economic adviser, Thomas Balogh, was arguing that as "full employment without an incomes policy is impossible", the government needed to hold "reserve powers . . . in order to deter selfish minorities who otherwise would use their more than average bargaining position to snatch sectional advantages against a patriotic majority" (PRO PREM 13/1875, Balogh to Wilson, 28 February 1967).

Both the proponents and opponents of incomes policy within the Cabinet claimed that their stance was based on a realistic understanding concerning the character of contemporary British trade unionism. The opponents of anything stronger than a voluntary incomes policy were emphatic that statutory wage control was incompatible with the voluntarist traditions of the trade union movement, and its concomitant suspicion of state interference in industrial relations or free collective bargaining. To persevere with a statutory incomes policy, therefore, was to risk alienating the trade unions, whilst also facilitating the transfer of power to the shop-floor, where shop stewards would benefit from the crumbling credibility and authority of the national-level union leaders.

By contrast, those Labour ministers most inclined towards some form of statutory incomes policy believed that it was precisely the voluntarist character of Britain's trade unions which rendered them unable or unwilling to exercise the degree of restraint which the government required for the successful operation of its incomes policy; ministers had relied upon voluntary wage restraint in the past, but the unions had failed to repay the trust placed in them by the government. Hence the apparent need for any incomes policy to incorporate a statutory element.

For their part, the trade unions, or, rather, the TUC, suspected that even a voluntary incomes policy would still be part of a deflationary programme, rather than being linked to "planned growth" as originally intended. Furthermore, the TUC was uneasy that a voluntary incomes policy would entail the delegation of responsibility for administering the policy to the TUC's General Council itself. Thus did the General Council insist, in November 1966, that:

> It is no more desirable or practicable for the TUC to attempt detailed control of wage determination at all levels than it is for the government. Nor does it imply that the aim would be to find an alternative means of perpetuating the policy of overall restraint which has too often characterized the approach of governments in recent years. (TUC Annual Report 1967: 323)

Although the TUC's General Council was willing to reactivate its own incomes policy committee (which had been suspended during the wage freeze) in order to "vet" the wage claims of affiliated trade unions, it continued to view incomes policy in the context of a longer-term "planned growth" of the economy, rather than the type of short-term deflationary measure that governments invariably deployed it for.

Government and unions drift apart

Consequently, by the spring of 1967, the TUC and the Wilson government – or, rather, those Cabinet ministers who favoured some form of statutory incomes policy – appeared to be drifting further apart with regard to future incomes policies. At a conference of executives from trade unions affiliated to the TUC, held in March 1967, the General Council declared that it would regard as "compatible with incomes policy claims for increases of up to £1.00 a week in national minimum rates which were less than £14.00 a week". At the same time, the General Council also insisted that any incomes policy "would have to have regard to the need to reward the acquisition of skills and the acceptance of responsibility", although it was immediately suggested that trade unions "should not interpret this as automatically justifying claims on the basis of traditional relativities" (TUC Annual Report 1967: 329). Meanwhile, The TUC's General Secretary insisted that:

> above all in this business we need flexibility. We need – I am not ashamed of the phrase at all – room for those shoddy, shabby, dirty compromises which are the essence of practical people trying to do a job. We do not rule out any . . . considerations . . . cost of living, comparability, the importance of the need to maintain proper differentials for skill and so on. (TUC Annual Report 1967: 539)

Faced with constant division within the Cabinet over incomes policy, hostility from a significant number of Labour backbenchers (particularly those on the Tribunite Left or with trade union sponsorship), and opposition from many trade unions themselves, it is not surprising that Wilson occasionally plumbed the depths of despair. On one occasion, he suggested that if the unions would not accept an incomes policy backed by statutory powers, then the government should cut public expenditure, on the grounds that: "If they take too much in real wages, we shall have to cut their schools, their hospitals and housing" (Crossman, 1976: 280, diary entry for 16 March 1967); while just a week later, he was half-heartedly ruminating on the possibilty of a "divorce" between the Labour party and the trade unions (Crossman, 1976: 287, diary entry for 22 March 1967).

When the government did publish its White Paper outlining the incomes policy to follow the period of "severe restraint", it was made clear that there was to be no specified pay norm, due to ministerial concern that any such figure was invariably viewed by the trade unions as the minimum increase to which they were entitled. Instead, wage increases were to be linked to a range of criteria similar to those stipulated by the 1965 incomes policy, with the government insisting that no trade union could assume that its members would automatically be entitled to a wage increase during the twelve months following the expiry of the period of "severe restraint". Furthermore, the White Paper revealed that the government intended to reserve the right to delay a wage increase for up to one month whilst ministers considered its merits or justifications, whereupon a further three-month delay might be imposed if the government considered that the increase ought to be examined by the National Board of Prices and Incomes. At the end of its period of deliberation, the Board itself would be entitled to impose a three-month deferment of the award, thus yielding a total period of delay of seven months in the case of apparently excessive or unwarranted pay increases (Department of Economic Affairs, 1967).

Ministers were thus extremely disappointed, though perhaps not surprised, when the TUC's annual conference in September supported (against the advice of the General Council) by 4,883,000 votes to 3,502,000, a motion critical of governmental interference in collective bargaining. These ministers did glean some comfort a few weeks later, though, when delegates at the Labour party's own annual conference voted 3,860,000 to 2,535,000 *against* a motion condemning the Wilson government's incomes policy for being detrimental to the "best interests of trade unionists and lower income groups" (Labour Party Annual Conference Report 1967: 163–201).

Any pleasure derived by ministers from such support was to prove short-lived however. After more than three years' resistance, the government finally, on 18 November 1967, devalued the pound by 14.3 per cent, yielding a reduction in sterling's parity with the dollar from $2.80 to $2.40. This in turn exacerbated the growing tension between the Labour government and the trade unions, for the two "sides" drew different conclusions about the implications of devaluation for economic strategy, particularly with regard to incomes policy.

Wilson and his ministerial colleagues were adamant that far from permitting a relaxation of economic policy, it was now more essential than ever to sustain the Labour government's strategy, in order that the potential benefits of devaluation were fully realized, not least of these being cheaper exports and a marked improvement in Britain's balance of payments (Labour Party Archives, Re.192/September 1967). Harold Wilson and George Brown therefore met the leadership of the TUC two days after devaluation to inform them that the government's immediate priority was to restrain domestic demand in order to promote an export drive. At the same time, the TUC was warned that whilst devaluation would result in price increases of up to 3 per cent, the trade unions should not insist on corresponding wage increases. In short, Wilson and Brown sought to persuade the trade unions that a short-term reduction in their members' living standards would provide the basis for higher wages and increased living standards in the longer-term, derived in part from a period of export-led growth.

Thus did the government proceed with incomes policies regardless of the trade unions' lack of support. Determined to take full advantage of the apparent window of opportunity afforded by devaluation, and eager to convince the international financial community that Britain was now in a position finally to conquer its economic problems, the Wilson government declared (via the Budget on 19 March 1968) that with immediate effect, pay increases for the next eighteen months would be limited to a maximum of 3.5 per cent per annum. Exceptions were to be permitted in accordance with the four criteria originally enshrined in the 1965 White Paper, namely: a significant increase in productivity; to assist the re-allocation of labour; exceptionally low pay; and a deterioration in pay compared to another group of workers undertaking similar work. However, it was clear that the government now saw increased productivity as the primary justification for exceeding the 3.5 per cent pay limit during the next eighteen months.

Proposing to monitor wage increases at local level

Prior to the formal announcement of this limit, the Cabinet Committee responsible for preparing the incomes policy – chaired by Harold Wilson, and consisting also of Anthony Crosland, Ray Gunter, Roy Jenkins and Peter Shore – had intended that wage increases would be monitored not just at national level, as was usually the case, but this time at plant and factory level too. This proposal, which was very much associated with Jenkins and Shore, caused considerable consternation when it was discussed by the full Cabinet at the end of February and beginning of March 1968, with a number of ministers, most notably George Brown, James Callaghan, Richard Crossman, Richard Marsh and Tony Greenwood insisting that control of wages at plant and factory level was not feasible (Castle, 1990: 191–5, diary entries for 29 February, 5 March and 7 March 1968).

Jenkins, however, was adamant that the controls were absolutely essential, warning that if the government failed to win back the confidence of the international financial community, then further devaluation was likely within three months, which would probably destroy the government completely. Indeed, Jenkins' attack on his critics in the government was "so terrifying that it was not recorded in the Cabinet minutes". Yet in spite of the vigour of Jenkins' exposition, and the dire warnings contained therein, "no member of the Cabinet could understand the proposal that wage decisions at plant level should be checked", whereupon Peter Shore – who "collapsed" when cross-examined about the proposal – was instructed to prepare an alternative scheme for the following week's Cabinet meeting (Crossman, 1976: 695, diary entry for 7 March 1968). Barbara Castle was among several ministers who were bemused that "Peter just doesn't seem to have taken in the impossibility for the Government itself, through a mass of civil servants, to vet thousands of wage increases at plant level" (Castle, 1990: 195: diary entry for 7 March 1968).

Aubrey Jones, chairman of the National Board of Prices and Incomes, was also hostile to the Jenkins–Shore proposal on the grounds that it was: "Wholly . . . absolutely impractical to have any control at plant level" (Crossman, 1976: 693, diary entry for 6 March 1968). Consequently, the proposal for control of wage increases at plant and factory level was abandoned by Shore at the next Cabinet meeting, leading Barbara Castle to conclude that "he was weakening . . . [as are] a number of members of the Cabinet" (Castle, 1990: 194, diary entry for 7 March 1968).

Another ministerial debate concerned the duration of the next incomes policy. Shore had originally recommended that it should operate from July 1968 to October 1970, but Wilson pointed out that this would take the government right up to the next general election, whereupon it would either have to try formulating a new incomes policy at a politically sensitive time, or explain why it was suddenly abandoning incomes policies with an election in the offing (the implication being that the government would be charged by its opponents either with cowardice or opportunism). Wilson therefore suggested that the policy should run for eighteen months, until the end of 1969 – a suggestion approved by the full Cabinet.

Jenkins nonetheless reiterated the need for a tough incomes policy in order to impress international financiers and the currency markets, thereby prompting Richard Crossman to enquire of the Chancellor:

> I can see that if you have a tough policy it will help you with the bankers for these critical next three months, but it may make the economy unworkable later on and it may precipitate a strike which ruins the Labour government. Which is the greater risk to you – the breakdown in the incomes policy in the next twelve months or a run on the pound in the next three?

Jenkins' reply was: "A run on the pound in the next three", although Crossman nonetheless suspected that at heart, Jenkins:

> Doesn't believe in a prices and incomes policy and he's rather have a free-for-all, like the strongish group in the Cabinet headed by Dick Marsh who've been routing against a statutory policy week in and week out. But so grave is the immediate threat to sterling that he [Jenkins] has to have a strong prices and incomes policy even if it causes catastrophe in a year's time. (Crossman, 1976: 720–21, diary entry for 14 March 1968).

In fact, Barbara Castle had noted after the previous week's Cabinet meeting that Jenkins "had some scepticism about it [the incomes policy] in the long term", but was convinced that for the immediate future, there was no alternative. "If we are not seen to deal strongly with wages we can't avoid a second devaluation, world monetary confusion and the destruction of this Government" (Castle, 1990: 195, diary entry for 7 March 1968).

It was partly to appease the financial community that the maximum of 3.5 per cent was specified for the new incomes policy, for the Cabinet had originally contemplated a figure of 4 per cent – mainly to assist the low paid – but it was feared that a higher limit might be interpreted by the City and overseas holders of sterling as indicative of the government's weakening resolve.

Peter Shore was also concerned that a clearer definition was needed as to which groups of workers were genuinely deemed to be exceptionally low paid, for he suspected that any exceptions permitted for such workers would be exploited by other workers whose real motive was to maintain their differentials. To overcome this problem, he suggested – to widespread agreement amongst his ministerial colleagues – that the new 3.5 per cent pay limit should be accompanied by improvements in the social wage, particularly family allowances. The Cabinet also agreed that consideration should be given to the introduction of a national minimum wage, "but that there should be no public reference to it" nor any discussion of it with the trade unions (although nothing more was heard about this particular initiative) (PRO CAB 128/43, 22nd conclusions, 18 March 1968 and 23rd conclusions, 21 March 1968; see also Labour Party Archives, Re.418/February 1969).

In fact, the notion of a National Minimum Wage had already been considered briefly elsewhere in the Labour party by this time, but dismissed due to the envisaged problems of agreeing on a specific figure, and then having to engage in potentially protracted negotiations every year over the rate at which it needed to be increased. Furthermore, it was also pointed out that the figure at which any National Minimum Wage was established would probably prove inflationary, and thereby "likely to contribute to its downfall", whilst simultaneously alienating those workers whose incomes were just above the level of a minimum wage (Labour Party Archives, Re.123/April 1967).

Opposition increases in the labour movement

In order to ensure adherence to the 3.5 per cent limit, the Wilson government declared that legislation would be introduced empowering it to defer a pay (or price) increase for up to twelve months, as compared to the existing seven-month maximum period of delay. The ensuing Prices and Incomes Bill (1968) reached the statute book in July, but only after suffering considerable criticism from a sizeable minority of Labour backbenchers.

Most of these Labour opponents of the Bill were on the left of the party, and objected in particular to the implication that the wage levels and pay increases of ordinary working people were largely responsible for Britain's economic problems. Following on from this, a number of left-wing Labour MPs were aggrieved that whilst ministers were seeking to regulate wages, there was no initiative to control the economy in general, thereby ensuring that whilst wages were to be constrained – by statutory means – capitalism itself was to remain unfettered (see, for example: Ian Mikardo, *HC Debates* 5th series, Vol. 765, col. 377 and Vol. 767, cols. 544–5; Mikardo, 1988: 176; Stan Orme, *House of Common Debates* 5th series, Vol. 765, cols. 354–63).

Indeed, such was the scale of hostility amongst such MPs that at Report Stage, an amendment tabled by the TGWU-sponsored Labour

MP, Trevor Park, calling for the deletion of penal powers over incomes (but not prices), was supported by 23 Labour MPs, whilst at least twenty abstained, thus causing the government's majority to fall to 18 (*House of Commons Debates*, 5th series, Vol. 767, cols. 343–50; *The Times*, 26 June 1968: *Financial Times*, 27 June 1968. Of the 23 "rebels", "almost all . . . were Tribune Group members" (Panitch, 1976: 158), again indicating the extent to which opposition to incomes policies, particularly those enshrining penal powers, emanated from the left of the Labour party, and from trade union-sponsored MPs.

Meanwhile, a less than fraternal meeting of the parliamentary Labour party, on 8 May, heard Roy Hughes complain of the conflicting loyalties which prices and incomes legislation was engendering amongst trade union-sponsored MPs, and which was having a highly damaging effect on relations between the Labour party and the trade unions. Manny Shinwell, meanwhile, warned that if he had to choose between saving the Labour goverment *or* the Labour party, he would choose the latter. Certainly, the backbench opponents of incomes policies shared Norman Atkinson's concern that through continued wage restraint, the Labour government appeared to be siding with employers against workers. Similar complaints were expressed at the following week's meeting of the parliamentary Labour party, when 42 MPs voted *against* a motion in support of the Wilson government's prices and incomes legislation.

The criticisms of the government's latest incomes policy which emanated from the Labour backbenches in Parliament were strongly echoed by the trade union movement outside. Whilst the trade unions had been generally supportive of the Wilson government with regard to devaluation, they were far less enamoured with the continued "jam tomorrow" rhetoric of Wilson and Brown; wage restraint today in lieu of improved living standards in years to come. As such, early in 1968, whilst the Chancellor was preparing his Budget, the TUC called for a programme of economic expansion intended to secure an annual growth rate of 6 per cent, which would in turn facilitate a wage "norm" of 5 per cent. Indeed, the TUC urged affiliated trade unions to seek wage increases of about 14 shillings (this constituting about 5 per cent of average earnings at the time), thereby ensuring that the greatest beneficiaries of this "policy" would be the low-paid, particularly as they would also be the hardest hit by the 3 per cent increase in the cost-of-living caused by devaluation. However, the TUC insisted that this proposed 5 per cent "norm" should be pursued on a voluntary basis by the trade union movement, rather than be imposed by the government.

Even if trade union leaders and the TUC's General Council had been more sympathetic to the government's demands for continued wage restraint via further incomes policies, the ordinary rank-and-file members of many trade unions were becoming extremely impatient with repeated ministerial attempts at holding down their wages. Thus did Frank Cousins declare at the TUC's 1968 annual conference that irrespective of "what political background the government has, it cannot get involved in the detail of industrial negotiation". He therefore implored ministers "to keep out before they destroy not only themselves, but us" (TUC Annual Report 1968: 555–6).

Cousins' stance was echoed by the recently elected leader of the AUEW, Hugh Scanlon, when he declared that the Wilson government's approach to wage restraint was merely "a policy on the traditional Tory lines, committed and perpetuated with the full approval of the Treasury" (TUC Annual Report 1968: 611). Delegates then voted by 7,746,000 votes to 1,022,000 against all statutory restraints on collective bargaining, whilst a subsequent motion recommending a voluntary incomes policy to be administered by the TUC itself was approved by a mere 34,000 votes.

The Wilson government desperately sought to defend its stance at the Labour party's own annual conference a few weeks later, where Barbara Castle, recently appointed as Secretary of State at the newly formed Department of Employment and Productivity (which replaced the Ministry of Labour), insisted that ministers had been searching for "something better than crude industrial power politics, whether practised by industrial tycoons or trade unions". In so doing, she warned delegates that if the labour movement destroyed the government's incomes policy without "being clear [about] what you put in its place, then you will share a very heavy responsibility" (Labour Party Annual Conference Report 1968: 152). Castle's plea was to no avail; delegates proceeded to vote 5,098,000 to 1,124,000 against the government's incomes policy. Consequently. with opinion inside the labour movement hardening against incomes policy, Wilson and Castle decided to embark upon a programme of industrial relations reform, with a view to tackling trade union irresponsibility, as manifested in unofficial strikes and allegedly excessive wage claims.

In Place of Strife

Back in March 1965, the Labour government had appointed a Royal Commission on Trade Unions and Employers' Associations (although it was universally recognized that the primary focus was to be on the unions themselves), its brief being:

> to consider relations between managements and employees and the role of trade unions and employers' associations in promoting the interests of

> their members and in accelerating the social and economic advance of the nation, with particular reference to the law affecting the activities of these bodies.

A major reason for launching such an inquiry was the growing political concern over the incidence of unofficial strikes in British industry (such strikes accounting for more than 90% of all industrial stoppages), a phenomena which had vexed the previous Conservative government, and subsequently caused considerable concern to the new Labour government. As the ensuing Report, published in 1968, made clear, there were significant implications for incomes policies, for it was noted that:

> Britain now has two systems of industrial relations. The one is the formal system embodied in the official institutions. The other is the informal system created by the actual behaviour of trade unions and employers" associations, of managers, shop stewards and workers. (Royal Commission, 1968: 12)

These "two systems", it was explained, were in conflict, because: "The informal system undermines the regulative effect of industry-wide agreements. The gap between industry-wide agreed rates and actual earnings continues to grow." However, the Report was quick to emphasize that: "Any suggestion that conflict between the two systems can be resolved by forcing the informal system to comply with the assumptions of the formal system should be set aside. Reality cannot be forced to comply with pretences" (Royal Commission, 1968: 36).

Herein lay a key explanation for the repeated failure of incomes policies to secure lower wage settlements and restrain increases in earnings. Whatever pay agreements might be entered into by trade union leaders, employers and government ministers at national level, these were invariably exceeded by agreements reached at local level, particularly when shop stewards invoked (unofficial) strike action. Hence the phenomenon of "wage drift", whereby actual, overall earnings increased in excess of official rates of pay determined at national level.

Paradoxically, incomes policies served to compound the problem, for the routine involvement of senior trade union leaders in negotiations with employers and Cabinet ministers merely reinforced the impression amongst employees at plant or factory-floor level that their union leadership was growing ever more remote and out of touch, and failing in their task of securing higher wages. Into the ensuing vacuum stepped shop stewards, who then secured the support of the work-force both by their proximity and visibility, and more importantly, their success in securing higher wage increases at local level than those agreed by the unions' senior leaders in London.

The CBI, in its written evidence to the Royal Commission, had emphasized precisely this point, insisting that plant or local-level pay bargaining "if widely resorted to, makes impossible any national planning with regard to incomes: that in conditions of full employment it cannot be other than inflationary; . . . that it increases the scope for unofficial strikes . . . and that it is calculated to weaken the organization of trade unions and employers" associations" (quoted in Royal Commission, 1968: 52).

The Donovan Report itself subsequently endorsed this perspective when it declared that:

> Incomes policy must continue to be a lame and faltering exercise so long as it consists in the planning of industry-wide agreements, most of which exercise an inadequate control over pay. So long as work-place bargaining remains informal, autonomous and fragmented, the drift of earnings away from rates of pay cannot be brought under control. (Royal Commission, 1968: 53)

Yet the Donovan Report was "convinced that incomes policies can make a contribution of outstanding importance to the economic growth of this country and a more ordered system of industrial relations", and therefore insisted that "any proposals which we make for the reform of industrial relations should assist an incomes policy to work effectively" (Royal Commission, 1968: 52).

However, the proposals enshrined in the Donovan Report were a serious disappointment to Harold Wilson and Barbara Castle. The Donovan Report shied away from recommending any significant legislative reforms, preferring instead to strengthen, as far as possible, the existing voluntarist system which had become established during the course of the twentieth century. For example, the Donovan Report not only declined to recommend that collective agreements between employers and trade unions should be legally binding, it also refrained from advocating strike ballots and "cooling-off" periods prior to industrial action. It also rejected the option of legislation to outlaw unofficial strikes, claiming that "the law could not in any circumstances assist in the reduction of unofficial strikes. It cannot do so in this country today – this is the point. To take steps in this direction today would not only be useless but harmful".

The caution which characterized the Donovan Report was widely seen to reflect the influence of two particular "groups" represented on the Royal Commission, namely the trade unions themselves, in the guise of the TUC's General Secretary George Woodcock, and the "Oxford school" of academics, personified on the Royal Commission by Hugh Clegg and Otto Kahn-Freund. Both "groups" favoured the voluntarist system, whereby the state and the law were kept out of industrial relations as far as practicably possible, thereby enabling trade unions and management to determine matters pertaining to pay and conditions free from political or judicial interference. For the trade unions themselves, of course, this was the essence of free collective bargaining.

The disappointment felt by Wilson and Castle over the timidity of the Donovan Report and its recommendations was due in large part to their original expectation that the Royal Commission would advocate a number of radical proposals, whereupon the government could "enact more modest proposals as an acceptable compromise" with the trade unions (Ponting, 1990: 352). However, the modesty of the proposals enshrined in the Donovan Report was such that virtually any recommendations which the Government subsequently put forward would appear radical in contrast and thus antagonize the trade unions.

Yet Harold Wilson was adamant that "the confessed failure of the [Donovan] Commission to find any short-term remedy for unofficial strikes could not be accepted" (Wilson, 1971: 591). What also rendered this "confessed failure" unacceptable to Wilson was the fact that at this time, the Conservative party was itself advocating a new legal framework for Britain's industrial relations, in which curbs would be placed on unofficial strike action, and collective agreements might be rendered legally binding. Wilson was acutely aware that the Conservative's proposals, as outlined in a document entitled *Fair Deal at Work* (discussed in chapter 5), were likely to prove electorally popular, thereby making it essential that the Labour government could put forward its own programme of industrial relations reform. He also assumed that the trade unions would prove rather more amenable to reform proposals which emanated from the Labour party than anything proposed by the Conservatives.

Consequently, in 1969, a White Paper entitled *In Place of Strife* was published, in which the government (or, rather, Barbara Castle, backed by Wilson) proposed a significant and systematic reform of industrial relations. In particular, the White Paper recommended that the Secretary of State for Employment be empowered to instruct a trade union to conduct a strike ballot, whilst also being entitled to impose a four-week "cooling-off" period when an unofficial strike was considered to be potentially damaging to the economic well-being of the country. Furthermore, it was suggested that a Commission for Industrial Relations be established, which would have the statutory power to impose fines on trade unionists or other workers who persisted with unofficial strike action after they had been ordered to desist.

Opposition from the trade unions was to be expected; what Wilson and Castle did not fully anticipate was the degree of opposition which *In Place of Strife* provoked within the Labour party, both at Cabinet level and on the backbenches. Wilson had envisaged that *In Place of Strife* would require just one meeting of the full Cabinet in order to be approved prior to being published, and then presented to Parliament. In fact, four Cabinet meetings were required, the first of these lasting all day. What these meetings reveal was that there were actually two "factions" within the Cabinet opposing *In Place of Strife*, albeit for different reasons (Ponting, 1990: 355).

One "faction", largely comprised of ministers with strong trade union backgrounds or links, was opposed to *In Place of Strife* as matter of principle, the argument being reiterated that the voluntarist approach should continue to be upheld, and that interference in industrial relations and trade unionism by government or the law would prove unacceptable to the unions and thus unworkable in practice. Callaghan insisted that penal sanctions against the trade unions would prove "futile and harmful", a perspective shared by Judith Hart, Fred Lee, Richard Marsh, and Roy Mason (Castle, 1990: 294, diary entry for 3 January 1969). Callaghan recalls that:

> From the moment I set eyes on it I knew such a proposal, which ran counter to the whole history of the trade union movement . . . could not succeed. Barbara galloped ahead with all the reckless gallantry of the Light Brigade at Balaclava.

Callaghan in particular advanced three specific objections to the "punitive" proposals enshrined in *In Place of Strife*. First, he insisted that the proposed legal sanctions would not stop unofficial strikes, and would thus prove ineffective. Secondly, they would not get through Parliament, due to opposition within the parliamentary Labour party. Thirdly, they would create serious tensions between the Labour government and the trade unions at a time when the morale of the labour movement was already low, in the context of successive incomes policies (Callaghan, 1987: 274).

The second "faction" – led by Richard Crossman and Roy Jenkins – actually endorsed the philosophy and contents of *In Place of Strife*, but believed that Castle's tactics were wrong, namely the publication of a White Paper in January whose legislative proposals would not be introduced until the new parliamentary session in the autumn. It was argued that this would provide the trade unions with the best part of a year during which to develop a campaign and mobilize the labour movement against *In Place of Strife*. Jenkins told Castle that he supported her proposals "only . . . on the understanding that we should ACT . . . at once" by introducing "a short interim Bill", an approach endorsed by Crossman (Castle, 1990: 295, diary entry for 3 January 1969).

Castle was initially opposed to such an interim measure, fearing that it would focus attention on the penal elements, and thereby further alienate the trade unions. Indeed, she was acutely aware that *In Place of*

Strife itself "may be the political end of me with our own people. I'm taking a terrific gamble, and there is absolutely no certainty that it will pay off". Castle's "only comfort is that I am proposing something I believe in" (Castle, 1990: 296, diary entry for 7 January 1969). Certainly, opposition within the parliamentary Labour party was such that after a Commons debate on *In Place of Strife* in March 1969, fifty Labour MPs voted against the government, whilst a further forty abstained, these dissentients and abstainers being "more than we had anticipated" (Castle, 1990: 310, diary entry for 3 March 1969).

A short Industrial Relations Bill

Undeterred, Wilson and Castle decided to proceed with the introduction of a short Industrial Relations Bill – a prelude to more substantive legislation to follow later in the year – in spite of Castle's strong objections to such a measure when it had been proposed in Cabinet by Jenkins and Crossman a couple of months earlier. This short Industrial Relations Bill comprised two main measures. First, when the TUC was unable to resolve an inter-union dispute, the Secretary of State for Employment would be entitled to impose a settlement, based upon recommendations made by the proposed Commission on Industrial Relations. Refusal to abide by the Employment Secretary's instructions would leave the trade union concerned liable to financial penalties. Secondly, the short Industrial Relations Bill was to grant the Employment Secretary with the power to order a twenty-eight day "cooling-off" period with regard to unofficial strikes. Again, refusal to comply would result in the imposition of fines.

Significantly, the imminent introduction of this "short" Industrial Relations Bill was announced not by Castle or Wilson, but by the Chancellor, Roy Jenkins, in his Budget statement on 15 April 1969. This was interpreted by some as an indication that the Bill's real purpose was not so much to secure a genuine improvement in industrial relations, but to persuade the financial markets and the City that a Labour government was prepared to be tough against the trade unions to compensate for the deficiencies of its incomes policies.

Once again, Wilson and Castle found themselves subject to widespread and vehement opposition, from both the trade unions and large sections of the Labour party. Initially, Wilson refused to back down, insisting that the legislation could only be abandoned if the trade unions were able to convince him that they would themselves deal effectively with inter-union disputes and unofficial strikes. With the TUC unable to offer the necessary assurances, Wilson resolved to proceed with the Industrial Relations Bill, declaring it to be "essential to this

Government's continuance in Office" (quoted in Jenkins, 1970: 134).

Yet Wilson and Castle were still unable to elicit sufficient support from their parliamentary and Cabinet colleagues, to the extent that in June, Wilson was finally compelled to abandon the Industrial Relations Bill in return for a "solemn and binding" commitment by the TUC's General Council that it would assume responsibility for intervening in serious unofficial industrial action by affiliated unions. This climb-down by Wilson undoubtedly prevented further splits both between the Labour party and the trade unions, and also within the parliamentary Labour party, but it also meant that the problems concerning incomes policies remained unresolved.

Facing up to futility

Indeed, during the course of 1969, the Labour government itself became increasingly disillusioned with incomes policies, partly because of the opposition being engendered within the trade unions and on the party's backbenches, but also because of growing doubts about the efficacy of incomes policy with regard to securing wage restraint. A report published by the National Board of Prices and Incomes the previous year had suggested that the government's incomes policies had only made a difference of about 1 per cent *vis-à-vis* increases in earnings since 1965 (National Board for Prices and Incomes, 1968), which finally persuaded many ministers that "it wasn't worth all the effort and disputes that it generated" (Ponting, 1990: 377).

Yet the abandonment of the Industrial Relations Bill meant that during its final year in Office, the Labour government was left with neither industrial relations reform nor an effective incomes policy. The Cabinet had already decided that when the statutory element in its current incomes policy ended in December 1969, it would not be renewed, but that instead powers would be retained merely to defer pay increases for up to four months pending investigation by the National Board of Prices and Incomes.

Furthermore, a White Paper published in December 1969 announced that during the following year, pay increases should be confined to a range of 2.5–4.5 per cent, although this "norm" could be exceeded in exceptional instances, most notably in industries with a high proportion of low-paid workers, and where significant increases in productivity were achieved. It was also proposed that comparability criteria be deployed more extensively between the public and private sectors in order to tackle low pay amongst the those employed in the former.

The specification of a 2.5–4.5 per cent norm reflected the divisions which existed in the Cabinet over the next phase of incomes policy. The

Chancellor, Roy Jenkins, had originally urged a pay limit of 3.5 per cent, but Barbara Castle insisted that this was "utterly unrealistic", and backed by Richard Crossman and Peter Shore, proposed "a realistic range of 2.5–5 per cent". With Jenkins baulking at an upper limit as high as 5 per cent, it was agreed that a range of 2.5–4.5 per cent be adopted for pay deals during 1970 (Castle, 1990: 366–7, diary entries for 17 November and 20 November).

Yet by this time, with various groups of workers seeking "excessive" pay increases, and very few price increases being blocked by the National Board of Prices and Incomes, there was a growing recognition within the Cabinet that to all intents and purposes, "the prices and incomes policy is in fact in ruins" (Crossman, 1977: 654, diary entry for 24 September 1969), and was seriously undermining the strength and unity of the Labour party (Labour Party Archives, Re.418/February 1969).

Certainly, as table 4.1 indicates, weekly earnings in 1968 had increased overall by 7.8 per cent, rising to 8.1 per cent the following year. This upward trajectory accelerated during 1970, reflecting the breakdown of the Labour government's incomes policy towards the end of 1969, when weekly earnings rose by 13.5 per cent. Indeed, one commentator has suggested that the increase in earnings during 1968 and 1969 was broadly similar to what it would probably have been in the absence of an incomes policy (Fels, 1972: 34–8).

Table 4.1 *Increases in prices and incomes, 1964–1970* (in percentage)

	Increase in weekly earnings	Increase in retail price index
1964	8.3	3.2
1965	8.5	4.8
1966	4.2	3.9
1967	5.8	2.5
1968	7.8	4.7
1969	8.1	5.4
1970	13.5	6.4
Average	8.0	4.4

Source: The Treasury, *Economic Trends.*

Prices, too, continued to rise during the same period, albeit not to the same degree, the retail price index increasing from 4.7 per cent in 1968 to 6.4 per cent in 1970. Meanwhile, taking the 1964–70 period as a whole, it is clear that whilst prices rose by an average of 4.4 per cent, earnings increased by 8 per cent on average.

Given the upward movement of earnings during the latter half of the

1960s, very few commentators have viewed the Labour governments' incomes policies as a notable success. One writer has observed that with regard to incomes policy: "The Wilson years . . . ended in failure as wage-push inflation began to threaten the economic gains achieved by the 1967 devaluation" and "demands for wage restraint in the wider interest of resolving the underlying crisis of the British economy had come into conflict with the fragmented character of so much of the country's wage bargaining system" (Taylor, 1993: 172; see also Taylor, 1982: 201).

Jones, meanwhile, suggests that the results of the Labour governments' attempts at labour market intervention "can hardly be described as satisfactory", bequeathing as they did "a legacy of rising unemployment, a wage explosion and an increasingly militant and unpopular trade union movement acutely sensitive to the most minor infringement upon the process of free collective bargaining" (Jones, 1987: 81–2).

As Towers explains, Labour's incomes policies were "always trying to operate 'against the tide' and alongside repeated packages of deflationary measures", whilst at the same time the "key problem of wage drift and shop floor control of earnings . . . was not effectively tackled: too much emphasis was placed on aggregate norms". Nonetheless, Towers does concede that "in spite of everything, the policy may have contributed towards dampening of the course of pay and price inflation (Towers, 1978: 13–14).

However, there is little evidence or agreement that the Labour governments' incomes policies succeeded in significantly enhancing productivity or eradicating poverty. The fact that earnings increased steadily during the 1964–70 period appears to have been in spite of, rather than because of, the productivity criteria enshrined in the various incomes policies, with some commentators observing that "in spite of the . . . conditions which the NBPI attempted to lay down, these were very frequently not observed". Indeed, during this period "the surveillance of the NBPI was weakened by insufficient and inadequate references, and productivity bargains became one of the main routes by which wage awards evaded control" (Blackaby, 1978: 396), and "a means to drive a coach and horses through the policy" (Jones, 1987: 83).

For example, according to a retrospective survey of 24 "productivity deals" reached under the Labour government's incomes policies, over half were deemed dubious or defective (Clegg, 1971: 38). Furthermore, local or plant-level productivity deals (genuine or otherwise) compounded the problem of "wage drift" with actual earnings increasing at a higher rate than envisaged in the government's various pay "norms".

Nor were the Labour governments' incomes policies any more successful in tackling poverty and low pay, in spite of their formal provisions for exemptions and exceptions *vis-à-vis* those earning the lowest wages (see, for example; Hyman and Brough, 1975: 101–7; Dean, 1978:

40–8; Towers, 1978: 25). Indeed, whereas the top 10 per cent of manual workers saw their gross weekly earnings (as a percentage of the median) increase from 143.9 per cent in 1965 to 147.2 per cent by 1970, the bottom 10 per cent of wage earners experienced a decline from 69.7 per cent to 67.3 per cent during the same period (Blackaby, 1978: 395; see also Field, 1975: 689).

A number of factors seem to account for the apparent failure of the 1964–70 Labour governments' incomes policies to eradicate poverty. First, although various incomes policies enshrined special provisions for productivity deals *and* more generous pay increases for the low paid, it would appear that for both the government and the National Board of Prices and Incomes, it was productivity which was viewed as the most important criterion, with pledges to the low-paid somewhat symbolic and rhetorical. Certainly, it has been suggested that "The productivity goal held sway", with the Board evincing "a general tendency to regard low pay as a very subordinate element in incomes policy" (Hyman and Brough, 1975: 102–3; see also Fels, 1972: 132).

Secondly, many of those on the lowest incomes were engaged in occupations or unskilled work where it was particularly difficult to achieve notable improvements in productivity. Conversely, those most capable of attaining greater output were generally skilled workers who already enjoyed higher wages. In this context, linking pay increases to higher productivity often served to widen differentials and deepen inequalities within the working class (Labour Party Archives, Re.418/February 1969; Labour Party Archives, Re.437/March 1969), whilst also widening disparities between the public and private sectors, due to the difficulties of effecting genuine or tangible productivity increases in the former.

One other factor which militated against any real distributive success with regard to the Labour governments' incomes policies concerns the increases in taxation, particularly indirect taxation, which were also invoked as part of the shift to deflation rather than expansion. Although indirect taxes were higher on luxury items than on basic items and essentials, they nonetheless obviated some of the increases in earnings obtained by the lower paid during this period (see for example Stewart, 1972: 95–8; Panitch, 1976: 217).

Ultimately, it appears that if the Labour governments' incomes policies were intended to improve productivity and eradicate low pay, then they enjoyed little overall success. Although it has been suggested that there was some alleviation of poverty whilst Labour was in power, this was due to improvements in welfare provision and the "social wage" for the non-working population, most notably pensioners (Stewart, 1972: 217–19). Yet even the original objectives attributed to incomes policy by the Labour governments were substantially revised in the context of external events and pressures. Having entered Office extolling "a policy for incomes" to increase productivity and reduce poverty, the Labour government was soon invoking incomes policies intended to secure wage restraint, in order to deflate the economy and avoid devaluation. When that failed, incomes policies were then pursued in order to make devaluation a success, which meant continued attempts at restraining wages. Indeed, by March 1969 a junior Minister at the Department of Employment and Productivity was insisting that: "It is not a primary function of the government's prices and incomes policy to redistribute incomes" (Harold Walker, *House of Commons Debates*, 5th series, Vol. 780, col. 1625).

Instead, it was suggested that the responsibility for tackling poverty and excessive inequality (and these themselves were subject to problems of definition and evaluation) resided in appropriate social and fiscal policies. Yet as we have already noted, integral to deflationary packages were increases in taxation and curbs on public expenditure, both of which severely constrained the government's ability to alleviate poverty.

The Labour party may originally have intended that any incomes policy would assist the lowest paid and thus contribute towards a slightly more egalitarian society, but it increasingly felt obliged to pursue pay policies in order to assuage the concerns of the business community and holders of sterling. Hence the Wilson governments' incomes policies became inextricably linked to wage restraint and deflation, not wealth redistribution and expansion, and as such, merely reaffirmed the trade unions' commitment to free collective bargaining, even if they wanted other aspects of the British economy to be subject to greater planning and regulation by government.

5

The U-turn beyond Selsdon: The Heath government, 1970–1974

Searching for a new approach

The election defeat of 1964, followed by another eighteen months later, prompted a fundamental review of Conservative policies whilst the party was in Opposition. The outcome was a marked shift towards neo-liberalism in the sphere of economic policy, coupled with the adoption of a legalistic approach towards industrial relations. There was a widespread feeling within the Conservative party, particularly amongst younger, newer MPs, that the last few years of the Macmillan and Douglas-Home administrations had been characterized by drift and indecision. What was thus deemed necessary was a reassertion of traditional Conservative principles and a renewed sense of purpose, with private enterprise and market forces once again ascribed primary importance. Indeed, writing immediately after the 1964 election defeat, a hitherto Conservative Minister even expressed his hope that the Party would *not* be returned to Office "too soon", so that it would have sufficient time to "search its own soul . . . decide its principles anew . . . base its politics on clearly seen principles" (Bevins, 1965: 159).

Of immense importance, and clearly linked to the reorientation of Conservative economic policy, was the insistence on curbing trade union power and apparent "irresponsibility" by imposing a new legislative framework on their activities. This marked a clear departure from the conciliatory approach and support for voluntarism which had prevailed in Office from 1951 to 1964. Indeed, by 1964 there were many Conservatives who believed that conciliation had degenerated into appeasement of the trade unions. Once again, it was amongst younger Conservatives especially that support for a tougher approach to the trade unions was most prevalent, although some senior figures, such as

Enoch Powell, were also impatient with what they perceived to be the pusillanimity of the Conservative leadership's previous stance towards the trade unions. Thus did Powell look back over the 1951–64 Conservative governments and wryly observe that: "the Party came into Office . . . without any specific commitment on trade union law and practice, and it faithfully carried that non-commitment out for thirteen years" (Powell, 1968: 5).

Back towards free collective bargaining

With regard to wage determination in particular, the Conservative Opposition moved steadily away from support for incomes policy, and instead, reasserted the principle of free – or "responsible" – collective bargaining. Thus, whilst the Conservative's 1964 election manifesto insisted that an incomes policy was "crucial to the achievement of sustained growth without inflation", the publication of the policy document *Putting Britain Right Ahead* the following year evinced only slight allusion to the issue of incomes policy. The emphasis instead was on such factors as competition, efficiency and incentives, with economic planning (under the auspices of the National Economic Development Council) receiving no mention whatsoever.

This shift away from economic intervention thus made a mockery of the claim by a senior Bow Group official shortly after the 1964 election defeat, that the issue facing Conservatives was no longer about whether to have an incomes policy, but about the details and administration of such a policy (Driscoll, 1965: 46). On the contrary, the debate after 1964 was precisely about whether or not the Conservatives should continue endorsing incomes policies, with party opinion hardening against them during the latter half of the decade. As a senior Conservative party official observed: "We are against a compulsory incomes policy but the alternative of a voluntary policy is not credible" (Sewill, 1967). From 1964 onwards, therefore, Conservative party policy therefore veered increasingly towards advocacy of the restoration of free, or *responsible*, collective bargaining.

The criticisms of incomes policy which underpinned the renewed advocacy of free collective bargaining focused on both economic and political factors. Two particular economic objections were articulated by Conservative neo-liberals, with Enoch Powell being the most frequent and eloquent critic. First, it was argued that incomes policies constituted an impediment to the natural functioning of the market. For neo-liberals in the Conservative party, labour power was viewed no differently to any other commodity, and was thus deemed to be subject to the same immutable laws of supply and demand. The market, it was insisted, would establish its own equilibrium with regard to both prices and wages. The demand by employers for particular types of workers would determine the level of wages received by particular occupational groups. Workers with rare or highly sought after skills would be able to command higher wages than those with few skills, or skills which were widely possessed. Freed from political interference and government determination, wages would find their own "natural" or market level (as would unemployment).

This obviated any consideration of such criteria such as comparability, equity, fairness or social justice. Conservative neo-liberals were adamant that such criteria could not be applied to the determination of pay; attempts by Westminster or Whitehall to determine wages were deemed futile, and, by impeding the operation of market forces, would merely compound Britain's economic problems (Bow Group, 1965: 4). As wages could only realistically be determined according to market criteria, and as the market was deemed by Conservative neo-liberals to be morally neutral, then it followed that seeking to determine pay by the application of subjective criteria based on social or ideological objectives was doomed to failure.

The second economic objection to incomes policy enunciated by Conservative neo-liberals, and which gained wider currency within the party after 1964, was that such policies derived from a misunderstanding of the root cause of inflation. Advocates of incomes policy saw the intimate link between wage increases and price increases as the basis of inflation, and hence it was assumed that the way to curb inflation was either to secure wage restraint workers and their trade unions, or occasionally to urge employers to restrain price increases instead.

This perspective, however, was roundly condemned by Conservative neo-liberals, insisting as they did that the real cause of inflation was excessive increases in the money supply, unmatched by correponding increases in industrial output and productivity. Furthermore, it was held that inflationary increases in the money supply were the consequence of excessive government expenditure, with politicians sanctioning the printing of too much money, invariably in order to finance social objectives (which governments ought not to assume responsibilty for anyway) or to maintain full employment (which was, in the long term, unsustainable).

The corollary of this perspective was that incomes policies were irrelevant to curbing inflation, and *inter alia* that the trade unions were not directly to blame. Instead, the blame for inflation rested ultimately with politicians themselves, for it was they who sanctioned the printing of more money, rather than facing up to the economic facts of life. As one Conservative opponent of wage control expressed it, "incomes policy is . . . in the last resort a bolt hole for politicians who, having failed in the job of managing the economy, seek to heap the blame on the trade unions" (Lewis, 1970: 64).

These economic criticisms of incomes policy were accompanied by political objections, not least of these being the allegedly corporatist consequences of such policies. Conservative neo-liberals argued that incomes policies not only entailed governments seeking to determine wages, but also meant the leaders of representative institutions, such as the trade unions, effectively policing their members to ensure that they abided by agreements entered into with ministers. The recourse of both Conservative and Labour governments to incomes policies during the 1960s prompted Enoch Powell to warn ominously that Britain was in:

> Imminent danger of slipping unawares into that form of state socialism which is known as fascism, whereby the control of the state over individuals is exercised largely through corporations which purport to represent the various elements of society, and particularly the employers and employees. (Powell, 1969: 164)

More generally, it was argued by Conservatives such as Duncan Sandys that in a free society, governments had no business seeking to fix wages. As such, he was adamant that incomes policies were wrong in principle, as well as unworkable in practice (*The Times*, 18 March 1968), the latter objection being endorsed by Jock Bruce-Gardyne when he characterized attempts by governments to control wages by legislative means as "the pursuit of the unattainable" (Bruce-Gardyne, 1969: 678). In similar vein was the claim that "in a free society it is impossible to prevent employers from paying higher wages if they wish to do so. A wage dictatorship would be a dictatorship indeed" (Lewis, 1970: 63). To those Conservatives still enamoured with incomes policy, Enoch Powell posed three pointed questions:

> Are employers to be forbidden to offer wages which they can pay and which are necessary to get or keep the workforce they need? Are employees to be forbidden to accept these wages? Are they to be punished if they do? (Conservative Party Archives, LCC(65), 42nd meeting, 13 April 1965)

In defence of incomes policy

Certainly not everyone in the Conservative party was being converted to neo-liberalism at this time; there were a number of senior Conservatives, such as Edward Boyle, Iain Macleod, and Reginald Maudling, who remianed convinced of the need for incomes policies. Indeed, one of the major reasons why such Conservatives continued to believe in incomes policy was precisely because of the power of the trade unions, who constituted "islands of monopoly in the economy". This power meant that it was "not practical politics to deal with monopoly elements directly". Instead, government had to rely upon the pressure of public opinion combined with persuasion. Only this approach could secure moderation by the trade unions, and facilitate a workable incomes policy (Conservative Party Archives, ACP, "Incomes policy; tentative thoughts on future policy", December 1964).

The ensuing debate within the Conservative party was lent added resonance due to the introduction of the 1966 Prices and Incomes Bill by the Labour Government. This legislation provided the Conservative protagonists with a particular focus for their arguments, whilst also highlighting the divisions within the Shadow Cabinet itself (Enoch Powell and Reginald Maudling having, at the beginning of the year, publicly expressed widely divergent views on incomes policy; see *The Times*, January 1966, *passim*).

More than a year later, it was privately acknowledged that "The [Conservative] Party is split about the desirabilty of an Incomes Policy . . . and will continue to be split" (Conservative Party Archives, CRD 3/7/11/1, Newton to Sewill, 2 March 1967). The extent of opposition to incomes policy within the Conservative party had been confirmed at a joint meeting, on 14 March, of the party's backbench labour committee, trade committee and finance committee. The backbenchers at this well-attended meeting had made clear to Iain Macleod their "disillusionment with prices and incomes policy and with the apparent lack of a clear-cut distinction between our policy and that of the Government" (Conservative Party Archives, LCC(67) 163rd meeting, 15 March 1967).

Virtually a year later, the Shadow Cabinet was acknowledging that the parliamentary Conservative party continued to be characterized by "a fairly even division between the 'doves' and the 'hawks'" with regard to incomes policy (Conservative Party Archives, LCC(68) 222nd meeting, 7 March 1968), whilst the Shadow Cabinet itself found it difficult to agree on how best to respond to the Labour government's prices and incomes policies (CPA, LCC(68) 224th meeting, 13 March 1968).

Furthermore, Edward Heath believed that many Conservatives at constituency level throughout the country were favourably disposed towards some form of incomes policy, so that there was something of a disjuncture between grass-roots Conservative opinion and the stance of the parliamentary party. This made it even more vital that the Shadow Cabinet articulate clearly and carefully its reservations about incomes policy in general, and the Labour government's prices and incomes policy in particular (CPA, LCC(67) 159th meeting, 27 February 1967).

Conservative divisions highlighted

Such was the division of opinion within the Shadow Cabinet that the Conservative's official response to the government's Prices and Incomes Bill was to table a "reasoned amendment", expressing qualified acceptance of an incomes policy, but deploring the compulsion and coercion which Labour's legislation was deemed to entail.

This compromise did little to quell the divisions which existed on the Conservative backbenches. On the contrary, one Conservative MP, Geoffrey Hirst, even resigned the party whip in protest at the leadership's refusal to vote against the Prices and Incomes Bill "in a straightforward manner", claiming that incomes policies constituted "a slippery slope" to ever increasing infringements of individual liberty (*The Times*, 11 July 1966). This view was echoed by another Conservative backbencher, Thomas Iremonger, when he warned that Labour's Bill represented "the first step down the slippery path of socialistic control of processes which were best left to the operation of the immutable laws of supply and demand" (*House of Commons Debates*, Vol. 731, col. 1742). Also urging that the laws of supply and demand be permitted to determine wages were Sir Keith Joseph (*House of Commons Debates* Standing Committee B, 1966–7, Vol. 3, col. 263), and John Biffen (*House of Commons Debates*, 5th series, Vol. 733, col.1807).

One further reason advanced by some within the Conservative party as grounds for opposing Labour's Prices and Incomes Bill was that merely by discussing the details of the Bill, Conservatives were effectively lending credence to the principle of incomes policy. They were, it was suggested, creating the impression that the party was unhappy about some of the *details* of Labour's incomes policy, rather than unhappy about incomes policy *per se*. Debate over the details of incomes policy was superseding what ought to be outright opposition to incomes policy as a matter of Conservative principle. In short, it was feared that the Conservative leadership was permitting itself to be drawn into a battle fought on the Labour government's terms and terrain (Reading, 1967). Indeed, there was concern not only that "we are now fighting the Government on grounds which they have made very much their own" but that "their efforts have been far more successful than ours ever were" (Conservative Party Archives, CRD, Newton to Sewill, 2 March 1967).

However, a number of Conservatives were not prepared to countenance the return to high unemployment which they insisted would follow the abandonment of incomes policy in favour of unfettered market forces. Like Cyril Osborne, they were emphatic that their could be no return to "the bad old days" when the "economic machine" was allowed to grind forwards regardless of the social consequences: there had to be some political control of the economic system (*House of Commons Debates*, 5th series, Vol. 731, cols. 1783–4). Indeed, Osborne had recently sought an assurance from the Labour government that it would *not* abandon its prices and incomes policy, constituting as it did Britain's only hope of economic salvation (*House of Commons Debates*, Vol. 730, col. 2171). Also refusing to countenance the high levels of unemployment which were associated with abandonment of incomes policy was Kenneth Lewis, who abstained from voting against Labour's Bill in several parliamentary divisions during the standing committee stage. Without an incomes policy, Lewis insisted, Britain would be faced either with high inflation, or high unemployment (*House of Commons Debates*, Standing Committee B, 1966–7, Vol. 3, cols. 274–5).

Further Conservative support for incomes policies emanated from the former Treasury Minister, Edward Boyle, as well as Terence Higgins, now the Opposition spokesperson on Treasury and Economic Affairs, and the former Chancellor, Reginald Maudling. Boyle was emphatic that an incomes policy was vital to any attempt at curbing the wage-cost spiral afflicting the British economy. Even if no incomes policy could ever be 100 per cent effective, he argued, this was no reason for abandoning such policies altogether (Boyle, 1966: 26–7). Maudling, meanwhile, reiterated that an incomes policy was essential due to the monopoly power of the trade unions, for this power invalidated the free-market assumptions subscribed to by Conservative neo-liberals. Maudling was convinced that an incomes policy was vital not only in combating inflation, but also as a means of ensuring that wage increases reflected such criteria as fairness, rather than being determined solely by the "brute force" of collective bargaining by trade union monopolies (*The Times*, 5 January 1966: *HC Debates*, Vol. 731, col. 1760 and col. 1765).

However, many of Maudling's Shadow Cabinet colleagues believed that it was precisely "the monopoly power of certain trade unions" which constituted "the nub of the incomes problem", for "unless it could be broken no real incomes policy could be achieved" (Conservative Party Archives, LCC(65) 42nd meeting, 1965). Yet if this monopoly power could be broken, some Conservatives believed, then surely there would no longer be any need for an incomes policy? The monopoly power of the trade unions might make incomes policies unworkable, but the breaking of that power would presumably render incomes policies unnecessary.

Disagreement sustains ambiguity

Faced with this dilemma, many Conservatives were initially inclined to "wait and see how things worked out with the [Labour] government's incomes policy". At the same time, the Shadow Cabinet decided that should Labour's incomes policy prove ineffective: "It would be a good idea if the cry of failure could come from the backbenches rather than our Front Bench" (Conservative Party Archives, LCC(65), 42nd meeting, 1965). Yet even by the spring of 1968, when Conservative opinion had hardened considerably against incomes policies (not least because of the problems encountered by the Labour government), the Shadow Cabinet was reluctantly acknowledging that "any Government in power in this country in the present situation would need to control incomes over the next eighteen months . . . if devaluation were to be made to work" (Conservative Party Archives, LCC(68) 224th meeting, 13 March 1968).

Indeed, Heath himself contributed towards the ambiguity over the Conservative party's stance at this time, making a speech in which his assertion that "compulsory controls are wrong in principle" was followed by the declaration that "I am quite prepared for a tough incomes policy" (quoted in Conservative Political Centre, 1968). It is also noteworthy that whilst Heath allowed the statement: "We utterly reject the philosophy of compulsory wage control" to be included in the 1970 Conservative manifesto, "he did not", his biographer alleges, "believe it deeply". Indeed, "rejecting the *philosophy* of compulsion did not say anything about rejecting the *practice*, if in the government's judgement it should become necessary" (Campbell, 1993: 232–3).

One approach suggested in some quarters of the Conservative party was to "bunch" annual wage claims, so that they were all submitted, and then settled, at a specific time of the year. This, it was envisaged, would help to overcome the constant problem of "leap-frogging" derived from comparison with a pay award secured by another trade union earlier in the year. If all wage claims were submitted – as a legal requirement – in the same month each year, then they could be examined by a new Monopoly Power Commission which would then be able to "add them all up and to point out that they totalled more than the likely increase in a national productivity, and that they would therefore lead to an increase in prices". If the trade unions subsequently continued to insist on excessive pay awards, then "the Government might threaten increases taxation to cancel out the increased purchasing power" (Sewill, 1967).

There was little support for this proposal in the Conservative party, though, partly on the grounds that a legal obligation on all trade unions to submit their pay claims at the same time jarred with the Conservative party's renewed neo-liberal emphasis on reducing the role of the state generally, and moving back towards free collective bargaining in particular. More importantly, however, were the practical objections, such as the fact that the bunching of pay claims could not possibly "take account of all the localized factors which may affect wages in a particular factory all through the year". There was also concern that bunching might actually result in a "further inflation of wage claims", whilst placing trade union leaders under greater pressure from the rank-and-file, because publication of an annual list of pay claims "could expose Union leaders to tremendous pressure along the lines of: 'Why are you not claiming for us as much as X is claiming for his men?'" (Conservative Party Archives, CRD, Newton to Sewill, 2 March 1967). Certainly, neither Edward Heath nor Iain Macleod considered it feasible to bunch wage claims and evaluate them in the manner suggested (Conservative Party Archives, CRD, Sewill to Barber, 17 March 1967), and thus the proposal was never pursued.

One further problem which emanated from deliberations within the Conservative party over whether or not to persevere with an incomes policy concerned the issue of productivity. Although all Conservatives could readily endorse the principle that wage increases should be closely linked to increases in productivity, it was pointed out that in most cases, "only at the plant level can genuine productivity agreements be made". In other words, any incomes policy which sought to link wage increases with improved productivity would "tend to push negotiations away from the national to the plant level" (Conservative Party Archives, CRD, Douglas to Sewill, 2 March 1967). Yet this would further strengthen the position of shop stewards and trade union officials at plant level by involving them more directly in wage negotiations, when the Conservative party (and the Labour government too) was becoming increasingly concerned at the extent to which trade union leaders and officials were being undermined by local-level bargaining and unofficial strikes in defiance of national-level agreements.

Indeed, the whole thrust of Conservative proposals for industrial relations reform in Opposition (see below) was to restore the authority of national level trade union leaders, curb unofficial strikes, and thereby ensure that wage agreements reached by these senior union officials were adhered to by their union members at plant level. There was also a distinct danger that encouraging plant-level wage deals ostensibly linked to productivity would merely exacerbate the growing problem of wage drift.

Fair Deal at Work

The Conservative party's increasing hostility to incomes policy whilst in Opposition cannot be viewed in isolation from its proposals for reform of industrial relations which crystallized during this period. The 1960s had witnessed increasing concern – across much of the political spectrum – about the incidence and impact of unofficial strikes, these accounting for over 90 per cent of all industrial stoppages. As noted in chapter 4, so serious was the problem that the Labour Prime Minister, Harold Wilson, felt obliged to establish a Royal Commission on Trade Unions and Employers Associations, chaired by Lord Donovan (even though Wilson had previously quipped that such commissions merely "took minutes and wasted years").

The Conservative Opposition, meanwhile, formulated its own programme for industrial relations reform, with proposals emanating from the party's policy review group on trade union law and practice, which had been established, along with several other policy review groups, in 1965. These were derived from the party's determination to re-evaluate and revamp its policies after thirteen years in Office. In identifying unofficial strikes as the number one problem of industrial relations (see, for example, Stephen Abbott, 1966: 8; Robert Carr, *House of Commons Debates*, Vol. 807, col. 633–4: Conservative Political Centre, *circa* 1966: 4–5), the Conservative party developed a series of proposals intended to facilitate a return to *responsible* collective bargaining in the sphere of wage determination, which, in turn, would obviate the need for incomes policies.

Although some Conservatives viewed unofficial strikes as symptomatic of "reds under the beds" and communist agitators within the trade unions seeking to sabotage industry in order to destroy capitalism, the dominant perspective within the Conservative party was that the incidence of unofficial strikes was primarily a reflection of the growing gulf between trade union leaders and their members in the work-place. This growing gulf was itself partly a consequence of the increasing scope, size and bureaucratization of modern industry, resulting in an ever-widening chasm between management and trade union leaders on the one hand, and employees on the other.

Yet, as many Conservatives pointed out, incomes policies themselves exacerbated this gulf between trade union leaders and their members, because the incorporation of these leaders into national-level discussions with ministers and employers' representatives reinforced the view amongst rank-and-file trade unionists that their leaders were becoming ever-more remote, and failing to represent their interests adequately. Indeed, such incorporation sometimes led to suspicion on the factory-floor that trade union leaders were effectively acting as agents of the state in seeking to hold down wages, thereby further undermining their authority or legitimacy in the eyes of their rank-and-file membership.

A dangerous consequence of this trend, many Conservatives believed, was that a vacuum emerged between ordinary trade unionists and their leaders, a vacuum which was subsequently filled by local union leaders and shop stewards, who could then win the support of the rank-and-file by pursuing higher wage claims than those being agreed by the national-level union leadership (Conservative Trade Unionists National Advisory Committee, 1966: speech by John Spence at 1966 Conservative party annual conference). If management failed to accede to these higher wage demands, the outcome would often be an unofficial strike, yet if employers at local or regional level did meet these demands, then the economy would continue to be affected by the phenomenon of wage drift.

In this respect, it was pointed out, incomes policies would not work because of the federal character of the TUC and CBI. As such, it was "not much use to get agreement from these bodies unless the have some control over their members which at present they do not" (Reading, 1967). Put another way, the problem was not that trade union leaders were too strong, but that they were too weak, and therefore unable to exercise sufficient authority over their ordinary members.

Consequently, the Conservative Shadow Cabinet, primed with the recommendations of the party's policy review group on trade union law, decided that reform of industrial relations should aim to enhance the authority of trade union leaders over their members, and thereby diminish both the incidence of unofficial strikes and the phenomena of wage drift. The attainment of such objectives would then obviate the need for an incomes policy.

However, throughout its time in Opposition, the Conservative party was bedevilled by disagreement over the specificities of its legislative proposals to reform industrial relations (Dorey, 1995: ch. 4; Moran, 1977: *passim*). Indeed, when the Conservative party's legislative proposals were published in the policy document *Fair Deal at Work* (Conservative Central Office, 1968), the effect was to reinforce the reservations harboured in some quarters of the Party and fuel the debates about what precisely the next Connservative government should – and could – do with regard to incomes policies and industrial relations.

Legally enforceable collective agreements?

One particular source of anxiety was the issue of whether collective agreements ought to be rendered legally binding. Those Conservatives who favoured such a policy argued that this would reduce, if not remove, the scope for unofficial strike action in defiance of nationally-agreed pay deals, and also eradicate wage drift. This, in turn, would facilitate greater industrial and economic stability, enabling employers and government to plan ahead with more confidence.

The Conservative party's policy review group on trade union law and practice had originally been compelled to compromise on this issue by stipulating that only procedural agreements should be enforceable in law. *Fair Deal at Work*, however, declared that all collective agreements should be deemed legally enforceable unless the parties to such an agreement expressly stated otherwise. This exemption clause was itself a reflection of the disagreement within both the Conservative party in general, and the review group in particular, for whilst some Conservatives wished to make all collective agreements legally binding, others were unhappy at bringing such agreements within the ambit of the law. Indeed, the Shadow Employment Secretary and thus a leading author of the subsequent Industrial Relations Bill, Robert Carr, pointed out that: "We have consistently said we believe in 'free' collective bargaining. It could hardly be this if agreements had to be legally binding regardless of the parties' wishes" (Conservative Party Archives, CRD, policy group on industrial relations, PG/20/66/130).

The Conservative case for making collective agreements legally enforceable (unless stated otherwise) derived from four particular arguments. First, it was claimed that such a measure would act as an incentive to both sides of industry (employers and trade unions) to give more careful consideration to the agreements which they entered into, whilst also encouraging trade union leaders to explain them more carefully to their members. Secondly, and following directly on from this point, it would encourage trade union leaders to maintain closer contact with their rank-and-file members, whilst also enabling the former more readily to identify problems on the shop-floor. Thirdly, it was envisaged that the role and functions of shop stewards would be more clearly defined. Fourthly and finally, it was anticipated that management would find it easier to take disciplinary action against individuals breaching collective agreements, because if a trade union intervened to obstruct such action, it would be deemed to be condoning the breach of agreement, and consequently become liable to be sued for damages itself.

Yet the question of damages was itself a source of disagreement amongst Conservatives who favoured making collective agreements legally enforceable. Keith Joseph, for example, believed that any damages incurred by a recalcitrant trade union should be "within limits so that no union can be deliberately bankrupted by its own militants", but this was scorned by John Boyd-Carpenter, who did not believe any limit should be set on the amount of damages for which a trade union might be deemed liable if it acted in defiance of a legally enforceable collective agreement (Conservative Party Archives, LCC(65)70, Keith Joseph, "Trade Unions and Industrial Efficiency", 8 December 1965; John Boyd-Carpenter, "Comments on LCC(65)70)", January 1966).

There was also the question of exactly who should sue in the case of such an agreement being breached, for it was recognized that employers themselves might be reluctant to initiate legal proceedings, for fear of exacerbating industrial conflict. On this basis, some Conservatives favoured the appointment of an official "analogous to the Registrar of Restrictive Trade Practices" to whom cases could be referred, although management and trade unions would still retain the right to sue for damages themselves if they so wished. Alternatively, a framework of Industrial Courts – national, regional and local – was mooted as another option. So vexatious was this whole issue that Keith Joseph admitted to his Shadow Cabinet colleagues that: "The policy group is silent on this" (Conservative Party Archives, LCC(65)70, 8 December 1965).

Such issues reaffirmed the reservations of those Conservatives who feared that the party was treading a dangerous path in its approach to industrial relations reform. A number of Conservative MPs shared David Madel's concern about the dangers of "bringing agreements between employers and employees into the framework of law". Speaking with remarkable prescience at the Conservative's 1967 annual conference, Madel warned that unless the party leadership "really thought out all the implications" of its policies, it would be "in danger of triggering off the greatest industrial unrest of the century". A further concern amongst some Conservatives was that when elected, the party would find itself introducing legislation which could not be properly enforced in practice, a mistake which "would bring the law into disrepute" (Conservative Trade Unionists National Advisory Committee, 1966: 6). For the self-proclaimed party of law-and-order, this would be politically disastrous.

Other Conservatives even wondered whether the party would be able to win a general election pledging comprehensive and far-reaching industrial relations legislation, even though opinion polls might indicate popular support for such measures. Although on different ideological wings of the Conservative party, both John Biffen and Hugh Dykes were concerned that the new-found penchant for industrial relations legislation could frighten away some working-class voters and trade unionists who might otherwise be inclined to vote Conservative (Biffen, 1965: Dykes, 1968: 32).

The Industrial Relations Act

The anxiety within the Conservative party over whether or not collective agreements between employers and trade unions should be rendered legally binding continued into Office after the June 1970 election victory. Indeed, the arguments were rehearsed once again when the newly-elected Heath Government immediately introduced its Industrial Relations Bill, based on the proposals outlined in *Fair Deal at Work*.

The Bill included a clause stipulating that all agreements between the two sides of industry would be deemed legally binding unless the two sides expressly and explicitly stated otherwise at the time. The Labour Opposition moved an amendment declaring that collective agreements should *not* be considered legally binding unless the two sides declared otherwise. This amendment, although defeated, nonetheless highlighted the tensions within the Conservative party over the issue (as the Labour Party doubtless intended it to do), for whilst Raymond Gower considered it "absurd" for collective agreements to be exempt from legal enforceability (*House of Commons Debates*, 5th series, Vol. 810, col. 1300), another Conservative backbencher, Robert Awdry, admitted that since the election, he had experienced growing doubts about the wisdom of rendering collective agreements legally enforceable, and as such, he urged his colleagues to give sympathetic consideration to Labour's amendment (*House of Commons Debates*, 5th series, Vol. 810, cols. 1300–1).

The recently-elected Conservative government clearly envisaged that by encouraging more orderly and responsible trade unionism via the Industrial Relations Act, the need for an incomes policy would be obviated. Certainly the official stance was one of restoring free collective bargaining, at least in the private sector. When introducing the Industrial Relations Bill to Parliament, Robert Carr, the Secretary of State for Employment, declared that the first principle upon which the Bill should be judged was the extent to which it restored collective bargaining, freely and responsibly conducted. This could only be achieved, however, by ensuring that wage agreements reached between national-level trade union leaders and employers were not subsequently undermined by unofficial strike action perpetrated at local or plant level by shop stewards and their ilk (*House of Commons Debates*, 5th series, Vol. 808, cols. 961–87).

Hence the proposals enshrined in the Industrial Relations Bill to render collective agreements legally binding, whilst also curbing unofficial strikes by making trade unions, as corporate bodies, liable in law for the actions of their officers and officials (including shop stewards). In this respect, it was hoped that the authority of trade union leaders would be restored over their rank-and-file membership, thereby ensuring that wage agreements entered into by those leaders would then be upheld at local or plant level, especially once these agreements were deemed legally binding. In other words, the Industrial Relations Act was intended to secure "more orderly collective bargaining" (Barnes and Reid, 1980: 142), although some Conservatives suggested that whilst reforms of industrial relations law "would have an effect" on collective bargaining and wage determination "we should not deceive ourselves into thinking that they would have a very large effect" (Sewill, 1967: 2).

At the same time, ministerial rhetoric *vis-à-vis* pay emphasized the importance of such criteria as productivity and efficiency in the sphere of wage determination. The Heath government was adamant that pay – or, rather, pay in the private sector – should no longer be determined by the state. In the public sector, however, the Heath Government committed itself to an N-1 pay policy, whereby pay increases were to be 1 per cent less each year than in the previous year. This approach reflected the view now held by many Conservative ministers that "the main cause of wage inflation arose from the demands in the public sector", which were financed from government expenditure and increases in the money supply, without any corresponding increase in productivity. If public sector pay deals could be restrained, then a solution would have been found to the problem of wage inflation generally (Maudling, 1978: 191).

The Cabinet also hoped that by standing firm when public sector trade unions submitted excessive pay claims, management in the private sector would be similarly encouraged to resist wage militancy. Thus, whilst formally eschewing incomes policy in the private sector, the Heath Government anticipated that its tough stance *vis-à-vis* public sector employees would indirectly serve to dampen down wage increases amongst *all* workers.

A siren voice

Reginald Maudling, however, remained unconvinced by the neo-liberal perspective subscribed to by many of his ministerial colleagues. Indeed, in the wake of various challenges to the Heath government's N-1 policy, Maudling became even more convinced that "a single coherent [pay] policy was required". Consequently, in the summer of 1971, he sought – unsuccessfully – to present a paper to the Cabinet outlining the case for greater government involvement in the realm of prices and incomes. Maudling wanted to reiterate his thesis that the monopoly power of the trade unions invalidated traditional neo-liberal assumptions about the operation of "the market" and the laws of supply and demand, particularly in the sphere of wages.

Furthermore, he was adamant that in a period of economic expansion, the most powerful trade unions would be able to obtain the largest pay increases, whilst in a period of recession, many employers would be likely to accede to union wage demands because they literally could not afford to endure strike action. Maudling therefore concluded that his ministerial colleagues had two options; they could either pursue a confrontational policy, involving a "show of strength" with the trade unions, in order to defeat inflationary forces in the economy, or they could seek to encompass organized interests by bringing them into the ambit of economic policy-making, which would clearly entail recourse to a permanent incomes policy. The former approach would no longer work, Maudling insisted, which therefore meant that the modern capitalist economy could only operate effectively and fairly by accepting a greater degree of government intervention (Maudling's paper was subsequently published, more than a year later, in *The Times*, 12 September 1972).

During 1970–1, though, Maudling was effectively a siren voice within the Cabinet, as his ministerial colleagues maintained their eschewal of incomes policies (N-1 notwithstanding). The official government line at this time continued to be that incomes policies reflected attempts by politicians to control aspects of economic activity which were outside their legitimate domain. Furthermore, many Conservatives believed that because of the impracticability of incomes policies, attempts at pursuing them invariably degenerated into meaningless verbiage or a form of totalitarian economic control (Conservative Political Centre, 1971: 1). In any case, as previously noted, the Industrial Relations Bill was intended to obviate the need for an incomes policy.

Selsdon Man is slain

However, this refusal to countenance incomes policy was to prove short-lived, due to the imminent failure of the Industrial Relations Act (for details see Dorey, 1995: 97–100; Campbell, 1993: 457–67; Dorfman, 1979: 58; Stewart, 1977: 127; Taylor, 1993: 199–202; Taylor, 1996: 172–6), coupled with an increase in unemployment towards the then politically unacceptable one million mark. These two phenomena contributed towards a dramatic U-turn by Heath, entailing the search for a *rapprochement* with the trade unions, and the establishment of a new partnership between trade union leaders, employers' representatives and ministers over economic affairs. What further underpinned this U-turn, though, was the six-week miners' strike which took place early in 1972.

Just as Conservative ministers had been surprised by the strength and scale of trade union opposition to the Industrial Relations Act, so too were they taken aback by the degree of resentment which had been building up amongst Britain's miners due to the widespread pit closures and redundancies which had begun in the early 1960s. The period from 1960 to 1972 had witnessed a reduction in the coal industry's workforce from 700,000 to 290,000. The resentment in the coalfields was enhanced by the relative decline in earnings (about 25 per cent according to some estimates) which Britain's miners had experienced during this period of contraction.

It was in this context that, during the winter of 1971–2, the National Union of Mineworkers (NUM) submitted a pay claim seeking a 47 per cent increase, coupled with a demand that the weekly wage of a coal-face worker be increased from the then maximum of £27 to a minimum of £35. Such a pay claim obviously conflicted dramatically with the Heath government's N-1 pay policy for the public sector, but it enjoyed considerable support amongst miners, to the extent that 55.8 per cent of them endorsed strike action when balloted by the NUM.

The miners were in a strong bargaining position at this time, not least because Britain's power stations only had about two months worth of coal stocks (itself an indication that strike action by the miners had not been envisaged by the government). What further strengthened their position, whilst adding to the bewilderment of the government, was the NUM's willingness to adopt a pro-active stance via the use of "flying pickets". This entailed large numbers of striking miners (and supporters from outside of the coal mining industry) being bussed to picket coal mines other than their own. More significantly, though, these flying pickets were also being transported to other strategic sites, most notably depots where coal was stored, and power stations.

The NUM's President during the 1972 strike, Joe Gormley, later acknowledged that the NUM had been "determined to make the battle as short and sharp as possible" (Gormley, 1982: 96). This objective was aided by the solidarity proffered by other groups of workers, most notably train drivers (some of whom refused to transport coal supplies to power stations) and road haulage employees. However, perhaps the most surprising source of support for the miners was public opinion, where there was a widespread perception that the miners' grievances were fully justified, and their consequent wage claim entirely legitimate.

For supporters and opponents of the miners' alike, the symbol of the 1972 strike was the closure of the Saltley coke depot in the West Midlands, due to arrival of 15,000 flying pickets, led by Arthur Scargill. It was the police who actually ordered that the gates of Saltley be closed, and lorries delivering coal be turned away, on the grounds that the maintenance of law-and-order was jeopardized by such large numbers of pickets.

The police were not alone in their concern over maintaining social order; ministers themselves were becoming afraid that continuation of the miners' strike might result in civil unrest, and even political upheaval. A senior Conservative official during this period acknowledged that many within the Heath Government were panic-stricken at the events unfolding around them, fearful that the miners' strike would precipitate riots and a complete breakdown of civil order: "At the time, many of those in positions of influence looked into the abyss and saw only a few days away the possibility of the country being plunged into a state of chaos not so very far removed from that which might prevail after a minor nuclear attack" (Sewill, 1975: 50).

On 8 February 1972, Heath declared a State of Emergency, whilst the following day, Robert Carr summoned the NUM leadership to the Department of Employment to offer them an improved pay deal. Sensing the government's desperation, the NUM rejected Carr's offer, preferring to hold out for the even better offer which they were by now confident would soon be forthcoming. They recognized, as did a Conservative Minister himself, that: "The Government is now vainly wandering over the battlefield looking for someone to surrender to and being massacred all the time" (Hurd, 1979: 103).

Desperate to secure an end to the miners' strike, the Heath gvernment established a public inquiry headed by Lord Wilberforce, who was instructed to report back as soon as possible. Indeed, such was the urgency of the situation that after only two days of public hearings, the Wilberforce Inquiry published its Report, in which it recommended that the miners be awarded wage increases of 20 per cent, to be phased in over 16 months. It was further suggested that: "if it cannot be paid for out of the NCB's revenue account . . . the public, through the government, should accept the charge" (Wilberforce, 1972: 10). Determined to exploit fully the Heath government's desire to settle the dispute immediately, the NUM once again rejected the improved pay offer, preferring to extract further concessions from exhausted ministers and exasperated NCB officials, before finally calling off the strike at the end of February.

Seeking a partnership

In the wake of the NUM's victory, occurring as it did amidst widespread and active trade union opposition to the Industrial Relations Act, and with unemployment rapidly approaching one million, Heath embarked upon a major U-turn, one which ascribed the utmost importance to seeking conciliation and cooperation with the trade unions, particularly in the sphere of pay determination. Less than two years of being elected on a programme which rejected incomes policies in favour of a return to free collective bargaining, Heath sought to facilitate a partnership between Government and trade unions *vis-à-vis* economic policy, which obviously included the crucial issue of pay. Heath himself insisted that there had to be "a more sensible way" of dealing with economic and industrial affairs, whilst the Secretary of State for Industry, Peter Walker, was proclaiming a "trialogue", whereby a three-way partnership would be launched, involving Cabinet ministers, trade union leaders and employers' representatives.

Whilst Heath initially remained sceptical about formal incomes policies, the summer of 1972 nonetheless witnessed the government seeking voluntary wage restraint by the trade unions, via a "concordat" with the TUC and the CBI. The unpalatable alternatives were deemed to be further legislative intervention, renewed industrial conflict, and/or continuing inflation. In response to Conservative neo-liberals who continued to insist that the solution to Britain's economic problems rested primarily with stricter control of the money supply, the Chancellor, Anthony Barber, speaking at the Conservative's annual conference, argued that whilst the government's new approach entailed some interference with market forces, rampant inflation – then running at 8 per cent and rising – would itself wreak far greater havoc with market forces that a prices and incomes policy.

The three options

By the summer of 1972, three broad options were being canvassed within the Conservative party with regard to wage determination. First, there remained the neo-liberal insistence that control of the money supply, not wages, should be the government's primary objective, for it was the former which underpinned inflation. For proponents of this approach, tripartism was undesirable in principle, and unworkable in practice (at least, in a free society). Quite apart from the fact that incomes policies were deemed to be based on a false premise (namely that it was wage increases which fuelled inflation, rather than increases in the money supply), this perspective also insisted that the trade unions were incapable of adhering to any incomes policy. As such, John Biffen argued that the notion of inviting a tame set of trade union moguls to 10 Downing Street or Chequers in order that they could agree to wage restraint on behalf of their members was "a proposition of the greatest political delusion" (*House of Commons Debates*, 5th series, Vol. 845, cols. 927–8). In similar vein, Wyn Roberts was warning that the inevitable failure of any voluntary incomes policy would lead, with equal inevitability, to the imposition of a statutory incomes policy. Roberts was therefore concerned that the Heath government was pursuing a very dangerous path (*House of Commons Debates*, 5th series, Vol. 840, cols. 99–100).

For many Conservatives subscribing to this perspective, opposition to incomes policies was also linked to concern about the role of Parliament, for it was suggested that the tripartite agreements which incomes policies invariably entailed were a short step from corporatism, with economic and industrial decisions increasingly taken by ministers and the leaders of organized interests and producer groups. This mode of decision-making – considered to be the inevitable outcome of pursuing incomes policies – was deemed to constitute a serious threat to parliamentary sovereignty (see, for example, John Biffen *House of Commons Debates* 5th series, Vol. 845, cols. 927–8; John Biffen: 1977; Nicholas Budgen, *House of Commons Debates*, 5th series, Vol. 914, cols. 1239–40; David Howell, 1972; Timothy Raison, 1979).

The extent to which neo-liberal ideas had gained intellectual credibility on the Conservative backbenches during the second half of the 1960s was confirmed by the degree of support which this approach now enjoyed among many of the party's MPs. Alarmed by the drift government economic policy, Richard Body urged every Conservative Minister to read Friedrich Hayek's *The Road to Serfdom* (Body, 1972: 8), whilst a meeting of the Conservative backbench finance committee during the summer of 1972 warned that if the Cabinet resorted to a statutory prices and incomes policy, then it would be opposed in the Division Lobbies by several of its own MPs (*The Times*, 13 June 1972).

The second option being canvassed in the Conservative party was to seek a voluntary agreement, between the TUC and the CBI, to restrain – or even freeze – pay and price increases for a given period of time. Not only was such interference with market forces deemed a lesser evil than rampant inflation and reduced economic competitiveness, it was also considered that the continued increase in unemployment which would be occasioned by pursuing the neo-liberal strategy might well pose a threat to the social and political stability of the United Kingdom. It was also pointed out that a more constructive, conciliatory approach to the trade unions and wage determination would provide a welcome contrast to the tough stance adopted by ministers during the previous two years (Bow Group, 1972: 5: see also Hurd, 1979: 105).

The third option canvassed by a few Conservatives, most notably Peter Tapsell, was to impose a statutory prices and incomes policy. In calling upon the government impose a statutory freeze on wages, prices and dividends, Tapsell claimed that there existed considerable support in the Conservative party for such an approach (*The Times*, 13 June 1972). This perspective held that the inability or unwillingness of the trade unions to exercise restraint meant that a voluntary policy was doomed to failure. At the same time, the imperfections of the labour market – largely due to trade union power – were now so great that neo-liberal objections to incomes policy no longer carried much conviction. Consequently, a statutory prices and incomes policy became a regrettable necessary, particularly as inflation could not be checked by fiscal or monetary policies alone. As such, those Conservatives who claimed that market forces and control of the money supply alone could tackle inflation were accused of believing in fairy tale economics, and of indulging in "a form of economic masturbation" (John Nelson-Jones/ The Bow Group, *circa* 1972).

Searching for a voluntary prices and incomes policy

Throughout the summer of 1972, Heath and his ministerial colleagues sought to pursue the second of the above options, namely the search for a voluntary agreement on prices and incomes, even though few ministers "believed we had much chance of arriving at any worthwhile and sustainable settlement with the unions". Yet with free collective bargaining not being pursued in a responsible manner, and a statutory incomes policy deemed inappropriate – "there were grave dangers in imposing more legislation on the unions" – ministers were convinced that there was little alternative but to "at least make an attempt to negotiate a voluntary deal" (Heath, 1998: 402).

According to the Special Assistant to the Chancellor of the Exchequer during this time: "Although almost all Conservative ministers detested it as much as their subsequent critics, it was clear that, if an avalanche of accelerating pay settlements was to be avoided, there was no alternative but to revert to some form of incomes policy" (Sewill, 1975: 51). Even a Conservative neo-liberal like Angus Maude came to the conclusion that whilst he was opposed to incomes policy and tripartism in principle: "We are in a situation where economic laws have virtually ceased to operate", and as such, he explained to Conservative delegates at the party's annual conference in October 1973 that: "In a mad world it may be that only the absurd can have a hope of success."

An incomes policy was also being urged upon the Government at this time by the Central Policy Review Staff, established by Heath himself in 1971 as a source of independent (from the civil service) advice, both for himself and for his Cabinet colleagues (Blackstone and Plowden, 1988: 86). Certainly, it is notable that a number of Cabinet ministers in Heath's government subsequently became proponents of voluntary incomes policy and tripartism, whereby ministers, trade union leaders and employers' representatives regularly met to discuss economic policies, including those pertaining to pay. Indeed, from 1972 onwards, Heath himself increasingly became an advocate of a voluntary incomes policy and tripartism, not merely as a short-term measure born of crisis, but as a permanent feature of economic management. Heath's conversion to incomes policy and tripartism, needless to say, fuelled further the anxieties of his neo-liberal colleagues, and was roundly condemned by a trenchant editorial in *The Spectator* (4 November 1972).

Whilst cognizant of the urgency of the circumstances which had engendered it, Conservative neo-liberals nonetheless viewed the Cabinet's sudden pursuit of a voluntary incomes policy (and the tripartite talks between ministers, the TUC and the CBI which it entailed), as a humiliating U-turn, and a repudiation of the principles on which the Conservative party had fought the 1970 election. Indeed, it was this

U-turn which prompted the formation of the Selsdon Group within the Conservative party, which depicted itself as comprising "classical liberals" who were convinced that only "a policy of economic freedom can give the individual the degree of choice and independence essential to his dignity", and who therefore wished to see a return to "those true Conservative policies" upon which the Party had successfully contested the 1970 general election (*The Times*, 8 October 1972).

Nonetheless, September 1972 heard a proposal from the Cabinet that pay increases be should limited to a maximum of £2 per week, and price rises to 5 per cent per annum, in return for a government pledge that it would pursue an annual rate of economic growth of 5 per cent over the next two years. The TUC, however, wanted stronger, statutory, measures on prices, but was not willing to offer anything more than voluntary pay restraint in return. The TUC also insisted that a prerequisite of any agreement with the Heath government over prices and incomes was the repeal of the Industrial Relations Act, a demand which was understandably unacceptable to Heath and his ministerial colleagues.

In spite of the TUC's intransigence – or maybe because of it – Heath persisted in his search for an agreement with the two sides of industry, whereby a series of often lengthy meetings took place throughout September, October and into the beginning of November. For example, a seventeen-hour session at 10 Downing Street on 26 October – "the most rancorous and difficult tripartite meeting so far" (Heath, 1998: 414) – was followed by a seven-hour meeting on 30 October, and an eight-hour session on 1 November.

Yet with the TUC continuing to insist on statutory price controls and the repeal of the Industrial Relations Act, and Heath equally consistent in rejecting these demands, the several months of tripartite talks ended without agreement on a prices and incomes policy, and were officially abandoned on 2 November. By this time, Heath and many of his ministerial colleagues "did not really believe it was practicable to fight on without statutory backing" (Heath, 1998: 414).

A statutory prices and incomes freeze

Consequently, on 6 November 1972, Heath announced a ninety-day freeze on prices, pay, rent and dividends, to be enforced by a Counter-Inflation (Temporary Provisions) Bill, given its First Reading just two days later, followed by its Second Reading after another two days. Price increases which had been announced but not actually implemented were to be suspended for the duration of the freeze, as were wage increases due to come into effect during the period covered by the standstill. The only price increases to be permitted were those of fresh food (such as fruit, vegetables and fish) which were subject to seasonable variations, and imported raw materials, whilst the only permissible pay increases were those "resulting directly from extra effort or output" (Treasury, 1972). Heath viewed this freeze as a short-term response in lieu of a longer-term agreement with the trade unions over wages.

Surprisingly, perhaps, there was very little dissent within the Cabinet in the wake of Heath's 6 November announcement. Even ministers who subsequently became committed neo-liberals and thus staunch critics of incomes policy, most notably Keith Joseph and Margaret Thatcher, did not display any dissent at the government's reversion to statutory wage control, to the extent that Heath enjoyed "support from . . . the entire Cabinet" (Howe, 1995: 75); see also Walker, 1991: 123–4). Nor did Geoffrey Howe, subsequently to become Margaret Thatcher's first Chancellor, demur from this major U-turn. Indeed, it was only on the day before Heath announced the freeze that Howe became a full member of the Cabinet, having just been appointed Minister for Consumer Affairs in the Department of Trade and Industry. Ironically, Howe's first task immediately upon taking up this new post was "to assume almost dictatorial control over prices throughout the nation's economy" (Howe, 1995: 70).

This lack of dissent within the Cabinet over Heath's reversion to statutory prices and incomes control can only partly be attributed to the convention of collective (ministerial) responsibility. What also accounted for the acquiescence of those ministers who subsequently espoused neo-liberalism and the eschewal of incomes policies was the fact that at the time of Heath's policy U-turn, Conservatives such as Howe, Joseph and Thatcher had not yet become fully converted to economic neo-liberalism. Indeed, it was precisely their experiences in Heath's Cabinet from late 1972 to 1974 which prompted their subsequent intellectual and ideological conversion to economic neo-liberalism, thereby bringing them closer to the views of an increasing number of Conservative backbenchers. Margaret Thatcher, for example, later acknowledged that: "As a member of [Heath's] Cabinet I must take my full share of responsibility for what was done under the government's authority." However, whilst acknowledging that Heath's errors were also "our errors, for we went along with them . . . some of us (though never Ted, I fear) learned from these mistakes" (Thatcher, 1995: 195–6).

Meanwhile, although Sir Keith Joseph had already evinced nascent neo-liberalism in his criticisms of incomes policy during the late 1960s, he subsequently claimed that it was his unhappy experiences as a Cabinet Minister in the Heath government which had finally and fully converted him to the alleged virtues of the free market, monetarism and "rolling back the state". At the time, however, he too apparently acquiesced to Heath's resort to a statutory prices and incomes freeze. Indeed, with the exception of Nicholas Ridley, "no other member of the Government dissented from the 180-degree reversal of policy and philosophy" (Hillman and Clarke, 1988: 113).

It is worth noting that the Conservative party's avowed opposition to incomes policy when it was elected in June 1970 may, to some extent, have been tactical, for Peter Walker recalls that when his Shadow Cabinet colleagues were finalising the Conservative manifesto, Iain Macleod suggested that:

> we might have to have an incomes policy, but to explain in a manifesto that you might have to do it in certain circumstances was grey. Manifestos had to be black or white. Either we said we were going to have an incomes policy and it would be superb or that we were not going to have one at all. We should say that we were not going to have one and if in a few years we changed our minds we would have to explain that there were special circumstances. As far as the manifesto was concerned it should not be blurred. No "Ifs" or "buts". Everybody said it was right and so it got into the manifesto. (Quoted in Walker, 1991: 52)

Divisions develop and deepen elsewhere in the Conservative party

This might explain, at least in part, the remarkable degree of ministerial acquiescence over Heath's U-turn on incomes policy, but such equanimity was certainly not reflected on the Conservative backbenches. Here, there was considerable anger amongst the party's neo-liberals, for not only did the freeze represent a complete suspension of the operation of market forces, it was also being presented as a prelude to a permanent prices and incomes policy. On the Floor of the House of Commons, Enoch Powell asked Heath whether he had "taken leave of his senses", and then proceeded to vote against the Second Reading of the Bill (*House of Commons Debates*, 5th series, Vol. 845, cols. 885–91). Scarcely less critical was Nicholas Ridley, who accused Heath of "economic Canutism" (*House of Commons Debates*, 5th series, Vol. 845, col. 1039), whilst Teddy Taylor insisted that this "crazy and impractical policy" was not a viable option due to Britain's reliance on imported goods and commodities, the price of which were determined by world markets (Taylor, 1972).

The Counter-Inflation (Temporary Provisions) Bill also revealed differences of opinion amongst Conservative neo-liberals themselves, for whilst some of them were outraged at the U-turn, others were prepared to offer Heath qualified support, insisting that he use the ninety days to fashion a proper monetary policy. It was also suggested that the prices and incomes freeze might have the "psychological" benefit of illustrating to trade unions just how serious Britain's economic problems had become. Thus, although four Conservative MPs abstained during the parliamentary Division on the Second Reading of the Bill, most neo-liberals were willing to give the government grudging support in the expectation that "something better" would ensue in ninety days' time.

Among those Conservative MPs offering such support was Norman Tebbit, who contemplated resigning as PPS (parliamentary private secretary) to Robin Chichester-Clark, but after much soul-searching, "knuckled under and shamefacedly supported the Government". However repugnant Tebbit found Heath's recourse to a statutory prices and incomes freeze, the prospect of following Labour MPs through the Division Lobbies induced even greater repugnance (Tebbit, 1988: 126). Towards the very end of 1973, however, Tebbit did resign as Chichester-Clark's PPS, having found the Heath government "harder and harder to support", and claiming that: "I have for some time felt increasingly restricted by the constraints imposed on my freedom to speak about industrial affairs and the related fields of incomes policy" (Tebbit, 1988: 129).

Tensions were also discernible within the right-wing Monday Club, for whereas one senior official was urging support for the prices and incomes freeze as an alternative to "economic anarchy and vaulting price rises", whilst also enabling the government "to tread water whilst seeking a better means of ordered economic progress", the Monday Club's economic policy group was bemoaning the abandonment of the policies on which the Conservative party had fought and won the 1970 general election (*Monday News*, November 1972). Furthermore, the chairman of the Monday Club was advocating both an incomes policy *and* a monetary policy entailing reduction in the money supply, warning that Enoch Powell without Heath spelt social tension leading to revolution, whilst Heath without Powell meant a futile attempt at tackling inflation solely by incomes policy alone (*The Times*, 17 November 1972).

In the event, only Enoch Powell voted against the Counter Inflation (Temporary Provisions) Bill at its Second Reading, with four Conservative MPs – Jock Bruce-Gardyne, John Biffen, Neil Marten and Anthony Fell – abstaining. Powell also voted against the Bill when it received its Third reading, but this time, only Biffen and Bruce-Gardyne abstained.

However, dissatisfied Conservative MPs were afforded another means of registering their unhappiness at the new direction of government policy – and with Heath's allegedly autocratic style of leadership generally (Norton, 1978: 221–55) – when they cast their votes in the annual ballot for the chairs of the party's backbench subject committees.

Availing themselves of this timely opportunity, they elected the distinctly neo-liberal Nicholas Ridley as chairperson of the Conservative finance committee (with Jock Bruce-Gardyne elected as one of the two vice-chairpersons), whilst John Biffen was elected to chair the party's backbench industry committee. Two weeks later, Edward Du Cann – "well known as a *bête noire* of the Prime Minister" – was elected chairperson of the Conservative's 1922 Committee. These results were widely seen to constitute "a slap in the face for the Government" (Campbell, 1993: 482–3).

The proponents of incomes policy within the Conservative party were, of course, very supportive of Heath's new approach. Certainly, having apparently been a solitary – and stifled – voice in Cabinet prior to 1972, Reginald Maudling felt vindicated about Heath's U-turn over pay determination. Whilst Conservative neo-liberals cited trade union power as a major reason why no incomes policy would work, Maudling insisted once again that it was precisely the power of the trade unions which rendered an incomes policy necessary. He pointed out that the increasing sophistication of modern industry, depending as it did on a skilled workforce, meant that trade unionists engaged in industrial action could no longer be replaced by volunteers or troops as readily as in former times. Nor could this enhanced trade union power be adequately countered through legislation. As such, Maudling insisted that the only alternative to conflict and confrontation was for government to seek agreement with the trade unions over the need for wage restraint (*House of Commons Debates*, Vol. 845, cols. 1065–6).

What also underpinned such support for an incomes policy was fear of the social and economic consequences which might follow if the neo-liberal strategy of combating inflation primarily through controlling the money supply was adhered to. According to Peter Tapsell, for example, such a strategy would only compound Britain's economic problems, by yielding further bankruptcies, higher unemployment and postponed investment. Such "unacceptable social and economic costs" rendered it essential that the government relied upon an incomes policy, rather than a drastic reduction of the money supply, as its chief weapon in the battle against inflation (*House of Commons Debates*, 5th series, Vol. 845, col. 878), a perspective also articulated by one of Tapsell's backbench colleagues, David Knox (*House of Commons Debates*, 5th series, Vol. 845, col. 1107).

From elsewhere within in the Conservative party came the warning that without an incomes policy, Britain was unlikely to remain a capitalist democracy (Nelson-Jones/The Bow Group, *circa* 1972: 19), an argument echoed by the Chancellor's Special Assistant and former Director of the Conservative Research Department, when (in looking back at the economic policies of the Heath Government) he declared that:

> one cannot escape the conclusion that if we were to rely on monetary policy alone, only permanent depression could keep inflation at bay. If the inescapable result of such a policy were permanent mass unemployment, it would be clear to all and sundry that the capitalist democratic system had failed. (Sewill, 1975: 40)

Furthermore, many Conservative proponents of incomes policies and tripartism viewed Heath's U-turn not as a betrayal of the party's principles and election pledges, but as evidence of British Conservatism's traditional pragmatism and flexibility, as well as the revival of its "one nation" tradition, which Selsdon Man had previously abandoned.

Beyond the ninety-day freeze

Neo-liberal anger on the Conservative backbenches was sustained early in 1973, when the Cabinet introduced the Counter Inflation Bill to succeed the ninety-day freeze. This Bill represented phase two of Heath's recourse to a statutory incomes policy, stipulating that maximum pay rises would be 4 per cent, plus £1 per week. Heath envisaged that this second phase would be operational until the autumn of 1973, by which time he hoped to have secured the support of the TUC for a third phase of incomes policy, but one based on voluntary consent.

A few days before the Second Reading of the Counter-Inflation Bill, the Chancellor, Anthony Barber, was sent to present the government's case to the party's backbench finance committee, whereupon over twenty MPs made their dissatisfaction with government policy abundantly clear, although once again, the dominant approach was one of pledging qualified or reluctant support in the Division Lobbies. Many of these neo-liberal critics only proffered support for the government's economic policy during 1973 on the understanding that Edward Heath was "on probation", and that if success did not ensue then "he is in very real trouble" (*The Times*, 19 October 1973). As such, when the Counter-Inflation Bill was given its Second Reading, only Enoch Powell voted against the Government, having condemned the Cabinet for contriving to pursue one of the "hoariest futilities" in the history of British politics, namely the use of coercion to prevent the laws of supply and demand from expressing themselves (*House of Commons Debates*, 5th series, Vol. 849, col. 977). This time, however, there were no Conservative abstentions.

The government did face problems, though, during the committee stage of the Bill, for John Biffen and Nicholas Ridley proceeded to move amendments limiting the duration of the prices and incomes policy to just one year, rather than three. Ignoring the pleas of the government's

Chief Whip, Biffen and Ridley then forced a Division on their amendments, whereupon they were supported by Opposition MPs, this ensuring a majority of two in favour of reducing the time limit on the government's policy.

The government reversed these amendments at Report Stage, thereby restoring the three-year provision, although John Biffen, Richard Body, Jock Bruce-Gardyne, Hugh Fraser and Enoch Powell voted against their government, whilst eight Conservative backbenchers abstained. Richard Body had already made clear his opposition to the drift of Heath's economic policy when he co-authored, with eight economists, a pamphlet entitled *Memorial to the Prime Minister* in which the money supply was identified as the underlying cause of inflation, thereby rendering any prices and incomes policy irrelevant, as well as constituting a betrayal of Conservative principles (*The Times*, 2 November 1972).

Continued neo-liberal hostility

Once the Counter Inflation Bill had reached the Statute Book, Heath turned his attention, during the summer of 1973, to formulating phase three, albeit amidst continued opposition both from the trade unions, and from neo-liberals on the Conservative backbenchers. His problems were compounded, though, by a motion passed at the annual conference of the National Union of Mineworkers in July, which called for pay increases of between 22 per cent and 47 per cent, an ominous portent of things to come.

October also witnessed the debate over incomes policy being continued via the Conservative's annual conference. An economic policy motion calling for partnership between Heath's Government, trade union leaders and employers' representatives was supported by an overwhelming majority, but not before it had been roundly condemned by Conservative neo-liberals irked at the corporatist ramifications. Such critics expressed considerable annoyance at the implication that the TUC represented all workers and that the CBI spoke on behalf of all employers.

Indeed, some neo-liberal critics of the Heath government's alleged drift towards corporatism portrayed themselves as guardians of the *petit bourgeoisie* and the embattled small entrepreneur, who were apparently being squeezed out of existence by big business and organized labour. Such Conservatives claimed that for a number of reasons, small businesses and the self-employed were particularly hard-hit by the Heath government's increasingly prescriptive approach to the determination of prices and incomes.

First, it was alleged that whilst domestic prices might be constrained by the Heath government's statutory prices and incomes policy, international prices were clearly beyond such control, and thus continued to rise regardless. This, it was alleged, made it profitable for larger firms to redirect their activities to foreign trade and exports, thereby maintaining profit margins in a manner which was beyond the capabilities of small firms whose markets were almost entirely local and domestic.

A second problem which small businesses were deemed to experience under Heath's statutory policy on prices and incomes was that although some of them had to import supplies and materials, and thus pay the higher prices which overseas manufacturers were charging, they were subsequently unable to recoup these higher costs from British customers via higher prices, as they would normally have been able to in a free-market economy.

The third problem which some Conservative neo-liberals specifically attributed to small businesses and the self-employed was that a recent upturn in demand and fuller order books had been accompanied by a shortage of certain supplies and materials, whereupon suppliers were giving priority to their larger customers. Once again, it was argued, the *petit bourgeoisie* – the traditional bedrock of Conservative electoral support – was suffering most, and in many cases being driven out of business completely, as a consequence of Heath's statutory prices and incomes policy.

The fourth and final problem which some Conservative neo-liberals ascribed to small businesses and the self-employed in this context was that unlike larger firms, they were unable to circumvent the pay policy by offering improved fringe benefits to their employees, which in turn rendered it difficult for them to retain staff or maintain morale. Once again, the solution urged by Conservative neo-liberals was for Heath to restore free-market forces, thereby permitting prices and incomes to be determined by the natural laws of supply and demand.

The government's economic policies (especially the reversion to incomes policy) were also being subject to criticisms in a number of other Conservative party forums during the latter half of 1973. For example, when the Chief Secretary to the Treasury, Patrick Jenkin, attended a Bow Group meeting to explain the government's economic strategy, he sought to remind his audience that the Conservative party had never been – and hopefully never would become – a party of unfettered economic *laissez-faire*, whereupon he was subjected to a bout of heckling. By contrast, the same audience warmly applauded John Biffen's eulogy to "Powellite economics", and his assertion that there could not be "any long-term future for the Conservative party if it is committed in perpetuity to this kind of [interventionist] policy" (*The Times*, 11 October 1973). At about the same time, Heath sought to defend his government's policies at a meeting of the party's 1922 Committee, whereupon he was subject to some tough questioning by a number of MPs (*The Times*, 19 October 1973). Meanwhile, Teddy Taylor was urging Heath to re-admit Enoch Powell to the Cabinet, claiming that Powell's views now enjoyed widespread support within the Conservative party (*The Times*, 16 October 1973).

Heath perseveres with "stage three"

None of these criticisms deterred Heath from proceeding with stage three of his statutory prices and incomes policy in October 1973. This phase entailed pay increases of no more than £2.25 per week, or 7 per cent per annum, up to a limit of £350 per person. It was left to workers and trade unions themselves to decide whether to opt for a flat-rate or percentage increase. This third stage also enshrined scope for productivity-linked pay increases of one per cent, or, where productivity increases were not deemed possible, one per cent increases in certain fringe benefits, such as sickness pay or holiday entitlement. Heath also proposed "threshold payments", whereby an additional 40 pence per week would be payable for every one per cent increase above 7 per cent in the Retail Price Index during stage three, which was intended to remain in force for twelve months. Overall, ministers envisaged that most workers would receive wage increases of about 8 per cent during this period.

One particularly significant feature of stage three was the provision for special payments to those who worked "unsocial hours". This was incorporated into stage three explicitly to assuage the National Union Miners, who had already (in July) submitted a claim for wage increases of between 22 per cent and 47 per cent. Heath had held a secret meeting with the NUM President, Joe Gormley, during July, the only other person in attendance being Sir William Armstrong, the Cabinet Secretary (and also Heath's main adviser on counter-inflation policy at the time). At this meeting, Heath and Armstrong believed that they had secured a pledge from Gormley that the inclusion of a special "unsocial hours" payment within stage three would be matched by a willingness on the NUM's part to settle within the proposed pay limit. Heath was therefore confident that Gormley, as President of the NUM, would be able to secure the support of the union's national executive for a pay deal which was within the parameters of stage three, but also included an additional sum in recognition of the miners' unsocial hours.

Another miners' strike

However, Heath was to become the unfortunate victim of both international events and internal NUM politics. On October 6 – two days before the formal announcement of stage three – the Yom Kippur war broke out in the Middle East. This, in turn, resulted in a quadrupling of oil prices by OPEC, at a time when Britain had yet to reap the full economic benefits of North Sea oil. This massive increase in oil prices in the Middle East was extremely damaging to Heath's anti-inflationary strategy, especially as it coincided with the start of stage three. It also, needless to say, significantly enhanced the bargaining power – critics would say "industrial muscle" or "potential for blackmail" – of the NUM.

Meanwhile, Heath's hope that Gormley would be able to secure the support of the NUM executive for a pay deal within the parameters of stage three, provided that a bonus for unsocial hours was added, faltered due to internal politics within the NUM at the time. On October 10, the National Coal Board offered the NUM a pay package which – including the unsocial hours bonus – amounted to more than 16 per cent. This offer was reckoned to be the maximum which the NCB could offer under the provisions of stage three. Indeed, the NCB informed the NUM that this pay package was their first and "final" offer, a declaration which unwittingly undermined the position of moderates on the NUM executive, for they were effectively being told that no improvements could be negotiated.

When he had discussed the ruse of a special unsocial hours payment with Heath back in July, Gormley assumed that the NCB would make an initial pay offer which deliberately excluded this bonus, whereupon the bonus would subsequently "be brought dramatically out from under the table at a late stage", thereby enabling Gormley to convince the NUM that he had secured this ingenious bonus through long, hard bargaining late into the night (Stewart, 1977: 180). This, he envisaged, would render such a deal more acceptable to his colleagues. However, by including the unsocial hours bonus in the first and "final" pay offer, the NCB left Gormley and NUM moderates without nothing to bargain over, thereby allowing the initiative to pass to the left, who exploited the situation to rally support for strike action.

A further problem for Heath – and Gormley – however, was that two members of the NUM's national executive were seeking re-election during the autumn of 1973, whereupon they had been "advised" by the Left that their re-election prospects would be seriously jeopardized if they decided to accept the NCB's pay offer. Gormley had originally calculated that with the support of these two members of the NUM executive, he would be able to secure a majority in favour of accepting the NCB's offer. In the event, however, the two executive members sought to ingratiate themselves with the left within the NUM, and voted against the NCB's pay offer, thereby committing the miners to industrial action (Walker, 1991: 123).

Initially, this industrial action was limited to an overtime ban, which commenced on 12 November 1973, but its impact was significantly and swiftly compounded by separate, but simultaneous, industrial action by electricity power workers, who started a ban on "out of hours" work in support of their own pay claim. Faced with industrial action by both coalminers and electricity power workers, Heath declared, on 13 November, another State of Emergency, along with restrictions on the use of electricity (in order to conserve diminishing fuel supplies). To add to the Heath government's woes, mid-December witnessed the start of an overtime ban by ASLEF, one of the train drivers' unions, which effectively meant that the transportation of coal from pit-head to power station would be seriously impeded.

On 28 November, Heath summoned the whole NUM executive to 10 Downing Street for a meeting with the full Cabinet, whereupon he intimated that more money might be made available for the miners via an imminent Pay Board report on wage relativities. Heath also promised a review of the coal industry, which might yield improved pensions and other fringe benefits for miners. Although Gormley was favourably disposed to Heath's conciliatory proposals, most of his colleagues on the NUM executive were less amenable, to the extent that they voted 18–5 *against* putting Heath's proposals to Britain's miners via a pit-head ballot.

The intransigence of many senior officials within the NUM increased suspicion amongst Conservative ministers that the miners' pay dispute was really a façade behind which lay a politically-motivated attempt to bring the government down. After all, the (communist) Vice President of the NUM, Mick McGahey, had told Heath to his face that he wanted to see the government defeated, and this lent credence to ministerial suspicions that the NUM was acting as the self-appointed vanguard of the British working class, aiming to overthrow a Conservative government through syndicalist means (Heath, 1998: 505).

On 13 December, Heath announced that in order to eke out the country's dwindling coal reserves, Britain would be put on a three-day working week in the New Year. At the same time, Heath appointed the emollient William Whitelaw as Secretary of State for Employment, evidently hopeful that if anyone could secure an amicable settlement with the NUM, then it was he. Indeed, Whitelaw and Joe Gormley very nearly did secure a breakthrough, the latter having suggested that an improved pay offer could be made to the miners by way of "compensation" for the time spent waiting for lifts to take them down the pit shafts at the start of their shifts, coupled with the time spent bathing at the end of each shift. Whitelaw intimated that "this did seem a possible way forward", subject to the agreement of the NCB and the Pay Board itself (Whitelaw, 1989: 128).

This possible solution was effectively sabotaged, though, when Gormley mentioned it – in confidence – to the Labour leader, Harold Wilson, who then put it forward, in the House of Commons, as if it were his own idea. This rendered it politically impossible for Heath and his ministerial colleagues to proceed with the initiative, much to the chagrin of both Whitelaw and Gormley. Indeed, Gormley later alleged that Wilson had deliberately wrecked the prospect of a settlement in order to secure political advantage for the Labour party, knowing that his action "would inevitably set the miners on another collision course with the Government". As such, Gormley described Wilson's behaviour as "completely despicable" (Gormley, 1982: 135). However, if some senior officials within the NUM were as intent on bringing down the Heath Government as many ministers believed, then it seems unlikely that the Whitelaw–Gormley initiative would have proved sufficient to end the miners' strike anyway, even if it had not been undermined by Wilson.

The next initiative to resolve the dispute emanated from the TUC itself, for many trade union leaders were themselves increasingly concerned at the impact of the three-day working week, particularly with regard to the implications for the jobs and earnings of their own members. Consequently, at a routine meeting of the National Economic Development Council on 9 January 1974, the TUC sought to assure the Heath government (via the Chancellor, Tony Barber) that the trade unions would *not* use any agreement reached between ministers and the miners "as an argument in negotiations in their own settlements" (TUC, 1974: 8). This assurance was rejected, however, with Heath and his colleagues not convinced that the TUC could genuinely guarantee the compliance of their affiliated members with such an undertaking.

The government's rejection of the TUC's initiative led some trade union leaders to suspect that it was actually Heath and his ministerial colleagues who were seeking to prolong the miners' strike for their own political ends, namely to call a general election in which they could secure re-election by being seen to stand firm against the NUM and trade union militancy. Other union leaders believed that the rejection of the TUC's olive branch was merely a result of Heath's own "pig-headedness" (Chapple, 1984: 136). Whichever explanation trade unions subscribed to, it was evident by January 1974 that there was a lamentable lack of trust on both sides.

One final opportunity to avert an all-out miners' strike presented itself on 24 January, the very same day that the NUM executive decided to proceed with a ballot of its members, in which they would be recommended to vote in favour of a national stoppage. A report on the issue of relativities was published by the Pay Board, wherein it was suggested that a new Relativities Board should be established, which would investigate whether certain groups of workers ought to be granted higher pay awards in the context of relativity and comparability. Heath immediately intimated that the miners might be the first case investigated by such a Board, but emphasized that this would only be after the resolution of the current dispute.

This pledge was too little, too late, for on 4 February, the NUM declared that its ballot had yielded a vote of 81 per cent in favour of an all-out strike by Britain's miners, to commence on 9 February. By this time Heath had already called a general election, to take place on 28 February, in which he would indeed ask the electorate: "Who governs Britain?", whereupon the voters were expected to answer: "the democratically-elected government, not militant trade unions". The Conservative's manifesto for the February 1974 election argued that acceptance of the NUM's demands would mean "accepting the abuse of industrial power to gain a privileged position", whilst also serving to "undermine the position of moderate trade union leaders".

The implications for incomes policy

The miners' strike also served to sustain the ongoing debate within the Conservative party over the issue of incomes policy, with both opponents and proponents citing the dispute with the NUM as a vindication of their respective perspectives. Conservative neo-liberals viewed the miners' strike as yet another example of the folly and futility of seeking to determine wages via incomes policies, with Enoch Powell foremost amongst those experiencing the "grim satisfaction" of seeing his repeated warnings being vindicated. The only viable method of determining wages, Powell reiterated, was through free collective bargaining, whereby the price of labour, like the price of any other commodity, would be determined by the immutable laws of supply and demand (*House of Commons Debates*, 5th series, Vol. 867, cols. 214–20). This "grim satisfaction" was shared by another backbench Conservative neo-liberal, Anthony Fell, who tartly observed that "chickens have a way of coming home to roost" (*House of Commons Debates*, 5th series, Vol. 864, cols. 725–7).

The miners' strike also served to win converts to economic neo-liberalism amongst some of Heath's ministerial colleagues. Certainly, as previously intimated, ministers such as Geoffrey Howe, Sir Keith Joseph and Margaret Thatcher subsequently became enamoured with the free market in the wake of their experiences in the Heath Government, and therefore became prominent opponents of incomes policies. The 1973–4 miners' strike persuaded them of alleged merits of the neo-liberal case against incomes policy, a conversion which was to have a profound impact on the Conservative party's subsequent approach to pay determination.

By contrast, Conservative proponents of incomes policies believed that the miners' strike provided yet more evidence of the need for a coherent policy on prices and incomes, one which ought, as far as practicably possible, to be based on agreement between government, trade union leaders and employers' representatives. Christopher Woodhouse was amongst those Conservatives convinced that it was necessary to develop a multilaterally agreed system for vetting and controlling prices and incomes (*House of Commons Debates*, 5th series, Vol. 868, col. 1298), whilst David Knox asserted that one of the most important questions facing government in contemporary Britain was whether to sustain full employment, and thus rely upon incomes policies to restrain wage increases, or, alternatively, to curb inflation via deflation of the economy, thereby reducing demand. Knox was adamant that the former option was the one which governments ought to follow, insisting that "in a full-employment situation, a prices and incomes policy is absolutely essential . . . indispensable" in order "to prevent people using to the full the bargaining power that a full-employment economy gives them" (*House of Commons Debates*, 5th series, Vol. 868, cols. 1255–60).

Yet just as Heath's conflict with the miners was serving to convert some Conservatives to economic neo-liberalism (and thus opposition to incomes policy), so too was the dispute finally persuading others on the backbenches of the need for such policies. Thus did William Shelton, a parliamentary private secretary, acknowledge that whilst he had been sceptical about incomes policies at the time of the first miners' strike in 1972, he had since become convinced of the need for such policies, due to the apparent failure of the Heath government's free market approach (*House of Commons Debates*, 5th series, Vol. 868, col. 1327).

The extent to which the miners' strike exacerbated disagreements in the Conservative party over whether wages should be determined by free collective bargaining or incomes policies was clearly illustrated by the sharp exchange which occurred on the floor of the House of Commons, between Enoch Powell and Patrick McNair-Wilson (*House of Commons Debates, 5th series*, Vol. 867, col. 125).

Yet in spite of the experiences with the miners, and the increasing opposition on the Conservative backbenches to incomes policy, Heath led the Conservative party into the February 1974 general election with a manifesto commitment to "renew our offer to the TUC and CBI to join us in working out an effective voluntary pay and prices policy, ultimately to replace the existing statutory policy, in the management of which both sides of industry would jointly participate".

In recognizing that, ultimately, neither a wages free-for-all nor state determination of incomes were desirable or feasible, Heath apparently accepted the argument outlined in a paper presented to his Steering Committee that:

> A policy which ultimately depends largely upon social pressures for its efficiency requires in the long-term the support of a good deal more than a half to two thirds of the people. As a temporary expedient to deal with a critical situation most people are probably prepared, if reluctantly, to submit their demands to the procrustean judgement of a statutory authority, but few people in the long term are going to be prepared to leave it to the government to decide the remuneration appropriate to their work. The prodigious extension of the powers of the state which this would represent would be distasteful to a large section of the middle class while that third of the working class on which we depend for success at the polls might well think if the government is going to settle their wages they would do better with a government of their own kind. (Fraser et al. 1973)

This paper was emphatic that "the responsibility for determining what is a fair basis of remuneration as between one occupation and another needs to rest on a broader base than a government ruling or even an Act of Parliament".

However, Heath and his colleagues were denied the opportunity of developing such a broader-based incomes policy due to the result of the February 1974 general election, for although the Conservative party won 1/4 million more votes than the Labour Party, they won four fewer seats. Heath initially sought to form a coalition government with the Liberal Party (who had fourteen MPs), but the Liberals rejected this proposition, due in large part to Heath's refusal to offer a firm commitment to electoral reform, but also because the Liberal Party was reluctant to be seen "propping up" a government which had lost its majority, and thus, arguably, its mandate to govern (Steel, 1980: 14–16). Having been spurned by the Liberals (and the Ulster Unionists, who had declined an invitation to take the Conservative whip in the House of Commons), Heath tendered his resignation to the Queen, whereupon Harold Wilson became Prime Minister, albeit presiding over a minority Labour government which was thirty-four seats short of an overall Commons majority.

6

Seeking to sustain a social contract: The Wilson–Callaghan governments, 1974–1979

The search for rapprochement

The Labour party's defeat in the 1970 general election meant that the trade unions found themselves facing a Conservative government committed to fundamental reform of industrial relations. Such a context compelled the Labour party and the trade unions to seek a *rapprochement* after the ill-will caused by *In Place of Strife* and the pursuit of incomes policies designed to restrain wage increases, rather than facilitate their planned growth as originally envisaged. The election of a Conservative government determined to give legislative effect to the measures enshrined in *Fair Deal at Work*, helped to bring the Labour party and the trade unions closer together again, a semblance of unity facilitated by their common opposition to the Heath government.

However, the degree of animosity engendered by both *In Place of Strife* and the Wilson government's various incomes policies meant that something more tangible was needed in order to re-establish a fruitful partnership between the Labour party and the trade unions. Mere opposition to the Conservatives was not quite enough; something constructive was required. Furthermore, Labour's leadership recognized that the party's prospects at the next general election would partly depend on the extent to which it could convince the electorate that it would enjoy a more harmonious working relationship with the trade unions in future.

Although *In Place of Strife* had been abandoned, and would no longer be a barrier to fraternity between Labour and the unions by the time of the next general election, there remained the trade unions' traditional opposition to incomes policies, derived from their commitment to free collective bargaining. This stance jarred with the Labour party's interventionist economic policies, and commitment to full employment, yet Labour's Shadow Cabinet recognized that the trade unions would reject further incomes policies, especially whilst the party was in Opposition.

Lest the Labour leadership was in any doubt about the implacable hostility of the trade unions to incomes policies, a number of union leaders made abundantly clear, right from the outset, their opposition to government determination of wages. At the Labour party's 1970 annual conference, the General Secretary of the TGWU (then Britain's largest trade union), Jack Jones, criticized those – including "some politicians" – who advocated wage restraint via incomes policies, but who themselves had "never been covered by a wage claim because . . . they never worked for a living". Jones' peroration, delivered in support of a motion declaring "total opposition to restrictions on collective bargaining", was endorsed by the president of the AEU, Hugh Scanlon, who declared that the Labour party should only talk about a "socialist incomes policy" when "we own the means of production, distribution and exchange".

Constructing a "social contract"

At the same time, however, Harold Wilson's former economic adviser, Lord (Thomas) Balogh, was expounding on the inflationary consequences of trade union wage demands, which also fuelled unemployment. Balogh was emphatic that the trade unions' commitment to free collective bargaining in the realm of wage determination was "incompatible with the achievement . . . of full employment". The solution, Balogh suggested, was the development of a *social contract* between Labour and the trade unions, which would determine the relationship between the industrial and political wings of the labour movement when the party was next in Office. However, he was emphatic that an incomes policy would be imperative if a Labour government was to achieve the economic and social objectives which both the party *and* the trade unions were committed to (Balogh, 1970: 34).

It was in the context of this conundrum that a *social contract* was indeed developed, emanating from a series of meetings between the Labour party–TUC Liaison Committee, formed in January 1972, and comprising senior members of the TUC's General Council, the Shadow Cabinet and Labour's National Executive Committee. Published in July 1972, the *social contract* delineated the main policies to which the next Labour government would formally be committed. In the realm of industrial relations, these policies would include immediate repeal of the Industrial Relations Act, the establishment of an Advisory, Conciliation and Arbitration Service (ACAS) to mediate when major industrial disputes arose, and employment protection legislation. There was also a proposal to develop a system of industrial democracy.

With regard to the vexatious issue of pay determination, the *social contract* studiously avoided advocacy of a formal incomes policy, even though some senior figures in the Labour party had originally wanted to make repeal of the Industrial Relations Act conditional on the TUC accepting "in advance the need for an incomes policy" (Benn, 1988: 407; see also Callaghan, 1971: 2–3; Castle, 1970: 356–7; Crosland, 1971: 3; Lever, 1971). Yet at one particular meeting of the Labour party–TUC Liaison Committee, Jack Jones warned that: "It would be disastrous if any word went out from this meeting that we had been discussing prices and incomes policy." Indeed, such was the apparent sensitivity of the trade unions on this issue that "any mention even of a voluntary policy was taboo" (Castle, 1980: 10). Instead, the emphasis was on voluntary wage restraint by the trade unions in return for a commitment by the Labour party to maintain full employment *and* improve the social wage, via higher welfare benefits and old-age pensions.

The Labour party leadership evidently hoped that improvements in the social wage would encourage – and enable – the trade unions to exercise voluntary restraint when seeking improvement "real" wages (although once Labour entered Office, Edmund Dell immediately began to harbour serious doubts about whether most trade unionists really cared about the "social wage", as opposed to "real" money wages (Dell, 1991: 148–9)). There would, it was hoped, be no need for a formal incomes policy and this, coupled with the promised repeal of the Industrial Relations Act and new employment protection legislation, was intended to procure a more harmonious relationship between the next Labour government and the trade unions.

The need for "responsible" collective bargaining

On this basis, James Callaghan informed the TUC at its 1974 annual conference that the *social contract* was a "means of achieving nothing less than the social and economic reconstruction of the country", whilst the Labour party's manifesto for the October 1974 general election decreed that the *social contract* lay at the "heart" of the manifesto, and formed the basis of "our programme to save the nation". The manifesto declared its opposition to "the authoritarian and bureaucratic system of wage control imposed by the Heath Government", and, instead, referred explicitly to "the newly restored right of free collective bargaining".

Indeed, the manifesto claimed that "the social contract . . . is not concerned even primarily with wages", but with a whole range of issues pertaining to social policy, wealth redistribution and full employment.

Yet the Labour party remained hopeful that the trade unions would exercise "responsible" collective bargaining in return for Ministerial commitments to full employment and improvements to the "social" wage. If the next Labour government could deliver its side of the social contract, and the unions delivered their side in the form of voluntary wage restraint, then the necessity for a formal incomes policy would be obviated.

A year earlier, at the Labour party's own annual conference, a motion had been endorsed declaring "opposition to any wage restraint or incomes policy designed to solve the problems of the economy by cutting the standards of living of workers". However, the same conference rejected an AUEW motion declaring opposition to incomes policy *in principle*. Labour's annual conference was, therefore, clearly acknowledging that some form of incomes policy might be acceptable, depending upon the circumstances in which it was introduced, the precise purpose it was intended to serve, and the format which it entailed.

Such was the faith placed by the Labour leadership in the *social contract*, coupled with voluntary pay restraint on the part of the trade unions, that James Callaghan informed delegates attending the TUC's 1974 annual conference that: "Rigid wage controls, statutory controls, interference with collective bargaining have all finished, whistled down the wind, a complete failure." Certainly, the senior Labour politicians and trade union officials involved in formulating the *social contract* "all agreed that a Labour government would never again introduce a statutory prices and incomes policy" (Castle, 1993: 441).

The apparent optimism of Labour's Front Bench that they would not need to resort to formal incomes policies might have been buttressed by the guidelines issued to affiliated trade unions by the TUC, in June 1974, via a document entitled *Collective Bargaining and the Social Contract*. These guidelines emphasized that "negotiators generally should recognize the scope for real increases in consumption are limited" whilst insisting that "a central negotiating objective . . . will to be ensure that real incomes are maintained" (TUC, 1974: 289).

Yet the allusion to maintaining "real incomes" was somewhat ambiguous, for whilst Labour ministers interpreted it as an indication of trade union willingness to exercise moderation when submitting pay claims, the fact that inflation averaged 16 per cent during 1974 suggested that the unions would need to seek comparable increases in order to "maintain the real incomes" of their members. Indeed, during 1974, average earnings increased by 20 per cent, thereby fuelling anxiety within the Cabinet right from the outset. In this context, the additional recommendation in *Collective Bargaining and the Social Contract* that trade unions should observe a twelve-month gap between their pay claims was of only limited comfort to Labour ministers.

Implementing the social contract

The Wilson government's immediate consternation at the trade unions' apparent failure to exercise wage restraint was compounded by the fact that the government had immediately set about delivering its side of the *social contract*. Although the Wilson government elected in February 1974 lacked a parliamentary majority, it immediately repealed the Industrial Relations Act (along with the National Industrial Relations Court), replacing it with a Trade Union and Labour Relations Act which effectively restored the legal immunities enjoyed by the unions prior to 1971.

The Wilson government also abolished the Pay Board – having first settled the miners' strike which had ostensibly prompted the Heath government to call the February general election in the first place – but retained the Price Code and the Price Commission, whilst also establishing a new Ministry of Prices, Consumer Protection and Fair Trading, whose Minister was included in the Cabinet. The new Labour government also fulfilled its commitment to establish an Advisory, Conciliation and Arbitration Service (ACAS).

Meanwhile, a rent freeze was introduced, as were food subsidies, in Dennis Healey's first two budgets. These budgets, in March and July 1974, also witnessed an increase in the value of social security benefits and old-age pensions, and an increase in income tax for high earners, coupled with a pledge to introduce, in the near future, new taxes on wealth and the transfer of capital. As Healey himself recalls, these measures not only represented Labour's adherence to its side of the *social contract*, they were also based upon the expectation that the trade unions would "respond by limiting their wage increases to what was needed to compensate for price increases in the following year" (Healey, 1989: 394). There was widespread recognition that ministerial haste in implementing many of Labour's *social contract* commitments was derived from the need to enhance the party's chances of securing a parliamentary majority in the imminent general election (although when the election was held in October 1974, the Labour government was re-elected with a majority of just three seats).

In the meantime, it was also significant that upon becoming Prime Minister following the February 1974 election, Wilson appointed Michael Foot as Secretary of State for Employment, even though in

Opposition, Reg Prentice had been Labour's employment spokesperson. However, Prentice was considered by many trade union leaders to be less sympathetic to the unions' aspirations than other senior Labour politicians, whilst also being a keen advocate of incomes policy. Thus was Michael Foot – to the delight of many trade unions and their leaders – appointed Employment Secretary. Incidentally, four years later, Prentice defected to the Conservative Party, alleging that the Labour party was being taken over by Marxists.

Towards a voluntary incomes policy

Having won the February 1974 general election, Cabinet ministers and trade union leaders alike immediately became concerned about the rate at which prices and incomes were increasing. A major problem derived from the "threshold" formula which had been enshrined in the third stage of the Heath government's incomes policy, whereby an additional 40p per week wage increase was permitted for *each* one per cent increase in the Retail Price Index above 7 per cent. By February 1974, when Labour entered Office, the RPI was recording an increase in the cost-of-living of more than 13 per cent, thereby triggering several "threshold" pay awards.

Obviously, Heath could not have foreseen at the time of formulating "stage three" the inflationary impact which would result from the quadrupling of oil prices by the OPEC nations in the autumn of 1973. Indeed, the full repercussions only began to manifest themselves after Labour had been returned to office, leading Wilson to acknolwedge that "with hindsight the thresholds were a disastrous mistake" for in circumstances "where world prices were rocketing, thresholds provided a major internal reinforcement to add to the already damaging external forces putting up prices" (Wilson, 1979: 43). For its part, by November 1974, the TUC was suggesting to its affiliated unions that it would be "far better to get prices rising more slowly, with money wages correspondingly not going up so fast, than to have prices and wages equating with each other at a higher and higher level which would inevitably be self-defeating for most trade unionists" (TUC, 1975: 349).

Yet during the first half of 1975, prices and incomes both continued their rapid upward trajectory. Whereas during the final quarter of 1973, the average increase in earnings stood at 12.5 per cent, by the final quarter of 1974 the rate of increase had risen to 25.5 per cent. By the second quarter of 1975, average wage increases were nudging 30 per cent, with the NUM having secured a 35 per cent pay increase at the beginning of the year. Such increases compelled Dennis Healey, in his April 1975 Budget speech, to observe that:

> The general rate of pay increases has been well above the increase in the cost of living . . . by February the retail price index stood 19.9 per cent over a year earlier, and the wage rate index was 28.9 per cent . . . pay has been running about 8 per cent or 9 per cent ahead of prices. I do not believe that anyone would claim that the TUC guidelines were intended to permit this result. (*House of Commons Debates*, 5th series, Vol. 890, cols. 281–2)

This observation led Healey to warn that:

> Bitter experience under many post-war Governments has taught most of us on both sides of the House that a statutory policy for incomes is unlikely to produce better results. Unless, however, the voluntary policy achieves stricter adherence to guidelines laid down by the trade unions of their own free will, the consequence can only be rising unemployment, cuts in public expenditure, lower living standards for the country, and growing tensions throughout our society. (*House of Commons Debates*, 5th series, Vol. 890, col. 282)

By this time, the TUC was itself acknowledging that "there had been undesirable gaps in the observance" of its own guidelines on pay (as stipulated in *Collective Bargaining and the Social Contract*), to the extent that:

> if settlements in the next round of negotiations were pitched at the level of some of those negotiated towards the middle of the year or if new settlements were made before the due date, the prospect of reducing inflation towards the end of the year and during the next year would be seriously threatened. (TUC, 1975: 354)

Phase One, 1975–1976

Throughout this time, a number of senior trade union leaders, most notably Len Murray and Jack Jones, were also imploring trade unionists to exercise restraint, but to no avail. Murray recalls:

> those union conferences passing resolutions calling for wage increases of 30–40 per cent. I also remember in tea rooms, in bars, the delegates – the same delegates who were voting the 30 per cent wage increases – saying to me directly: "Look, we've got to do something about this. We can't go on like this." (Quoted in Whitehead, 1975: 148–9)

Sharing Murray's consternation, and recognizing that ministerial patience with the trade unions was already starting to wear thin, Jack Jones seized the initiative in developing a formal incomes policy. In May 1975, Jones – with the support of Len Murray – persuaded the TUC's

General Council to endorse a policy whereby pay awards during the next twelve months would be limited to a flat-rate increase of £6 per week, but with no increase at all for those earning more than £8,500 per annum.

It was envisaged that such an incomes policy offered three particular advantages. First, a flat-rate pay increase of £6 per week appeared to avoided the ambiguities associated with traditional percentage increases and pay norms; with a flat-rate cash limit, all groups of workers would know exactly what they were entitled to.

Secondly, it was envisaged that a flat-rate cash increase – coupled with a pay freeze for those earning above £8,500 per annum – would imbue the incomes policy with an egalitarian element, ensuring that the main beneficaries would be those on the lowest wages, for whom a £6 per week increase represented a significant improvement at that time. Such a redistributive or egalitarian dimension was also envisaged as a means of securing the support of the left, both in the parliamentary Labour party, and in the trade unions. Thirdly, of course, it was anticipated that this incomes policy would presage a downward trajectory in the rate of inflation.

These considerations did not prevent criticism of the incomes policy from a variety of sources. On the contrary, the egalitarian and redistributive component was irksome to many of those trade unions representing skilled workers, who resented the erosion of pay differentials which it entailed. The incomes policy also incurred the wrath of many on the left, for whom free collective bargaining – in a predominantly capitalist society – remained sacrosanct. For such critics, recourse to an incomes policy – even if imbued with egalitarian or redistributive components – constituted an attempt by government (in this case a Labour Government) to make ordinary working people and their trade unions bear the sacrifices deemed necessary to curb inflation.

To opponents of incomes policy on the left of the labour movement, trade unions pursuing "excessive" pay increases each year were merely seeking to protect the incomes and standards of living of their members in the face of escalating prices. As such, it was believed that the cure for inflation ought to be governmental curbs on prices (and, by implication, profits) so that trade unions would not need to press for correspondingly high wage increases. Indeed, included in a six-point set of guidelines approved by the TUC's General Council on 25 June was a call for government action to limit price increases. This was linked to a call for a "price target" to be set for twelve months hence (i.e., June 1976), to which future pay increases would be linked.

Although the TUC's General Council did endorse the proposal that pay rises should be limited to £6 per week, with "nil increases" for those earning more than £8,500 per annum, it did so only by a majority of six, with nineteen in favour, thirteen against, and six abstentions. Amongst the trade unions whose representatives on the TUC voted *against* the £6 pay policy were the ASLEF, AUEW, AUEW-TASS, ASTMS, NALGO, NUM, NUPE, NUT and USDAW.

The narrowness of the majority, coupled with the range of trade unions and occupational groups opposing the proposed £6 pay limit, led Dennis Healey to doubt whether such an incomes policy would be adhered to voluntarily by the trade union movement. Certainly, some of the trade unions opposing the £6 pay limit did so on the grounds that they preferred a percentage pay "norm". As such, they insisted that the flat-rate cash figure should *not* be "envisaged as a permanent policy for continually eroding differentials either between or within negotiating groups" (TUC, 1975).

Considering a statutory incomes policy

Indeed, by early summer of 1975 "the debate within the Government was not whether there should be an incomes policy, but how far it should have statutory elements" (Dell, 1991: 160). At one stage, there were two Cabinet committees considering the options, along with an official (civil service) committee. There was also a one-day seminar held by Downing Street's Policy Unit, from which there emerged a recommendation similar to that being canvassed by the TUC's General Council, namely a flat-rate wage limit of £6 per week. It was further proposed that such a policy should be voluntary, but with a "battery of sanctions" held in reserve, whereby "any private employer breaking the policy would have tax penalties imposed, as well as being discriminated against in Government contracts, regional subsidies, investment allowances, etc." (Donoughue, 1987: 63–4). Clearly, the TUC's General Council and senior government officials were coming to similar conclusions, which in turn suggested that overall agreement on an incomes policy might more readily be secured than ministers had originally dared to hope.

Yet within the Cabinet itself, there was less agreement over precisely what form an incomes policy ought to take. Indeed, no less than three versions of an incomes policy were being mooted during June. The Employment Secretary, Michael Foot, was arguing in favour of an entirely voluntary incomes policy, whilst the Policy Unit at 10 Downing Street was a adhering to its call for a voluntary policy backed by the threat of sanctions. The third version being canvassed was a statutory incomes policy, this being urged on the Chancellor by the Treasury, which took a pessimistic view of the trade unions' ability or willingness to adhere to a voluntary policy (Donoughue, 1987: 65–6; see also

Blackstone and Plowden, 1988: 94). On 30 June 1975, at a meeting of one of the Cabinet committees examining incomes policies, the Chancellor sought support for the Treasury line, namely a statutory incomes policy permitting wage increases of no more than 10 per cent. Failure to adopt such a policy, it was argued, would result in a disastrous run on sterling in the financial markets. Wilson himself appeared to be persuaded of this line of argument – having previously been emphatically opposed to any element of compulsion *vis-à-vis* incomes policy – to the extent that "he said he would after all support a statutory pay policy, providing the legal sanctions were directed only against employers who conceded too much, and not against workers who demanded too much" (Healey, 1989: 395). Other ministers present, however, remained unconvinced and it was therefore left for a meeting of the full Cabinet to resolve, the following morning.

Wilson's apparent acceptance of the need for an element of compulsion caused such concern to Joe Haines and Bernard Donoughue (Wilson's Press Secretary and Senior Policy Adviser respectively) that at a little past midnight, and with the full Cabinet due to meet later that morning, the two of them drafted a minute to be sent immediately to Wilson, in order that he could read it before he went to bed. Haines and Donoughue reiterated their view that "the Cabinet is being faced with an attempt by the Treasury to stampede it into a statutory pay policy", a view which they claimed was validated by "the knowledge that no money was spent in defence of the pound on Monday". The clear implication was that the Treasury was deliberately permitting, if not tacitly encouraging, the collapse of sterling in order to "bounce" the Labour government into accepting a statutory incomes policy (Haines, 1977: 59), although this interpretation has been challenged by Edmund Dell, Labour's Paymaster General, who claims that Haines and Donoughue "naively adopted a conspiracy theory about Bank of England behaviour in managing the exchanges (Dell, 1991: 165).

When the full Cabinet met on 1 July, the Chancellor reiterated his argument that a statutory 10 per cent incomes policy was needed immediately in order to prevent any further run on the pound, whose value against other currencies was now dangerously low (Castle, 1980: 439, diary entry for 1 July 1975). Healey also pointed out that when he and Wilson had met Len Murray and Jack Jones the previous day, the two trade union leaders had declared their support for an inflation target of 10 per cent by September 1976, this to be reduced to single figures by the end of that year. What most concerned Murray and Jones, however was the issue of compliance, given that some trade unions might well resist an incomes policy designed to reduce inflation down to 10 per cent during the next fourteen months. Meanwhile, to the consternation of many of his Cabinet colleagues, Wilson let it be known that he favoured applying a "wage fund in the public sector, where people would have a choice between jobs or pay", whilst Roy Jenkins "favoured a total wage and price freeze for three months" (Benn, 1989: 411, diary entry for 1 July 1975).

What the Cabinet finally agreed upon was "a voluntary policy, but with statutory powers held in reserve if there was any widespread attempt to breach it" (Haines, 1977: 60). When this incomes policy was formally announced in the House of Commons on 11 July 1975, via a White Paper entitled *The Attack on Inflation*, Harold Wilson explained that the government would reserve the right to introduce statutory controls if voluntary wage restraint was not adhered to, although such compulsion would be directed at *employers* who breached the pay limits. Yet this proviso was not enough to prevent thirty-four Labour MPs from abstaining in a Commons vote on White Paper, whilst the ensuing legislation, introduced ten days later, also occasioned various abstentions and hostile amendments by disgruntled Labour MPs (Fishbein, 1984: 165; Wilson, 1979: 121). Wilson himself was relatively unperturbed, however, having previously reasoned that:

> The Tories will go along with our measures, they have to; and if the Left of the [Labour] Party votes against us, we therefore can rely on Tory support, but if the Tories move a motion of No Confidence, then of course the Labour party would no doubt unite to defend the Government. (Benn, 1989: 412, diary entry for 1 July 1975)

Wilson similarly reckoned that the trade unions would cooperate with the Cabinet's incomes policy partly on the grounds that if they failed to do so, and the government fell, they would almost inevitably be confronted with the return of a Conservative party now led by the increasingly anti-trade union Margaret Thatcher. In fact, Jack Jones cited another reason for his own support at this time, namely that "Harold Wilson, Barbara Castle and others had told me that there were members of the Government who were looking for a break-up, and were ready to move towards a coalition", leading Jones to fear that "the betrayal of 1931 could happen again" because "the Macdonalds, the Snowdons, the Jimmy Thomases are lurking around" (Jones, 1986: 299–300).

In January 1976, with the Cabinet considering what sort of incomes policy would follow the expiry of "phase one" at the end of July, the Central Policy Review Staff produced a forty-page memorandum on the need for a statutory prices and incomes policy, insisting also that: "Counter-inflation policy should be presented not simply as a temporary device, involving short-term sacrifice to get through a crisis, but as a permanent necessity . . . an incomes policy had to be seen as a vital ingredient in faster-rising real incomes in the medium to longer-term" (Blackstone and Plowden, 1988: 94).

Phase Two, 1976–1977

In May 1976 – by which time Harold Wilson had resigned and been replaced by James Callaghan – the government announced that "phase two" of its pay policy would commence in August. The figures stipulated for "phase two" actually emanated from the TUC itself, the government agreeing that the average pay increase for the twelve months starting in August should be 4.5 per cent. More specifically, it was proposed that pay rises should be no more than £2.50 for those earning up to £50 per week, and 5 per cent for those whose weekly wage was between £50–£80. For those earning more than £80 per week, the permitted wage increase was to be £4 per week.

To render "phase two" more palatable to the trade unions and their members, whilst also seeking to alleviate the plight of the lowest-paid, the Chancellor promised the TUC that acceptance of this incomes policy would be rewarded by an increase in tax relief and allowances. ministers were also at pains to emphasis that they attached "the highest importance to maintaining the principle of a voluntary policy" (Treasury, 1976: 8). Meanwhile, the incomes policy was to be accompanied by continued controls on prices, as stipulated in the Price Code, and enforced via the Price Commission.

The government further intimated that "phase two" would be followed by a return to more traditional methods of wage determination, namely free collective bargaining. Whether the Labour leadership seriously believed that this was feasible, or merely alluded to it in order to make "phase two" more palatable to the trade unions, is a matter of conjecture. It was doubtless a cause of concern to the Labour Cabinet that Jack Jones, who had been the staunchest trade union ally of the government during its recourse to incomes policy, was himself, by June 1976, calling for "a return to free collective bargaining towards the end of next year" (*The Times*, 18 June 1976).

In the meantime, though, Jones, along with David Basnett and Hugh Scanlon (leaders of the GMWU and AUEW respectively) issued a joint statement pledging support for "phase two" of Labour's incomes policy. This was not surprising, given that these three trade union leaders had been those most intimately involved in the discussions with ministers over the content of "phase two". Like many other trade union leaders during the spring of 1976, they had not disputed the need for a second year of incomes policy; their concern, rather, was over the details of such a policy.

With many of their union members being amongst the lowest paid, Jones and Basnett both favoured another flat-rate cash increase, on the grounds that this would benefit the low-paid far more than a percentage norm. Scanlon, however, desired a percentage norm because of his concern over the erosion of differentials which a flat-rate cash increase entailed. This stance was certainly understandable given that the engineers who Scanlon represented were amongst the most skilled, and thus better-paid, of the working class, and thus most resentful of any incomes policy which effectively favoured the lower paid.

Also concerned at the loss of differentials experienced by skilled workers was Frank Chapple, leader of the Electrical, Electronic, Telecommunication, and Plumbing Union (which merged with the Amalgamated Engineering Union to form the Amalgamated Engineering and Electrical Union in 1992). His "long-standing doubts and anxieties about pay policy grew", and although he refrained from directly rejecting the government's approach, he suspected that "the Government really needed the policy because it would otherwise be unable to resist the demands of its own employees", who Chapple thought "always seemed to be well cushioned, compared with the skilled workers that I represented" (Chapple, 1984: 141–2).

When announcing "phase two", the Labour government published figures to illustrate the net increases which would – in principle – accrue to workers according to their income. It was hoped that these figures would render "phase two" acceptable to the low-paid and higher-paid alike, for they suggested that – taking the proposed associated tax changes into account – a married couple earning £30 per week would receive a net weekly increase of £2.36, equivalent to 9.7 per cent, whilst another married couple on £150 per week would accrue a net increase in weekly income of £4.69, equivalent to 5 per cent (Treasury, 1976: 13; see also TUC Annual Report 1976: 410). In other words, the lowest paid would gain the largest percentage increases, whilst the better-off would continue to obtain higher cash increases. There were, it seemed, to be no losers.

Trade union endorsement of "phase two" was provided at a special conference of the TUC held on 16 June 1976, when the General Council's report entitled *The Social Contract 1976–77* – and which included the declaration that: "The pay guidelines reflect the view of the General Council that the package agreed with the Government is at a level and of a form which will be acceptable to the trade union movement" – was approved by 9,262,000 votes to 531,000. However, in spite of such overwhelming support, some trade unions were already making it clear that this second year of incomes policy was to be the last; the Labour government could not rely upon their support in a year's time.

This was confirmed at the TUC's annual conference in September where delegates voted for a composite motion moved by USDAW, and seconded by the TGWU, calling for "a planned return to free collective bargaining" ("planned" in order to "avoid a wages free-for-all") at the end of "phase two", whilst also declaring that "in a return to free collective bargaining", one of the issues which ought to receive the highest priority was "the recognition and payment of satisfactory differentials to reward ability, effort, skill and responsibilty". Yet this effective call for a restoration of differentials was also accompanied by a demand for "a continued and developing emphasis on improvements in basic rates and other special measures in order to assist workers on low pay and implement a TUC minimum wage policy" (TUC Annual Report 1976: 637).

The reference to a "planned" return to free collective bargaining offered ministers hope that a deal of some kind might be secured with the trade unions the following year. Such hope was raised a little further when, in December, Len Murray informed Labour ministers that the trade unions might well accept a third year of wage restraint *if* the Government could respond with a satisfactory package of policies concerning price controls and lower unemployment. For Jack Jones, such a "package" would need to include "import deposits or controls, a measure of reflation, a prices freeze, and very substantial increases in old-age pensions. We need an alternative economic policy . . . " (*The Times*, 23 May 1977).

Tensions within the trade unions

Although such a policy was not forthcoming, Jones still appealed to his members to accept a third year of formal wage restraint. However, his appeal was in vain, for at the TGWU's annual conference in the summer of 1977, delegates voted against a third year of wage restraint. A similar pattern emerged elsewhere during the summer of 1977, whereby trade union leaders – including such senior figures as Hugh Scanlon, David Basnett and Len Murray – urged their members to accept a third year of pay restraint, only to have their exhortations rebuffed by delegates voting at the annual conference of their respective unions, or by senior officals on the governing bodies of the unions.

By 1977, it was becoming increasingly apparent that whatever trade union leaders felt about the desirability or necessity of continued wage restraint, their members in the work-place were growing increasingly restless and resentful. Indeed, some trade union leaders at the TUC's 1976 annual conference had called for a return to free collective bargaining precisely because they recognized that their members would not tolerate a "phase three". As the leader of the Furniture, Timber and Allied Trades Union had argued when moving a motion opposing "the continuation of wage restraint in any form", if any attempt was made at imposing another incomes policy after the expiry of "phase two" in July 1977, "We shall have a revolt on our hands by the rank and file", for whilst "we can sit in this cosy and comfortable hall and take a decision . . . there are several million workers outside in offices and factories . . . who will by then probably have a different point of view" (TUC Annual Report 1976: 522).

Phase Three, 1977–1978

In spite of – or perhaps because of – the clear signals emanating from the trade unions that they wanted a return to free collective bargaining after the expiry of "phase two", several Labour ministers spent much of the spring and summer of 1977 seeking to persuade the TUC of the need for a third year of wage restraint. For example, when meeting the Economic Committee of the TUC's General Council in April, the Chancellor – accompanied by the Secretaries of State for Prices and Consumer Protection, Employment, and Industry – insisted that he could manage the economy only by making assumptions about the likely movement of earnings during the next twelve months, and whilst he avoided "making explicit what he thought a satisfactory agreement on a future round of pay policy might be, he made clear his belief that the state of the economy and his own actions hinged on such a pay agreement being attained" (TUC Annual Report 1977: 224).

The trade unions remained unpersuaded, though, leaving the Cabinet facing the dilemma that whilst "we knew there must be some kind of a deal with the TUC . . . the TUC were strongly opposed to any figure for pay" (Barnett, 1982: 135). Callaghan, though, remained cautiously confident that with many trade union leaders (as opposed to their activists and conference delegates) and public opinion recognizing the continuing case for an incomes policy, "the Government could count on understanding for its policy, if not positive agreement, provided we showed ourselves sensitive to trade unions' attempts to remove the distortions that pay policy had brought about" (Callaghan, 1987: 469). Yet the most that the TUC was able or willing to offer was that it would urge affiliated trade unions to adhere to the twelve month "rule" after when "phase two" expired on 31 July, intended to facilitate an "orderly" return to free collective bargaining, and thereby avoiding a wages explosion at the end of "phase two".

For his part, the Chancellor announced, on 15 July, the government's intention that inflation should be reduced to single figures by the following year (1978), which required that earnings should not increase by more than 10 per cent. This was to constitute the basis of "phase three", along with a corresponding 10 per cent limit on dividends. This policy was supported by most of the Cabinet, although Tony Benn was concerned that too much emphasis was being placed on a formal pay policy, whilst Stan Orme – although willing to acknowledge some of the drawbacks of free collective bargaining – maintained that incomes policies were incompatible with a market economy. The Employment Secretary, Michael Foot, meanwhile, was of the opinion that ministers ought to accept a declaration by the TUC that they would "recognize" the government's 10 per cent guideline, whilst Eric Varley was concerned that without some expressed figure laid down by the Cabinet, the government would be faced with a trade union free-for-all on the wages front, and constant leapfrogging.

At the same time, one of the Treasury ministers was concerned that the 10 per cent maximum for increases in *earnings* which the government was stipulating would be treated by many trade unions as a target for *wage* increases, whereupon the actual increase in *earnings* would be rather higher (Barnett, 1982: 134–6). This was because other payments, over and above actual wage rates and increases, such as overtime and bonuses, for example, tended to boost the level of overall earnings, to the extent that increases in earnings were invariably greater than increases in wages. Thus did the White Paper heralding "phase three" assert that "the general level of pay settlements should be moderate enough to secure that the national earnings increase is no more than 10 per cent . . . This means that the general level of settlements should must be well within single figures" (Treasury, 1977: 3).

Calling for an "orderly" return to free collective bargaining

The TUC's response to the government's announcement was the publication (via its Economic Committee), on 19 July, of a statement which reiterated the need for a return to free collective bargaining, with five main reasons advanced to justify its eschewal of further wage restraint after 31 July. First, it was claimed that in spite of the trade unions' acceptance of incomes policy since 1975, "the policy has fallen short of its objectives of containing inflation and reducing unemployment". Secondly, the TUC cited "the government's inability to check the rise of prices in the shops". The third reason was a direct consequence of these two factors, namely the decline in living standards which millions of workers and trade unionists had endured as a consequence of accepting wage restraint whilst prices and inflation increased at a higher or faster rate. Fourthly, and following on from the last point, the TUC pointed to the growing grass-roots revolt against further incomes policy, which was becoming increasingly apparent "in the swell of criticisms and justified complaints" emanating from ordinary trade unionists. The fifth reason cited by the TUC for rejecting a "phase three" of incomes policy was that the previous two years of pay restraint had yielded a variety of anomalies, discrepancies and grievances concerning wage structures and differentials; "Incomes policy has created some new problems and it has exacerbated some old and deeper-seated ones." These, the TUC insisted, could only be satisfactorily rectified "through the processes of voluntary collective bargaining", for there was "no other method by which the necessary adjustments can be made to meet the complex and ever changing requirements of industry and commerce" (TUC Annual Report 1977: 227–8).

However, in spite of such criticisms, the Callaghan government gleaned a glimmer of hope from the TUC's reiteration of the need for an *orderly* return to free collective bargaining, whereby trade unions should permit a full twelve months to elapse between their pay deals. The TUC's Economic Committee also stipulated that pay deals due to be completed, or come into effect, before 31 July (when "phase two" officially ended) should not be deferred. In other words, wage claims settled towards the end of "phase two" would remain in effect for a full twelve months. This too, it was envisaged, would prevent a wage explosion during the late summer and autumn of 1977. Furthermore, the Economic Committee urged the trade unions to consider carefully the inflationary consequences of pursuing wage increases in excess of 10 per cent (TUC Annual Report 1977: 227–8). As the Prime Minister himself observed: "In the absence of an agreement, the Government could hardly have asked for more" (Callaghan, 1987: 470).

The Economic Committee's insistence that the expiry of "phase two" should be followed by an *orderly* return to free collective bargaining, whereby each trade union was to abide by the twelve month "rule", was endorsed at the TUC's annual conference by 7,130,000 votes to 4,344,000. One of the most trenchant speeches in favour of this stance was provided by the leader of the AUEW, Hugh Scanlon, when he declared that:

> There is no need for excuses or alibis. The grass roots of our Movement have made perfectly plain their revolt against any question of a phase 3 and therefore there must be return to free collective bargaining. But free collective bargaining means what it says. It means that each union or industry will negotiate with its own employers increases in and terms thereto on which they can mutually agree, or take such action that they consider necessary in the event of a disagreement . . . The demand for free collective bargaining is overwhelming . . . free collective bargaining, with all its irrationality, with all its imperfections, must be the order of the day . . . (TUC annual Report 1977: 467–8)

A few trade unions – including ASTMS, NUM, SOGAT, and TGWU – urged an immediate return to free collective bargaining entailing the complete abandonment of the twelve month "rule", arguing that this still constituted a constraint on the trade unions' right to negotiate with employers, and therefore an impediment to free collective bargaining (TUC Annual Report 1977: 471–84 *passim*).

From a number of other delegates, meanwhile, came the argument that an incomes policy could only be acceptable if it was linked to a more explicitly socialist programme; until such time, incomes policy merely represented an attempt at holding down workers' wages and living standards in order to increase employers' profits and shareholders' dividends. Thus did Ken Gill, on behalf of AUEW-TASS (and backed by NUPE) move a motion which rejected "the theory that wage rises are a major contributory factor towards inflation", whilst arguing that "no incomes policy can be successful until an alternative economic strategy is initiated", one which included such measures as "a large-scale re-distribution of incomes and wealth", a substantial extension of public ownership, more effective controls on prices, imports and the movement of Capital, and "vastly improved social services by the injection of necessary resources" (TUC Annual Report 1977: 478). Such demands, however, left Frank Chapple of the EETPU "dumfounded" and led him to accuse Ken Gill of advocating "a siege economy".

Yet as already noted, delegates voted by a majority of almost 2.8 million to accept an "orderly" return to free collective bargaining, whereby the twelve month "rule" would be upheld. Support for this policy was provided by such trade unions as APECCS, AUEW, COHSE, EETPU, ISTF and USDAW, although the government would doubtless have been extremely concerned that unions such as the TGWU and the NUM were opposed to this policy, favouring as they did the immediate abandonment of the twelve month "rule".

One of the reasons why a number of trade unions were willing to proffer their support for such a policy was that by this time, many ministers themselves were acknowledging the need for "an orderly return to free collective bargaining", albeit one which avoided a "free-for-all or pay explosion". Some ministers apparently persuaded a number of trade unions that "phase three" was intended "to facilitate a phased return to normal collective bargaining" (Treasury, 1977: 2). If "phases" one and two of the Labour government's incomes policy were meant to have been temporary, then "phase three" was assumed to be transitional; an incomes policy intended to presage the end of incomes policies. Except that this proved not to be the case.

Phase Four, 1978–1979

On the contrary, the Cabinet was already contemplating "phase four" of its incomes policy at the end of 1977, even though ministers recognized that the trade union's were unlikely to provide even the degree of tacit support that had been proffered for "phase three". At a Cabinet meeting on 22 December 1977, Callaghan suggested that when "phase three" expired the following July, a pay norm of 5 per cent ought to be stipulated, which, allowing for wage drift, ought to limit overall increases in earnings to 7–8 per cent (these figures also representing the government's inflation target for the end of 1978).

The next couple of months entailed the Chancellor, along with the Secretaries of State for Employment, and Trade & Industry (Albert Booth and Eric Varley respectively) holding a series of informal talks with TUC leaders, although no substantive agreements were reached. Admittedly, the government was not really surprised, given the trade unions' insistence on a return to free collective bargaining, but what did cause additional consternation for the ministers involved was that by early 1978, the leaders of Britain's two largest trade unions were about to retire. Jack Jones stood down as leader of the TGWU in March 1978, to be replaced by Moss Evans, whilst Hugh Scanlon's retirement, in May, led to Terry Duffy becoming leader of the AUEW. Callaghan recalls that these changes "materially weakened" the hitherto constructive role played by the so-called "Neddy 6", namely the most prominent trade union leaders serving on the NEDC.

Until their retirement, Jones and Scanlon had, along with Alf Allen, David Basnett, Geoffrey Drain and Len Murray constituted the "Neddy 6", meeting on a monthly basis, with the Prime Minister and two or three of his Cabinet colleagues, usually including the Chancellor and the Employment Secretary. These meetings enabled ministers and trade union leaders to exchange information, and thereby facilitate an appreciation of each side's point of view. Callaghan lamented the retirement of both Jones and Scanlon in the spring of 1978, for Evans was opposed to incomes policies of any kind, whilst Duffy, although more sympathetic to the government's approach, "had not then acquired Hugh Scanlon's background knowledge or experience" (Callaghan, 1987: 520). Consequently, once Jones and Scanlon had retired, the "Neddy 6" was prone to greater division over economic issues such as incomes policies, thereby rendering it even more difficult for ministers to secure trade union acquiescence for further wage restraint.

The government's difficulties were compounded during the summer of 1978 by the Report of the Top Salaries Review Board, which was concerned with the pay of senior civil servants, heads of nationalized industries, and judges. Published in June, the Report recommended salary increases averaging 30 per cent, and as such, with "phase three" about to expire, Jones and Scanlon having retired, and the trade unions insisting upon a return to free collective bargaining, it could hardly have occurred at a worse time for the government.

Naturally, it was a cause of considerable consternation to Cabinet ministers when they met on 22 June, with the Chancellor, Denis Healey, inclined to accept the recommended increases, albeit phasing them in over two years, whilst Shirley Williams considered three years to be more desirable. Michael Foot, on the other hand, was unhappy about accepting the proposals at all, irrespective of how they were phased in, whilst David Owen was of the opinion that the government should not accept the recommended increases in full. Most other ministers, however, including the Prime Minister, and the Chief Secretary to the Treasury, believed that the Chancellor's option of phasing the full increases in over two years was the best one (Benn, 1990: 315, 317–18, diary entries for 22 June and 29 June 1978).

Yet when the Cabinet next met the following week, "it was evident that some . . . colleagues had got cold feet, and . . . were now fairly equally divided". Those ministers having second thoughts about accepting the recommendations of the Top Salaries Review Board had apparently been persuaded by Michael Foot's argument that "granting the increases would cause a serious outcry and a bitter response from our own supporters and the TUC" (Barnett, 1982: 161). Yet Callaghan remained unpersuaded, and declared that irrespective of the Cabinet split over the issue, the government's official policy would continue to be that endorsed the previous week.

In spite of having accepted the recommendations enshrined in the Report of the Top Salaries Review Board, Callaghan remained quietly hopeful that the trade unions might prove amenable to "phase four", if only on the grounds that he was widely expected to call a general election in the autumn of 1978, in which case, he assumed, the unions would wish to ensure the Labour party of their support for fear of paving the way for a Conservative Government.

Callaghan may have been further encouraged by the relative lack of opposition to "phase four" from within the Cabinet itself. Certainly, when ministers met on 13 July 1978 to discuss the government's incomes policy for the next twelve months (following the imminent expiry of "phase three"), few ministers were overtly critical, even though some of them harboured serious reservations about the viabilty of a fourth year of wage restraint, whilst others were simply unenthusiastic, viewing such a policy as something of a necessary evil. The criticism of incomes policy which traditionally emanated from left-wing ministers was partly muted because Michael Foot himself offered support for "phase four" (although he did believe that 5 per cent was too low), but it was also the case that those ministers who were normally critical of incomes policies simply lacked a viable alternative (see, for example, Barnett, 1982: 162; Donoughue, 1987: 155).

Callaghan was therefore able to conclude the 13 July Cabinet meeting by declaring that ministers were in support of a fourth successive incomes policy, although the 5 per cent limit was only given formal ministerial approval when the Cabinet next met one week later, and even then, a number of ministers expressed doubts about either the fairness (to the low paid) or efficacy of such a low figure (Benn, 1990: 326, diary entry for 20 July 1978). That such ministers formally approved the 5 per cent limit probably owed much to their own assumption that Callaghan would call a general election in the autumn, after which a new, more realistic or acceptable, policy on incomes would be developed (Barnett, 1982: 163).

Yet having secured Cabinet approval for "phase four", Callaghan met the TUC's General Council on 18 July, and reluctantly acknowledged that due to trade union insistence on a return to free collective bargaining "there would not be a formal agreement or possibly even an understanding on the pay policy" although he did express his hope that the unions would appreciate the need to secure lower inflation, an objective whose achievement "would depend on pay settlements". Indeed, Callaghan warned the General Council that if pay increases "remained at the current level, inflation would almost certainly reach double figures, with consequent adverse effects on sterling, interest rates, investment, output and jobs". Callaghan therefore suggested that the way forward might be an annual review whereby "the Government, the unions and the employers [would] reach an agreed view about the level of wage increases which would be appropriate". The General Council's responded by claiming that the government appeared to be "preoccupied with pay", and therefore failed to appreciate "the difficulties arising from continued pay restraint" (TUC Annual Report 1978: 289).

The Callaghan government's White Paper heralding "phase four" was published on 21 July. Entitled *Winning the Battle Against Inflation*, it formally declared that earnings should not increase by more than 5 per cent in the twelve months commencing on 1 August, although there were to be the usual exceptions for the low-paid, and in cases of "self-financing productivity schemes". The Government also urged that each trade union adhered to existing settlement dates (thereby effectively continuing the twelve month "rule"). The White Paper made clear the government's intention of applying the 5 per cent maximum to the public sector, whilst securing compliance from the private sector through "exercising its discretion in the fields of statutory assistance and other discretionary powers". The pursuit of a 5 per cent incomes policy was endorsed not only by the Treasury, but also the Central Policy Review Staff, and the Policy Unit at 10 Downing Street (Blackstone and Plowden, 1988: 94).

TUC opposition to further wage restraint

As expected, the response of the TUC's General Council to the government's White Paper was less than encouraging for ministers. Whilst maintaining that the TUC shared their determination to defeat inflation, "it does not accept the government's view on how this can be achieved". Instead, the TUC was adamant that "achieving a real rise in living standards in the coming year will depend not on pay guidelines or norms, but on the government's general economic and social policies". It was made clear that the trade unions "do not see the future in terms of the continuation of restrictive policies on current lines", to the extent that the General Council reiterated its call for the restoration of free collective bargaining, thereby rejecting "policies that concentrate on restricting pay" (TUC Annual Report 1978: 290–1).

This stance by the trade union movement was confirmed at the TUC's annual conference in September 1978, when there was widespread support for the NUM's motion urging that "after three years of restraint, trade unions must now negotiate freely in their members' interests", and thus declaring "opposition to Government policies of intervention and restraint in wage bargaining . . . and to any form of restrictive Government incomes policy". This call for "a return to normal and responsible collective bargaining" entailed a demand for the restoration of "just and adequate differentials" (which had been eroded during the previous three years of incomes policies), along with the "elimination of anomalies". Yet at the same time, the motion also called for "meaningful low pay targets" to be attained in order to eradicate poverty (TUC Annual Report 1978: 678). In the subsequent vote, the motion was supported by, among others, ASTMS, AUEW-TASS, COHSE, CPSA, NUGMW, NUPE, SOGAT and TGWU. Such breadth of trade union opposition clearly boded ill for the government's determination to persevere with a fourth year of wage restraint, as did Ken Gill's prophetic warning that:

> When a Labour Government disagrees with the trade union movement, then it is also certain that the Government is wrong. History has always shown this to be the case, and when as a result of that disagreement clashes have occurred, Labour suffers and those clashes end in disaster. (TUC Annual Report 1978: 550)

However, the Labour government remained convinced that its economic and social policies could only be successful if the trade unions exercised wage restraint via an incomes policy. Indeed, by the summer of 1978, it was evident that some ministers were actually thinking in terms of a permanent incomes policy whereby:

> collective bargaining is based each year on a broad agreement between Government, unions and employers about the maximum level of earnings which is compatible with keeping inflation under control . . . The policy for next year has been shaped so as to permit a transition to such longer term arrangements. (Treasury, 1978: 3)

James Callaghan himself was by now particularly keen on instituting some such method of pay determination, whereby:

> tripartite discussions [would] take place each year between the Government, unions and employers, in an attempt at creating a national consensus about the national level of earnings that would be compatible with keeping inflation at a low level; both sides would then work within such an understanding in their pay negotiations. (Callaghan, 1987: 521)

This approach reflected Callaghan's growing admiration for the (West) German system of "concerted action", whereby two key private sector wage claims near the beginning of the annual pay round "received intensive discussion at all levels of industry and government before they were finalized, and were then generally regarded as setting the pattern for the remainder". Callaghan viewed this as a possible means "by which the unions might return to . . . free collective bargaining without ill effects, provided they exercised an enlightened self-interest" (Callaghan, 1987: 474).

The government's strategy was lent qualified support by a few trade unions, most notably NALGO and the NUR, both of whom supported a motion at the TUC's 1978 annual conference which opposed "unilateral policies of wage restraint which are implemented without adequate consultation and bear most heavily on the public services", but did call for "a new approach to pay . . . within the framework of an economic contract with the Government". This approach should "be of a long-term nature and not simply a further extension of incomes policy", and would entail "agreement on flexible pay guidelines determined by discussion between the Government, employers and unions".

In moving the motion, the NALGO delegate explained that there was a need for a new approach to wage determination which avoided the extremes of free collective bargaining – the alleged virtues of which were not enjoyed by public sector employees – and government-imposed incomes policies. Instead, it was suggested that the "most rational system" would be for the trade unions to grant the TUC's General Council "some authority . . . .to negotiate a flexible norm". To continue with the existing approach, the delegate warned, would merely exacerbate "the frustration, annoyance and difficulties which are building up in our [public] services" (TUC Annual Report 1978: 551–2). In supporting the motion, Sid Weighell, on behalf of the NUR, insisted that: "We should be prepared to sit down with the Government to discuss a joint economic plan" (TUC Annual Report 1978: 553–4). However, the scale of trade union opposition to any form of incomes policy was, by now, so pronounced that this "compromise" was rejected in favour of the NUM's motion.

It was therefore apparent that the Labour government's approach was in sharp contrast to that of most trade unions, amongst whom there was a widespread determination to return to free collective bargaining after three successive years of wage restraint. Not only did incomes policy conflict with their *a priori* commitment to free collective bargaining, there was also a widespread feeling amongst the trade unions by 1978 that the Labour government had failed to deliver its side of the bargain, for having committed itself to increases in the "social" wage, as its side of the "social contract", ministers had presided over significant cuts in public expenditure, and thus a diminution of the social wage (although much of this had been unavoidable due to the conditions laid down in 1976 by the IMF). For example, the public expenditure White Paper for 1978–9 revealed plans for reductions totalling £3 billion.

However, ministers had always overestimated the extent to which ordinary trade unionists would happily accept improvements in the "social" wage *in lieu* of "real" increases in their wage packets. The latter were visible and tangible, whereas the former were, for many trade unionists, hypothetical or indiscernible. For the Government to claim that it was improving old-age pensions in return for wage restraint, for example, was usually of little consequence to a low-paid worker who would not be retiring for another 20 or 30 years. Trade unions and their members were, first and foremost, concerned about immediate or imminent improvements in take-home pay, what they considered to constitute "real" wages.

Three successive years of incomes policies – pursued by a government which had pledged, when elected, to reject incomes policy in favour of a return to free collective bargaining – had bred frustration and resentment amongst virtually all sections of the working population. Skilled workers resented the erosion of differentials which they had experienced, and were eager to use their industrial "muscle" or superior market position to secure the higher wage increases that they knew would be available to them under free collective bargaining. At the same time, many low-paid workers, often employed in the public sector, believed that incomes policies were merely perpetuating their impoverished position, especially when those incomes policies (with the exception of "phase one") entailed percentage increases, rather than flat-rate cash increases. As Alan Fisher, the leader of NUPE, graphically pointed out at the TUC's 1978 annual conference, "100 per cent of nothing is bugger all". Meanwhile, Charlie Donnett, of the GMWU, warned James Callaghan that "this winter we are saying enough is enough . . . we are not masochists, but we are getting desperate . . . I implore you, Prime Minister, before we are forced into a situation that we would rather not be in, please give us a sign that you are listening on behalf of the low paid". Public sector workers were also irked by the fact that the productivity exemptions applicable to some private sector workers were not appropriate or applicable to those employed in the public services; how could teachers, nurses, or social workers, for example, increase their productivity in order to improve their pay? And even if they somehow managed to do so, how would this actually generate the extra revenues required to finance a productivity payment?

By the autumn of 1978, therefore, the Callaghan government was facing a trade union movement increasingly united and uncompromising in its opposition to a fourth year of incomes policy; affluent and low-paid workers alike hankered after a return to free collective bargaining, convinced that they had gained little, if anything, from three years of government-imposed wage restraint. Indeed, many skilled workers were emphatic that they had experienced a relative decline in their earnings, whilst low-paid workers were convinced that their poverty had been compounded by wage restraint. Yet as some trade unions were quick to point out, profits and dividends had not been subject to any such restraint. Even the few trade union leaders who were still willing to countenance – in principle – a fourth year of incomes policy, decreed that the government's 5 per cent limit for "phase four" was too low, thereby rendering it unacceptable.

Such was the gravity of the situation for the government that Dennis Healey implored the TUC delegates to pledge their support for one more round of pay restraint, insisting that the outcome of the imminent general election might well depend upon it. Ministers evidently envisaged that the spectre of an anti-trade union Conservative government would be sufficient to induce trade union compliance with a fourth year of incomes policy.

What those ministers did not envisage, however, was that many trade union members would themselves vote Conservative in the general election, not least because the Conservative party, under Margaret Thatcher's leadership, was pledging a return to free collective bargaining, coupled with the restoration of differentials. For many trade unionists, therefore, the possibility of a Conservative government did not constitute the "threat" which Labour ministers implied, and hence most trade unions maintained their opposition to a fourth year of incomes policy and wage restraint.

Ministerial mistakes and misjudgements

A further blow to the Callaghan government was delivered the following month, when the Labour party's own annual conference voted – 4,017,000 to 1,924,000 – against "phase four". With the benefit of hindsight, Healey himself (the Chancellor at the time, no less) acknowledged that "we in the Cabinet should have realized that our five per cent norm would be provocative as well as unattainable". Indeed, Healey subsequently suggested that: "If we had been content with a formula like "single figures", we would have had lower settlements, have avoided the winter of discontent, and probably have won the election too" (Healey, 1989: 462–3).

The Labour government might also have secured a degree of tacit, *de facto* trade union support for "phase four" had Callaghan called the general election during the autumn of 1978, as most commentators had expected. Indeed, Callaghan himself had led the trade unions to believe that the election was about to be called, in which case, they might have been expected to quell some of their reservations about "phase four" so that ministers could conduct their campaign for re-election free from a backdrop of industrial conflict over pay. At the same time, some of Callaghan's Cabinet colleagues suppressed their own reservations about the viability of a 5 per cent pay policy on the grounds that a general election would be held in the autumn, with Joel Barnett subsequently doubting whether "it would have been agreed so easily if we had not all been so certain of an autumn election, before the pay round really got under way" (Barnett, 1982: 163).

Callaghan's subsequent decision *not* to call a general election during the autumn of 1978 was to prove fatal in two respects in the context of "phase four". First, there was considerable annoyance amongst many trade unions, who felt that they had been deliberately misled and manipulated by Callaghan and some of his Cabinet colleagues. There was a suspicion within the trade union movement that the various hints at an autumn election had merely been a ruse by Labour ministers to secure the trade unions' support for "phase four".

The second reason why Callaghan's decision *not* to call a general election during the autumn of 1978 was to prove fatal was that the Labour government would have to endure the next round of pay negotiations *before* the election (which had to be held by the autumn of 1979 at the latest). Given the trade unions' rejection of "phase four", and their annoyance at apparently being misled over the date of the general election, the government could no longer expect much sympathy or support from the trade unions: it had forfeited their trust. The conflict which was rapidly brewing over pay was to have fatal repercussions for the Labour government by the time that Callaghan did go to the polls the following spring, for the intervening period witnessed what became known as "the winter of discontent".

The 1978–1979 "winter of discontent"

Recognizing the hostility of many trade unions and their members to a fourth year of pay restraint, particularly when the proposed limit was just 5 per cent, November 1978 witnessed a frantic, last-ditch efforts by ministers to secure a deal with the TUC. A "Joint Agreement" (actually drafted for ministers by senior TUC representatives) was proposed, whereby the government, in return for TUC support for a fourth year of wage restraint, would grant a number of concessions to render such restraint more palatable. Amongst these concessions were special rewards for productivity, and the extension of "pay comparability" to the public sector. Furthermore, the Joint Agreement carefully omitted any specific reference to the figure of 5 per cent, opting instead to declare that:

> the fundamental objective of economic policy in 1978–79 is to keep the annual rate of inflation at not more than the present level and indeed to bring it down further . . . policies affecting incomes . . . must be related to this objective.

However, although the TUC's Economic Committee endorsed the Joint Agreement on the morning of 14 November, it was rejected later the same day by the General Council of the TUC. To add to the government's exasperation, this rejection was by just one vote, with two members of the TUC's General Council who were known to be in favour absent from the fateful meeting – one of them on holiday in Spain (Donoughue, 1987: 170).

Meanwhile, it was in the private sector that the first proper challenges to the Callaghan government's latest incomes policy emanated. In September, Ford car workers had embarked upon strike action after rejecting a 5 per cent pay offer by management. The strike ended nine weeks later when Ford increased their offer to 15 per cent. Not only was this settlement vastly in excess of the 5 per cent "norm", it also exposed Ford to government sanctions, although as the Chief Secretary to the Treasury, Joel Barnett, later admitted, the ensuing sanctions were largely symbolic:

> Ford had few direct contacts with the Government, other than supplying a small number of cars, ambulances and vans. There was . . . an agreement to provide large cash grants to build an engine plant in South Wales, but to cancel that would lose many jobs in an area of heavy unemployment.

> In any event, we could not cancel if we had wanted to, as the money was already legally committed. Still, we felt we must be seen to be taking some action, if sanctions, and possibly the whole pay policy, were not to collapse . . . we imposed a fairly ineffective sanction of not buying Ford cars. It was hoped that other companies, who would be more seriously hit by sanctions, would take heed. (Barnett, 1982: 164)

What really rendered the Callaghan government's sanctions policy obsolete, however, was Parliament's rejection of it after a Commons debate on the issue on 13 December. With the Liberals no longer supporting the Labour administration (the Lib–Lab pact having been terminated in the Summer), and four left-wing Labour MPs abstaining, the government lost the vote on its sanctions policy by six votes. Although the Labour government managed to win a vote of confidence in Parliament the following day, Callaghan openly acknowledged at the outset that the sanctions policy had been abandoned.

By the winter of 1978–9, Callaghan's 5 per cent pay policy was crumbling, as was the Labour government's political authority. With Ford having settled vastly in excess of 5 per cent, and Parliament rejecting the deployment of sanctions against private sector companies who breached the government's "pay norm", it was petrol tanker drivers who next posed a serious challenge to the government, threatening an all-out strike in pursuit of a 25 per cent wage increase. So eager was the government to avoid such a strike – recognizing that not only would it have caused widespread disruption, but also necessitated a State of Emergency – that it was quietly relieved when the petrol tanker drivers subsequently accepted a 20 per cent pay increase, thereby averting the threatened strike action.

Government relief was extremely short-lived, however, for the success of the petrol tanker drivers spurred road haulage lorry drivers into embarking (on 3 January 1979) upon strike action in support of a pay claim of more than 20 per cent. What enhanced the effectiveness – and the controversy – of the road haulage drivers industrial action was the deployment of secondary picketing, in order to limit further the movement of raw materials and supplies around the country. Although Labour ministers implored the TGWU leader, Moss Evans, to persuade his striking members to allow the transportation of "essential" supplies, Evans was impotent in the face of grass-roots militancy. Both the government and senior trade union leaders appeared powerless in the face of determined industrial action by rank-and-file trade union members and shop stewards. As Callaghan's Senior Policy Adviser expressed it: "The TUC, like the Government, was totally impotent before this anarchy" (Donoughue, 1987: 176).

By the time that the road haulage drivers had accepted a 21 per cent pay offer after three weeks on strike, it was the turn of public sector workers to embark upon industrial action, and it was this which really prompted the epithet "the winter of discontent", whilst also intensifying public hostility towards the trade unions in general. On 22 January, a number of unions representing public sector workers – led by the National Union of Public Employees – embarked upon a co-ordinated programme of industrial action in pursuance of a £60 per week minimum wage for manual workers in local government and the health service, many of whom constituted the lowest-paid workers in Britain. For them, a 5 per cent wage increase would be negligible; their sense of grievance and injustice was clearly fuelled by the level of pay awards being won by many private sector employees. As such, public sector workers were not only aggrieved at their poverty-level wages, but also at the widening gap between the public and private sectors in terms of pay. Yet however justified may have been the grievances of low-paid public sector workers at the time, their pursuit of industrial action gained little public sympathy. On the contrary, such action became the target of widespread public hostility and condemnation for two particular reasons. First, the groups of workers involved meant that industrial action had an extremely serious impact on sections of the public. For example, funerals were cancelled because local authority grave diggers were amongst those public sector employees on strike, whilst similar industrial action by dustmen meant that piles of household rubbish accumulated in gardens and streets, which in turn gave rise to concern about risks to public health.

The second reason why the industrial action pursued by public sector workers courted so much public hostility and condemnation was precisely that it was ordinary members of the public themselves who suffered. Indeed, it was often the most vulnerable or poorest who seemed to be hardest hit by public sector industrial action; the bereaved who could not bury their dead; the sick whose operations were cancelled; the poor without cars who were stranded by the absence of public transport, etc.

In this respect, industrial action by public sector workers seemed qualitatively different to such action by their counterparts in the private sector, for whilst the latter were ostensibly "harming" their employers, strike action by public sector workers unavoidably caused most hardship to the general public. Furthermore, whereas industrial action by private sector workers was usually targeted against a particular company, a strike by public sector workers was ultimately directed against the government (via the public) itself, thereby imbuing such action with constitutional and political ramifications. Indeed, during the "winter of discontent" the NUPE specifically targeted the constituencies of various Cabinet ministers for picketing.

Further disagreements within the Cabinet

The industrial action by public sector workers during early 1979 was rendered even more problematic for the Labour government because a number of Cabinet ministers were sympathetic to NUPE's case, whilst being appalled at the impact their action was having on the public, especially the most vulnerable sections of the community. Even James Callaghan himself, although declaring that he "had never in fifty years been so depressed as a trade unionist" (quoted in Barnett, 1982: 175), was reluctant to be too condemnatory or critical of the trade unions because: "His whole career had been built alongside the trade union movement, and he seemed to find it quite impossible to fight against it" (Donoughue, 1987: 177). This perspective was endorsed by one of Callaghan's Cabinet colleagues, William Rodgers, when he recalled that Callaghan "was a prisoner of his trade union past" (Rodgers, 1984: 178). The divided loyalties of certain Cabinet ministers was illustrated by the fact that when it was suggested that a State of Emergency be declared to counteract the impact of the strike by road haulage drivers, "the ministers in greatest opposition tended to be those sponsored by the Transport & General Workers Union" (Donoughue, 1987: 177).

By January 1979, the Treasury was urging the government to impose a statutory twelve-month pay freeze, but Callaghan "told the Treasury not to bother with pursuing it; he knew he could not get it through Parliament, and probably not even through his own Cabinet" (Donoughue, 1987: 176). Yet having rejected outright the imposition of a statutory pay freeze, the Cabinet was effectively left with three options. First, it could pursue a policy of "calculated capitulation", whereby the government settled the current pay disputes at almost any price, but then called a snap general election on the basis that victory at the polls would provide it with a mandate – and a sufficient parliamentary majority – to take a tougher stance *vis-à-vis* the trade unions and incomes policies thereafter.

Secondly, it "could make the present policy more flexible by reaching a quick settlement of the disputes which could not be won" whilst simultaneously "toughening our stance overall by introducing a stricter prices policy and vigorous monetary measures", the latter ensuring that pay increases of more than 9 per cent were financed from cuts in jobs and services.

The third option available to the Government by this time was for the Cabinet to seek a new pay agreement with the TUC, entailing a revised inflation target to be attained over a three-year period, coupled with a greater emphasis on the principle of comparability, especially for public sector workers (Donoughue, 1987: 177–8).

It was this third option which proved most attractive – or realistic –

to ministers, and thus it was that the government and the TUC sought to reach a new understanding in order hastily to repair the damage wrought by the "winter of discontent". For its part, the government established a Standing Commission on Pay Comparability, chaired by Professor Hugh Clegg, one of Britain's most senior and distinguished academics in the sphere of industrial relations. Establishing the Commission effectively constituted a humiliating public abandonment of the government's 5 per cent norm, as the criterion of comparability was to be invoked as a major means of determining pay awards, particularly in the public sector. Indeed, a number of disputes involving public sector workers were immediately submitted by the government to the Clegg Commission, with the expectation that it would report by August. In lieu of the Commission's recommendations, ministers granted a number of pay awards significantly in excess of 5 per cent – sometimes in excess of 10 per cent, in fact.

To little, too late; the damage done

There was also, in February 1979 (by which time the Conservative party was 18–19 per cent ahead of Labour in the opinion polls), the publication of *The Economy, the Government and Trade Union Responsibilities: A Joint Statement by the TUC and the Government* which represented a desperate attempt by ministers and TUC leaders at concocting some kind of new agreement which "at least give us a piece of paper on which to fight an election" (Barnett, 1982: 176). The Joint Statement stipulated that the government and the trade unions would seek to reduce inflation to 5 per cent "within three years from now", with an annual "economic assessment" taking place each Easter to ascertain the scope for pay increases, whilst also seeking some co-ordination or synchronization of certain pay awards. In the meantime, there was tacit agreement that a "norm" of 9 per cent would henceforth replace the 5 per cent pay policy.

At the same time, the TUC, partly under pressure from ministers, but also because it had itself become deeply concerned at the militancy and apparent callousness of some of its constituent unions and their members during the "winter of discontent", published its own guidelines on the conduct of future industrial action, suggesting, for example, that strikes should not only be considered as a measure of last resort, but ought also to be subject to a ballot of the workers involved. The TUC further urged trade unions to exercise greater responsibility and restraint with regard to picketing and secondary action.

Yet such initiatives were too little, too late. The damage was done. The trade unions had, via the "winter of discontent", inflamed public opinion against them, and this unprecedented hostility rebounded fatally on the Labour party itself in the general election held on May 3. As Callaghan himself later acknowledged: "The serious and widespread industrial dislocation caused by the strikes of January 1979 . . . sent the government's fortunes cascading downhill" (Callaghan, 1987: 540) whilst Dennis Healey declared that: "The cowardice and irresponsibility of some union leaders . . . at this time, guaranteed her [Margaret Thatcher's] election (Healey, 1989: 462; see also Donoghue, 1987: 187). Certainly, in the first volume of his recent biography of Margaret Thatcher, Campbell notes that: "Not only was Callaghan's credibilty destroyed, but public anger at the unions' indiscipline silenced the objections of her Tory critics and gave Mrs Thatcher's incoming Government the mandate to tackle the abuses of union power which she had lacked the previous autumn" (Campbell, 2000: 414–15). It was to take the Labour party eighteen years fully to recover, by which time, it too had steadily moved away from any commitment to incomes policy.

7

Back to free collective bargaining and beyond: The Thatcher–Major governments, 1979–1997

Initial ambiguity

Having evinced sharp disagreements over the issue of incomes policy in Office, the Conservatives in Opposition from 1974 to 1979 initially seemed mired in ambiguity, as the leadership sought for much of the time to steer something of a middle way in order to pacify the different wings of the party. It should also be borne in mind that although Margaret Thatcher became Conservative leader in 1975, she was not then a fully-fledged neo-liberal; Margaret Thatcher had not yet become a Thatcherite (Kavanagh, 1987: 97), although as noted in chapter 4, her experiences during the latter stages of the Heath government had disillusioned her about the efficacy of state intervention in, and regulation of, economic affairs. With regard to the issue of incomes policy, therefore, although Thatcher initially expressed opposition to statutory pay policies, she refused to state categorically that she would *not* pursue an incomes policy in Office.

A further reason why the loss of the February 1974 election did not result in an immediate abandonment of incomes policy by the Conservative party was the narrowness of Labour's "victory", which made it inevitable that another general election would be called in the near future, as Wilson sought to obtain a working parliamentary majority. In this context, there was no immediate change in Conservative party policy, and hence no immediate eschewal of incomes policy by the parliamentary leadership. This was partly because Heath remained Conservative leader until the following year, and was by now convinced that an incomes policy was an essential tool of economic management which no British government could dispense with. He was supported in this view by a number of his closest Shadow Cabinet colleagues, such as Robert Carr, James Prior and Peter Walker. Meanwhile, William Whitelaw was arguing that "our prices and incomes policy was remarkably successful", and believed that "there is still goodwill towards the prices and incomes policy" amongst the general public (Conservative Party Archives, LCC/74/8). Indeed, shortly afterwards, Whitelaw declared that before the Conservative party sought to determine its approach to industrial relations overall, "it is essential that we should have evolved a doctrine on incomes policy", for "no industrial relations policy can be coherent without supplying an answer" to the question about the most appropriate method of pay determination (Conservative Party Archives, LCC/74/10, "Industrial Relations Policy: Conservative Tactics and Strategy", 1 May 1974).

At this time, even Keith Joseph was still talking of the need for an incomes policy, albeit one which was "selective and involves as few decisions and as little bureaucracy as possible". He also suggested that: "We should make it our policy always to pass the results of wage increases through to the consumer . . . [for] only when the public feels the result of wage claims will they turn against them" (Conservative Party Archives, LCC/74/11).

However, most of the Conservative party leadership recognized that with another general election likely before the end of the year, not only was there insufficient time to develop new policies – even if there was agreement on what these policies should be, which there clearly was not – but a sudden and dramatic change of programme in such circumstances would probably be perceived by the voters either as pure panic or blatant opportunism. It simply was not feasible for the Conservative party immediately to disavow the policies pursued during the previous two years, along with the programme upon which it had fought the February election. As William Whitelaw noted with specific reference to the Party's prices and incomes policy, "any significant abandonment . . . in the short-term would be seen as opportunism . . . It would also be as good as an admission that the conflicts of last winter were misconceived" (Conservative Party Archives, LCC/74/11).

During most of its period in Opposition, therefore, the Conservative party oscillated between rejection of all incomes policies, and intimations that a Conservative government might seek an informal or voluntary incomes policy, possible as part of an annual economic forum. During this time, the Shadow Chancellor, Geofrey Howe, was among those Conservatives who favoured a "middle way" between complete rejection of incomes policies and recognition that a pay policy of some sort might play a valuable role in the battle against inflation. "If not an incomes policy", Howe suggested, then at least "a policy for incomes" (Howe, 1976).

Support for this approach was offered by Peter Walker, who argued that the strength of the trade unions was such that free collective bargaining was not a viable option (Walker, 1977: 67), whilst the Shadow employment minister, James Prior, was lamenting that the debate on wage determination in Britain was too often seen in simple black-and-white terms, whereby the issue was polarized into a stark choice between rigid pay control or a complete free-for-all (*Conservative News* October 1978).

Most of those Conservatives continuing to advocate incomes policy were from the "one nation" section of the Party. They considered themselves to be "realists" because they recognized that the power of the trade unions was such that a Conservative government would have to secure their cooperation, rather than seek to destroy their power through legislation, confrontation or permitting a significant rise in unemployment. Whilst acknowledging that there were invariably difficulties in pursuing incomes policies, Conservatives such as Peter Walker insisted that these were "nothing compared with the difficulties created by having no incomes policy", for these were "unsurpassable" (*House of Commons Debates*, 5th series, Vol. 909, cols. 495–501). On another occasion, Walker declared that "such is the strength of union power at the present time that a policy of free collective bargaining cannot successfully be pursued" (Walker, 1977: 67; see, also, Maudling, 1978: 266–7).

Similarly, Peter Tapsell claimed that it would "never again be possible anywhere in the Western world efficiently to maintain an industrialized parliamentary democracy without an incomes policy" (*House of Commons Debates*, 5th series, Vol. 914, cols. 1236–42). This view was endorsed by Edward Heath, who was now of the opinion that incomes policies had become an "inevitable and inescapable . . . part of economic management" (*House of Commons Debates*, 5th series Vol. 891, cols. 1707–8), whilst Robert Carr was claiming that those who believed that incomes policies could or should be abandoned were living in a fool's paradise (Carr, 1975).

This "realism" was by no means the only reason why "one nation" Conservatives remained committed to an incomes policy, however. Also of signal importance was their firm belief that incomes policies offered a means through which industrial partnership could be secured, thereby facilitating the development of "one nation". Dialogue over pay (and other economic issues, perhaps) would help to overcome distrust and division, not only between a Conservative government and the trade unions, but also between management and labour.

The ambiguity in the Conservative party's stance on the issue of incomes policies led Peter Walker to demand that the shadow Cabinet clarify its position (*The Times*, 19 January 1976). Walker's call went largely unheeded, however, for the 1976 policy document *The Right Approach* blandly suggested that whilst previous experience of incomes policies had not proved particularly favourable, it would be unwise to reject incomes policies outright (Conservative Central Office, 1976: 37). This anodyne assertion merely encouraged Timothy Raison to echo Peter Walker's call for a clarification of Conservative policy with regard to wage determination (Raison, 1977: 12).

Partly in response to these calls for clarification, a further document, *The Right Approach for the Economy*, was published in October 1977. Prepared by Geoffrey Howe, David Howell, Keith Joseph and James Prior, under the editorship of Angus Maude, *The Right Approach for the Economy* stressed the need for "realistic and responsible" collective bargaining, this to take place in the context of fiscal and monetary policies and a determination to curb both the money supply and public expenditure. It was suggested that a Conservative government "must come to *some* conclusions about the likely scope for pay increases if excess public expenditure or large-scale unemployment is to be avoided", these "conclusions" to be determined after discussions with the "major participants in the economy" in some kind of forum, such as the National Economic Development Council.

At this time, Geoffrey Howe was favourably disposed towards the (West) German system of "concerted action", and sought to persuade Margaret Thatcher of its apparent merits, via a paper outlining how the system operated. Howe need not have bothered. Instead of allaying Thatcher's fears, he increased them, her written reply declaring that: "This paper frightens me to death even more" (Thatcher, 1995: 404).

Consequently, although *The Right Approach for the Economy* was originally written as an official Shadow Cabinet policy document, such was Thatcher's unhappiness about the proposals for tripartite discussions between government, trade unions and employers' representatives, that she insisted the document be published only under the names of its authors, rather than as a Shadow Cabinet position statement (Howe, 1995: 101; Prior, 1986: 109). Furthermore, when asked by a television interviewer about the allusion to incomes policy enshrined within *The Right Approach to the Economy*, Keith Joseph retorted that this only applied to the public sector (Halcrow, 1989: 128). Yet even by 1978 there remained considerable ambiguity over the Conservative party's stance on incomes policies, to the extent that a *Spectator* editorial on the topic was entitled "Fifty-seven varieties", a wry reference to the apparent plethora of approaches discernible within the party (*The Spectator*, 14 October 1978).

The Conservative party's neo-liberal wing – growing both in number and confidence, as the intellectual tide by now appeared to be running in their favour – were also impatient with the opacity of the Shadow Cabinet with regard to incomes policy. What the neo-liberals sought was an unequivocal rejection by the Conservative leadership of incomes policies, and, instead, a commitment to free collective bargaining, with wages determined solely by economic or commercial criteria. In so doing, they reiterated their thesis that incomes policies reflected an invalid conception of the underlying cause of inflation, this erroneously seeking to conquer inflation by restraining wages rather than the money supply.

However, Conservative neo-liberals also maintained that incomes policies served to politicize the whole ambit of pay determination, rendering the government the focus of anger or frustration from aggrieved workers, and making it increasingly difficult to discern whether industrial action in support of a pay claim was a genuine industrial dispute or was politically-motivated (see, for example, Tebbit, 1975).

Following on from this objection was the concern that incomes policies, when they "inevitably" failed, had a damaging impact on both the rule of law, and on the authority of government itself. The rule of law was deemed to be undermined by the failure of statutory incomes policies, whilst the failure of a voluntary incomes policy was detrimental to the authority of the government. By contrast, it was suggested that as free collective bargaining does not entail the setting by government of a pay "target" or limit, "it cannot ever be proved on any objective basis to have failed". Instead, "the outcome of free collective bargaining may disappoint a government . . . fail to satisfy the Cabinet", but this does not constitute failure, and therefore does not undermine the rule of law, or the authority of government (Brittan and Lilley, 1977: 177). In this respect, the Conservative's gradual move away from incomes policy from 1975 onwards can be seen as a means of restoring the authority of government and the state, whilst bolstering the rule of law.

A crucial feature of the neo-liberal case against incomes policy during the latter half of the 1970s was the explicitly-stated view that a return to free collective bargaining would be far more effective in curbing trade union power, for in the context of "the market", pay rises not earned through increased productivity or efficiency would invariably result in job losses. In other words, those who insisted on "excessive" wage increases would probably price themselves out of work, whereupon the ensuing rise in unemployment could be blamed on the trade unions. In this context, it was suggested that free collective bargaining would act as a far more potent restraint on excessive pay demands than any incomes policy agreed between government and trade unions (Price, 1977).

According to Conservative neo-liberals, "people must be made to suffer the consequences of their actions, or inaction, once more" (Ridley, 1974), a view wholeheartedly endorsed by Keith Joseph when he declared that trade unions ought to be "free to price their people out of jobs, or bankrupt their employers, if their members really wished them to" (*The Times*, April 1976; see, also, Howell, 1974; Ridley, 1976).

As such comments implied, Conservative neo-liberals had few qualms about permitting higher unemployment. Not only did they view unemployment as a means by which trade union power could be curbed, they believed, too, that inflation itself fuelled unemployment in the long-run by virtue of undermining profitability and deterring investment, both of which had a detrimental impact on jobs. Conservative neo-liberals also inclined to the view that Britain had acquired a paranoia about unemployment ever since the Great Depression and Jarrow marches of the 1930s. According to Keith Joseph:

> Our post-war boom began under the shadow of the 1930s. We were haunted by the fear of long-term mass unemployment, the grim, hopeless dole queues and towns which died. So we talked ourselves into believing that these gaunt, tight-lipped men in caps and mufflers were round the corner, and tailored our policy to match these imaginary conditions. For imaginary is what they were. (Quoted in Halcrow, 1989: 72)

It was also during the latter half of the 1970s that Conservative neo-liberals began drawing a distinction between voluntary and involuntary unemployment. The former was deemed to occur when people priced themselves out of work, either by demanding "excessive" pay increases, or refusing to accept lower paid jobs once they were unemployed. In either case, the unemployed were deemed ultimately responsible for their own plight, and as such, it was suggested that only mass "involuntary unemployment" need give cause for concern (Bourlet and Roots, 1974). It was further suggested that inflation was actually a greater social evil than unemployment because everyone suffered the effects of inflation – particularly those on low or fixed incomes – whilst the effects of unemployment were much more localized or individualized, and thus limited in impact (Hodgson, 1975).

Towards the very end of the Conservative's period in Opposition, party opinion did harden considerably against incomes policies, as the neo-liberal perspective became more firmly entrenched. What emboldened the neo-liberals was the experience of the incumbent Labour government in seeking to impose wage restraint on the trade unions. Although the Labour leadership had secured trade union acquiescence between 1975 and 1977, the unions made it clear that they would not support further pay restraint, particularly as inflation was in double figures throughout this period. The tension between the Labour government and the trade unions over the Cabinet's insistence on pursuing, not merely a third, but also a fourth consecutive year of pay restraint, culminating in the notorious "winter of discontent", proved a major fillip to the Conservative party, for not only did it render the unions even more unpopular, and therefore endorse the Conservative case for trade union reform, it also destroyed Labour's hitherto claim that it alone could work harmoniously with the trade unions.

The "winter of discontent" undoubtedly served to confirm the neo-liberal case against incomes policies, to the extent that by the time of the 1979 general election, Margaret Thatcher herself had become unequivocally opposed to incomes policy. Furthermore, Conservative neo-liberals recognized that a pledge to restore free collective bargaining would enjoy a populist appeal amongst many trade unionists themselves, along with those skilled manual workers who resented the narrowing of differentials which Labour's incomes policies had entailed. Thus did the Conservative's 1979 election manifesto promise that "effort and skill [will] earn larger rewards".

Consequently, having won the May 1979 general election, the Conservative party presided over six main trends with regard to pay determination during its subsequent eighteen years in Office. First, it adhered to the principle that in the private sector, pay should be determined on the basis of negotiations between employers and employees, rather than being imposed or determined by government. In other words, free collective bargaining was to be restored in the private sector, albeit accompanied by ministerial exhortations to employees and trade unions to exercise responsibility and moderation when seeking higher pay.

Secondly, the Conservative governments adopted a tough stance *vis-à-vis* the public sector, which not only imposed stringent cash limits on public sector services and institutions, but also entailed "standing firm" when faced with industrial action over pay by public sector employees. This stance was derived not only from the Conservative's new approach to conquering inflation, namely controlling the money supply, and curbing public expenditure, but also from the party's hostility towards the public sector, which was seen as unproductive and parasitic, in sharp contrast to the wealth-creating and self-reliant private sector (see, for example, Bacon and Eltis, 1976).

Thirdly, although the Conservatives won the 1979 general election pledging a return to free collective bargaining, from the second half of the 1980s onwards there was increasing advocacy of *individual* pay bargaining (as opposed to *collective* bargaining), and also, to some extent, localized pay-bargaining.

Fourthly, the Thatcher governments successfully implemented a number of significant trade union and industrial relations reforms to weaken the trade unions. These legal reforms were intended, among other things, to weaken the ability of trade unions to extract "excessive" wage increases from employers. In this respect, the extent to which the Conservative governments of Margaret Thatcher and John Major really permitted *free* (from state interference) collective bargaining is a matter of considerable conjecture.

Fifthly, the Thatcher–Major governments proved willing to preside over high levels of unemployment, envisaging that this would further reduce the alleged power of the trade unions, and thus lead to lower pay claims and wage increases.

Sixthly, and finally, the 1979–97 Conservative governments absolved themselves of responsibility for the pay of millions of employees by privatizing nationalized industries, and also deregulating many of those industries or services which remained in the public sector, thereby opening them up to private sector involvement and market forces.

Each of these six facets warrants further examination, before considering other trends, such as de-industrialization and declining trade union membership, which underpinned the eschewal of incomes policies.

Restoring free collective bargaining in the private sector

From the outset, the Thatcher–Major governments insisted that in the private sector, pay was a matter to be determined "freely" between management and trade unions (or individual employees themselves), on the basis of economic and commercial criteria such as productivity and profitability. This insistence did not preclude Conservative ministers from repeatedly warning workers and trade unions of the dangers of seeking "excessive" pay increases, with unemployment frequently portrayed as a consequence of employees "pricing themselves out of work" through their insistence on being paid a higher wage than their company could afford. Yet in spite of such exhortations, the 1979–97 Conservative governments did refrain from directly intervening in pay bargaining conducted between private sector employers and their employers or trade union representatives, and as such, adhered to their commitment *not* to resort to incomes policies.

The Thatcher–Major governments' eschewal of incomes policy also enabled private sector managers to be confident that if they resisted a pay claim from their workforce, they would be fully supported by the Cabinet, rather than undermined by ministerial intervention or encouragement to yield to an excessive pay claim in order to secure industrial peace. Similarly, private sector management could rest assured that Thatcher and her ministerial colleagues would not seek to resolve a pay dispute by summoning a senior or semi-retired judge to head an inquiry which would subsequently recommend a much higher pay award than that offered by management. Although ministers insisted that pay determination in the private sector was entirely the responsibility of employers and employees, it was always crystal clear whose side the Thatcher–Major governments were on when a pay dispute occurred.

Standing firm vis-à-vis the public sector

Whilst the Thatcher–Major governments formally eschewed incomes policies, they did apply rigorous cash limits to the public sector, which effectively amounted to a *de facto* incomes policy because these cash limits stipulated the amount of pay increase which could be afforded each year. Any additional increase in pay would, Conservative ministers repeatedly insisted, have to be financed from cutbacks in jobs; one person's "excessive" pay rise would mean a colleague's redundancy. As such, the public sector pay increases allowed for by the cash limits were invariably in line with inflation only, the proviso usually being added that any extra – unless financed from job losses – would have to be earned from increased productivity or efficiency. Such a proviso was never particularly sincere or convincing, of course, for even if doctors and nurses treated more patients, or social workers dealt with more clients and took on bigger caseloads, for example, this did not in itself yield more revenue from which "productivity bonuses" could be paid to them.

Indeed, if various public sector workers did increase their productivity, the response of the Thatcher–Major governments was to seek further cutbacks in staffing, on the grounds that the same output could now be achieved by compelling the remaining staff to work harder (thereby providing Britain's taxpayers with greater "value for money"). Furthermore, the financial savings yielded by such staff cutbacks were rarely translated into the much-vaunted "productivity bonuses", but, instead, were invariably appropriated by the Treasury, obsessed as it was with cutting back on public expenditure as far as possible, irrespective of the longer-term damage wrought on Britain's public services. The overall result of such a strategy was an increasing disparity between private and public sector pay during the 1980s and 1990s, coupled with plummeting morale amongst those employed in the public services.

The Conservative governments' determination to hold down pay in the public sector – whilst insisting that this did not constitute an incomes policy – was clearly illustrated by their willingness to stand firm in the face of industrial action by employees in this sector. Ministers also envisaged that by refusing to yield when faced with industrial action by its own employees in the public sector, managers and employers in the private sector would be encouraged to adopt a similarly tough stance against their employees and trade unions. The government could hardly espouse the principle of "management's right to manage" if it was itself seen to "give in" to those who were, ultimately, its own employees. Standing firm when faced with industrial action by public sector workers was thus intended to set an example, and provide encouragement, to management in the private sector.

However, this "standing firm" was also linked to the emergence of a number of high-profile "macho" managers who readily – often with ministerial approval or even encouragement – confronted the trade unions in their particular firms or industries. Hence the 1980s witnessed (Sir) Michael Edwardes at British Leyland (although he had actually been appointed in 1977), Lord King at British Airways, Ian MacGregor at both British Steel and then the National Coal Board, and Rupert Murdoch and Eddie Shah (newspaper publishers), all implementing managerial decisions or policies which were bound – doubtless intended – to provoke a confrontation with the trade unions in their respective industries. When such confrontations occurred, the employers involved enjoyed the full and public support of the Conservative governments, as well as the judiciary and most of the press. Such employers were invariably portrayed a courageous men valiantly seeking to implement measures which would restore the competitiveness of their industries (and of the British economy generally) in the face of Luddite-like opposition from the trade unions. Thus, for example, Margaret Thatcher's selection, in 1981, of Lord King to "take on British Airways" was because "he was the sort of man she admired, a tough and determined bully, but very successful" (Ridley 1991: 45). Indeed, Thatcher herself recalls that right at the outset of her premiership: "I knew that whatever we decided to do about BL [British Leyland] would have an impact on the psychology and morale of British managers as a whole, and I was determined to send the right signals . . . we had to back Michael Edwardes" (Thatcher, 1993: 114–15).

The Thatcher–Major governments' determination to stand firm when faced with industrial action by public sector trade unions and employees was also inextricably linked to the objective of restoring the authority of the state. It was part of the Thatcherite critique of Britain's post-war economic and moral decline that successive governments had acceded far too readily to demands from organized interests, especially trade unions. As a result, not only had this proved deeply damaging to the British economy, it was also deemed to have undermined the authority of the state itself. Whilst the security and stability of the state has always been a cardinal component of Conservatism (talk of a minimal state, or of "rolling back the state", never implied a weak state), it was an objective ascribed particular importance Margaret Thatcher and her adherents (Bulpitt, 1986; Gamble, 1988).

For all of these reasons, therefore, various groups of public sector workers from 1979 onwards found themselves engaging in industrial action which was met with undisguised derision by the Thatcher–Major governments. Thus did steelworkers in 1980, civil servants in 1981, train drivers, London Underground workers, and health service employees in 1982, coal miners in 1984–5, and teachers during 1985–7 discover that the Thatcher governments were fully prepared to stand firm and not yield an inch when faced with industrial action by public sector employees.

Furthermore, when public sector workers did go on strike, the Thatcher governments were keen to emphasize that the only people who really suffered were those who relied upon the provision of public services. In other words, striking public sector workers were reminded that it was their own customers, clients and consumers – often some of the most deprived or vulnerable sections of society – who were harmed by industrial action, not the government itself (as if Thatcherite Conservatives really cared about such people). This, of course, was intended further to fuel populist prejudice and public opinion against trade unions and workers on strike whilst enabling Thatcher and her ministerial colleagues to portray themselves as "out there" on the side of ordinary people.

However, whilst applying rigorous cash limits to the public sector, and thereby placing strict limits on levels of pay, the Thatcher–Major governments insisted that this did not constitute an incomes policy, partly on the grounds that the limits did not apply to those employees in the private sector, but more importantly, because ministers did not seek trade union approval or cooperation for wage restraint in the public sector. By such semantics and sophistry did the Thatcher–Major governments simultaneously seek to limit public sector pay whilst strongly denouncing incomes policies and government interference in wage determination.

Encouraging individual, not collective, bargaining

The Thatcher–Major governments' eschewal of incomes policies was both reflected and reinforced by the trend away from collective bargaining towards individual bargaining, with each employee's pay increasingly linked to their performance. This was a trend which the Conservative governments enthusiastically encouraged, particularly from the late 1980s onwards, it being increasingly maintained that employees' remuneration should "reflect their own skills, efforts, capacities and circumstances" rather than being "solely the outcome of some distant negotiation between employers and trade unions". To achieve this objective, Conservative ministers were adamant that:

> many existing approaches to pay bargaining, beloved of trade unions and employers alike, will need to change . . . In particular, "the going rate", "comparability", and "cost of living increases", are all outmoded concepts – they take no account of differences in performance, ability to pay or difficulties of recruitment, retention or motivation . . . National agreements . . . all too often give scant regard to differences in individual circumstances or performance. (Department of Employment, 1988: 18–24)

These arguments were confidently reiterated just two months before the Conservative's April 1992 general election victory, when a White Paper entitled *People, Jobs and Opportunity* declared that:

> There is a new recognition of the role and importance of the individual employee. Traditional patterns of industrial relations, based on collective bargaining and collective agreements, seem increasingly inappropriate and are in decline. Many employers are replacing outdated personnel practices with new policies for human resource management which put the emphasis on developing the talents and capacities of each individual employee. Many are also looking to communicate directly with their employees rather than through the medium of a trade union or formal works council. There is a growing trend to individually negotiated reward packages which reflect the individual's personal skills, experience, efforts and performance. (Department of Employment, 1992: 6)

The increasingly enthusiastic encouragement of individual pay bargaining was inextricably linked with an attack on *national* wage determination which gathered pace during the second half of the 1980s. By this time, Conservative ministers were becoming ever more confident in their attempts at marginalizing the trade unions, to the extent that they now felt able to challenge what the unions had traditionally seen as their *raison d'être*, namely collective bargaining itself. Thus it was that when TUC representatives attended a meeting of the NEDC in November 1986, they were informed by the Chancellor, Nigel Lawson, that the pattern and extent of *national* pay bargaining were incompatible with the need for greater labour mobility and flexibility. Then, at another NEDC meeting in February 1987, Kenneth Clarke, in his capacity as Paymaster-General, expressed the government's hope that automatic annual pay increases, along with the criterion of comparability, would eventually disappear. It was against this backdrop that the TUC's 1987 annual conference endorsed the Union of Communication Workers' motion opposing "government attacks on national pay bargaining" and expressing "grave concern at Government inspired moves to promote a trend towards regional pay levels and merit pay arrangements", especially when these measures were clearly "designed to reduce living standards" and undermine "trade union bargaining strength" (TUC Report 1987: 519).

As noted at the beginning of this chapter, prior to 1979, the Conservative party oscillated between support for free *collective* bargaining and incomes policies, yet variously pursued either of these options on the grounds that it was seeking to acknowledge or accommodate the power of the trade unions in an era of full employment. By the 1990s, all of these phenomena – free collective bargaining, incomes policies, strong trade unions and full employment – had been rejected by the Conservative party. The Conservative principle of *individualism* had been incorporated into the sphere wage determination. Conservative ministers no longer felt obliged to choose between free *collective* bargaining *or* incomes policies, because by this time, *both* were being rejected.

Trade union and industrial relations reform

The programme of trade union and industrial relations reform implemented by the Thatcher–Major governments has been well-documented (see, for example, Dorey, 1995b: 156–94; Dorey, 1999a: 179–98; Dorey, 2001a; Hanson, 1991: 15–29; Marsh, 1992: 64–81; McIlroy, 1991; Taylor, 1993: 265–325), and therefore requires only brief mention here. Six items of legislation were introduced, namely:

1980 Employment Act

- New closed shop agreements to require the support of at least 80 per cent of the workforce, as expressed via a secret ballot.
- Compensation to be payable to employees who lose their jobs as a consequence of their refusal, on grounds of personal conscience or conviction, to join a trade union.
- Public (government) funds to be made available to trade unions to cover the administrative costs of conducting postal ballots prior to strike action, or for union leadership elections.
- Picketing to be curbed, so that only six pickets may lawfully gather at the entrance to a firm whose employees are engaged in strike action. Secondary picketing prohibited, as are other forms of sympathy action, such as refusing to handle the goods of a firm whose employees are engaged in strike action.

Employment Act 1982

- Existing closed shop agreements to be balloted upon to ensure that they command the continued support of at least 80 per cent of the workforce.
- Increased compensation payable to those employees losing their jobs as a consequence of refusing to join a trade union.
- Legal definition of a trade dispute significantly narrowed, thereby removing immunity from all forms of sympathy action, politically-motivated strikes, and industrial action against non-union firms.

Trade Union Act 1984

- Strikes to be considered lawful only if they have been supported by a majority of the workforce in a secret ballot.
- Strikes called without a ballot, or not enjoying majority support, to lose legal immunity for tort or damages.
- Trade unions obliged to hold ballots for the election of leaders and other senior officials if their members request such ballots.
- Trade unions to hold a secret ballot of their members at least once every ten years in order to gauge support for maintaining or establishing a political fund.

Employment Act 1988

- Unlawful for an employer to sack an employee for refusing to join a trade union, even if 80 per cent of the workforce have voted in favour of a closed shop.
- Unlawful for trade unions to engage in industrial action in support of closed shops.
- Unlawful for trade unions to take disciplinary action against members for refusing to participate in strike action, even if that strike has been supported by a majority of the workforce via a secret ballot.
- A new institution established, the Commission for the Rights of Trade Union Members, to provide trade unionists with legal advice and financial support if they are dissatisfied with the behaviour of, or their treatment by, the trade union to which they belong.

1990 Employment Act

- Unlawful for an employer to reject a job applicant on the grounds that they are not a trade union member.
- Trade union officials must repudiate unofficial industrial action by their members, or else be deemed liable.

- Employers permitted to dismiss any employees participating in unofficial strike action.
- Legal immunities removed from industrial action taken in support of workers sacked for taking part in unofficial strikes.

1993 Trade Union Reform and Employment Rights Act

- Automatic deduction from their wages of employees' trade union membership fees by employers – the "check-off" arrangement – unlawful unless each employee gives written authorization every three years.
- Employees given the right to join the trade union of their choice (rather than be directed to the "appropriate" trade union in accordance with the TUC's 1939 Bridlington Agreement).
- All strike ballots to be postal, and subject to independent scrutiny. Furthermore, if strike action is endorsed by the ballot, the trade union is required to give the employer at least seven days' notice before actually commencing the strike.
- Members of the public entitled to seek an injunction when employees in the "public services" engage in unlawful industrial action.
- The Advisory, Conciliation & Arbitration Service (ACAS) given a new remit, so that it is no longer expected to encourage and promote *collective* bargaining.
- All Wages Councils abolished, thereby ending the setting of a minimum wage in certain industries and occupations.
- Employers permitted to reward financially those employees who renounce trade union membership.

As already intimated, reference to this legislation is essential in placing the Conservative's post-1979 rejection of incomes policy in proper context, for these legislative reforms not only reflected the hostility of the Thatcher–Major governments to organized labour in general, they were also intended seriously to weaken the bargaining power of trade unions *vis-à-vis* employers, thereby seeking to ensure more "realistic" pay deals and more "responsible" trade union behaviour generally. In the context of high unemployment, this legislation was clearly intended to ensure that the balance of power in industry and the economy shifted decisively in favour of capital.

High unemployment

It would be a mistake to see the Thatcher–Major governments' attack on trade unionism solely in terms of legislative reforms and restrictions, vitally important though these were. It is also necessary to consider, however briefly, the significance and impact of high unemployment on trade unions and wage determination since 1979. Two particular factors are of significance in this context. First, high unemployment was thought, by many Conservative ministers, likely to dampen down wage claims, as employees accept lower pay increases and remuneration out of fear that they too might otherwise lose their jobs. In such circumstances, even a small pay increase may be gratefully accepted, particularly if ministers were preaching the doctrine that "low pay is better than no pay".

Secondly, high unemployment serves to weaken the organizational and financial strength of trade unions by depleting their membership, for as unemployment rises so union membership will fall (unless those losing their jobs are not members of a trade union in the first place, of course), along with the unions' revenues derived from members' fees.

Certainly British trade unionism experienced a considerable loss of members during the 1980s; in 1979, out of a national employment total of 23,173,000, there were 13,289,000 trade union members (57.3 per cent of those in work). By 1997, however, there were just 7,100,000 trade union members out of a total workforce of 23,000,000, which enabled Conservatives to claim that trade unionists were now a minority of the working population, to the extent that the unions represented less than 30 per cent of all employees in Britain

However, the notion that high unemployment automatically dampens down wage demands does need to be qualified somewhat, for during the 1980s some of those in work did continue to experience significant increases in their incomes and standards of living. This, though, owed much to factors such as income tax cuts, lower inflation, and the relative ease with which credit or loans could be obtained in the context wake of low interest rates and deregulation of the financial markets during the mid-1980s.

Nonetheless, it does seem plausible to suggest that high unemployment will exert an overall downward effect on pay increases for many groups of workers, particularly those who are unskilled or semi-skilled, partly because of their fears about losing their jobs, and partly because employers will be aware of their employees' lower expectations in such circumstances, and offer lower pay rises accordingly.

Furthermore, caution should be exercised when perusing economic statistics in this context, for whilst official figures indicate that *average* earnings increased steadily during the 1980s, these conceal the extent to which enormous salary increases for high earners were accompanied by pay freezes or even wage cuts for some of those at the other end of the socio-economic hierarchy. Indeed, the poorest 10 per cent of the population saw their share of national wealth decline by 3 per cent during the

1980s and early 1990s, to the extent that by the mid-1990s the gap between the highest-paid and lowest-paid workers was discovered to be wider than at any time since such statistics were first compiled back in 1886 (Commission on Social Justice/Institute for Public Policy Research, 1994). In short, the Conservative's eschewal of incomes policies, coupled with their toleration of high unemployment and abolition of Wages Councils (see below), was accompanied by an ever-widening chasm between those at the top and the bottom of the earnings hierarchy.

Privatization and deregulation

Although we have just noted the most important or explicit measures implemented by the Thatcher–Major governments *vis-à-vis* the trade unions, the role of privatization in reducing the scope and strength of trade unionism – and, therefore, collective bargaining – ought not to be overlooked or underestimated. The privatization programme which developed – it had hardly featured in the 1979 Conservative manifesto – under the Thatcher governments during the 1980s had a number of political and economic objectives (see, for example, Ascher, 1987; Dorey, 2001b; Heald, 1989; Richardson, 1994), but one of the advantages soon discerned was a further diminution in the scope and strength of the trade unions, coupled with a means by which ministers could further extricate themselves from responsibility for wage determination *vis-à-vis* millions of public sector employees.

There was a recognition that the most powerful or militant trade unions were frequently those representing workers in the public sector and the nationalized industries. The power and militancy of such unions was derived not only from the vital importance of their industries or services to the British economy and society, but also from their privileged position as monopoly providers of these goods and services. This was deemed to make it relatively easy for such unions to "hold the country to ransom", and thereby compel governments to accede to their demands when they flexed – or merely threatened to flex – their industrial muscle. As John Moore remarked whilst Financial Secretary to the Treasury in 1983: "Public sector trade unions have been extraordinarily successful in gaining advantages for themselves in the pay hierarchy by exploiting their monopoly collective bargaining position" (quoted in Kay, Mayer and Thompson, 1986: 82).

Furthermore, previous post-war governments had invariably found that, when pursuing incomes policies, it was trade unions representing employees in the nationalized industries and public sector with whom they frequently came into conflict. Whilst the Thatcher–Major governments eschewed incomes policies, this did not obviate the need to tackle public sector trade unionism. Consequently, although this power was to be curbed, in large part through legislation and high unemployment, coupled with "standing firm" in the face of industrial action, the Thatcher–Major governments also sought to undermine trade union power further via privatization.

This would simultaneously absolve the government from responsibility for determining wages and other conditions of employment in previously publicly-owned industries, whilst also exposing those employed in such industries to the alleged virtues of market forces and competition. Once in the private sector, Conservative ministers reasoned, workers would be compelled to recognize that their jobs and wages depended upon such criteria as competitiveness, customer satisfaction, effort, efficiency and their employers' profitability, rather than on industrial militancy, political pressure or social justice.

This last consideration would become even more important, the Thatcher governments reckoned, where employees purchased shares in the industries in which they worked. In such circumstances, these share-owning employees would acquire a personal interest in the commercial success of "their" firm or company, and as such would be less inclined to engage in restrictive practices or industrial action which would compromise its competitiveness and threaten its profitability. In turn, it was suggested by Conservatives such as John Moore that privatization might serve to improve industrial relations, for:

> As we dispose of state-owned assets, so more and more people have the opportunity to become owners . . . So these policies also increase personal independence and freedom, and by establishing a new breed of owners, have an important impact on attitudes. They tend to break down the divisions between owners and earners. (Quoted in Abromeit, 1988: 71)

One other aspect of the Thatcher–Major governments' privatization programme was the expectation that it would facilitate the development of smaller, localized bargaining units, a feature which would offer three advantages from the Conservative's perspective. First, the fragmentation of industries or services into smaller units – such as "cost centres" – would undermine collective, national-level pay bargaining, and enhance the development of local or regional wage determination and pay awards. This, it was hoped, would further weaken the role of trade unions, particularly their national leaders and officials.

Secondly, Conservative ministers sometimes claimed that localized pay bargaining would enable employers to offer wages more commensurate with local labour market conditions, so that pay was more closely linked to local circumstances, rather than being determined in accordance with the national "going rate".

Thirdly, Conservatives envisaged that by fragmenting industries and services, privatization would prevent trade unions from causing *national* disruption through industrial action, because a dispute over pay would be *vis-à-vis* an employer at local or regional level. For example, it has been noted that the Major government's privatization of the railway industry led to the establishment of an extremely complex and fragmented structure, entailing almost 100 individual units, with different companies responsible for specific functions, such as signalling or track maintenance, and trains themselves run by a range of regional companies, licensed via 25 franchises (Hindmoor, 2000: 272). With such a complex, fragmented and regionalized framework, the scope for a national rail strike is correspondingly lower, thereby further reducing the power of the trade unions representing workers in the rail industry, and concomitantly weakening their ability genuinely to pursue national-level collective bargaining.

Even in those services or sectors which were not fully or formally privatized – such as the NHS – there was a clear and conscious attempt to determine pay at local level, via the NHS Trusts, for example. Meanwhile, in the civil service, the implementation of the Next Steps programme, with its ever-expanding network of agencies, meant that pay was formally determined, not through direct, national-level negotiations with the Treasury, but via management within the agencies, with the Chief Executives of these agencies being empowered to determine the levels of staffing and pay within their own particular agency, albeit in accordance with the budget allocated to them by the Treasury.

For all these reasons, therefore, it can be seen that privatization, coupled with the spread of cost centres and market-testing within those services which remained in the public sector, was viewed by the 1979–97 Conservative governments as a further means by which trade union power and collective bargaining could be undermined, and wages thus constrained, whilst obviating the need for ministers to resort to an official incomes policy.

In similar vein, deregulation, particularly of services formerly provided by local government, was also of significance in the context of the Thatcher–Major governments' determination to restrain wage increases without recourse to formal incomes policies. With memories of the "winter of discontent" constantly in mind, Conservative ministers recognized that a major advantage to be gleaned from the reform of local government was the further undermining of public sector trade unionism, and of the "monopoly" power possessed by local authority employees providing public services.

A variety of reforms were thus pursued, such as compulsory competitive tendering, deregulation of public transport, and the opting-out of schools, all of which had the effect of further weakening public sector trade unions, and exposing local authority employees to market forces and competition of some kind, whilst linking pay and (continued) employment to such criteria as affordability, efficiency, productivity and profitability.

Abolition of Wages Councils

One additional feature of the Thatcher–Major governments' determination to exert a downward pressure on wage increases which ought to be noted concerns the abolition of Wages Councils. These bodies had long been established in a number of industries, with some of the relevant legislation dating back to 1909. Their scope and powers had subsequently been periodically enhanced, so that by 1983 there were 25 Wages Council (and two Agricultural Wages Boards) covering three million workers, most of whom were employed in just four industries, namely agriculture, catering, retail and textiles.

To the Thatcher–Major governments, however, Wages Councils represented an attempt at artificially fixing the wages of workers in certain industries, so that such workers would be paid a statutory wage in excess of that which they would receive if exposed to market forces. According to Conservative ministers, Wages Councils thus constituted a distortion of the market in the realm of wage determination, and meant that wage levels were higher than they would be if the price of labour was determined by the laws of supply and demand. As such, it was maintained, Wages Councils rendered some companies and industries uncompetitive, compelling them to pay higher wages than they could really afford, and consequently reducing profitability, or even forcing some firms out of business altogether.

Ministers also claimed that Wages Councils served to raise or sustain unemployment through pricing some employees out of work, by virtue of the fact that various employers could not afford to recruit new staff due to the level of wages which they would be required to pay. According to this Conservative critique, therefore, the attempt at protecting the low paid was actually counter-productive, and harmed the very people it purported to help; instead of providing them with employment at a certain level of remuneration, it prevented them from obtaining employment altogether. Once again, therefore, Conservative ministers readily invoked the mantra that "low pay is better than no pay".

A further objection directed by many Conservatives against Wages Councils was that they impacted negatively on many workers who were not themselves under the jurisdiction of such bodies. The argument here was that by artificially raising wages in certain industries, it encouraged other workers in other industries to seek higher wages in order to maintain differentials, thereby undermining competitiveness elsewhere in the economy, and increasing unemployment further.

A final Conservative objection to the Wages Councils was that industry-wide wage agreements were in direct conflict with the objective of moving away from collective bargaining and nation-wide wage deals, and towards local-level or individual pay awards.

Such a critique led inevitably to one particular policy, namely the abolition of Wages Councils, although like trade union reform in general, this was pursued in stages, rather than in one all-out attack. Young workers (those between 18 and 21 years of age) were the first, in 1986, to be "liberated" from the jurisdiction of Wages Councils, a measure which Conservative ministers proclaimed would lead to a reduction in youth unemployment. At the same time, the Factory Inspectorate, which had the responsibility for ensuring that employers abided by Wages Councils' pay awards, had its staff reduced, a further indication that the Government was not concerned about protection for the lowest paid. It was not until 1993, however, that Wages Councils were finally abolished, this being presented as a further means of increasing competitiveness and flexibility in Britain's labour market, whilst helping the unemployed to "price themselves back into work".

The rejection of corporatism

The Thatcher–Major governments' explicit rejection of incomes policies was also part of a more general eschewal of corporatism from 1979 onwards. After all, the development of a singularly British variant of corporatism – Middlemas prefers to speak of "corporate bias" (Middlemas, 1979: *passim*) – during the post-war era had been inextricably linked to the pursuit of incomes policies by successive Labour and Conservative governments (see, for example, Brittan, 1975: 58–63; Carpenter, 1976: 1–16; Cox, 1989: 198–223; Crouch, 1982: *passim*; Dorey, 1991: 24–7; Dorey, 2001c; Harris, 1972; Pahl and Winkler, 1974: 72–6). Yet under Margaret Thatcher's leadership, the Conservative party moved steadily away from this tripartite model of state–employer–trade union partnership *vis-à-vis* economic policy-making, to the extent that by the late 1980s, the former Trade and Industry Secretary, Lord Young, was cheerfully proclaiming: We have rejected the TUC; we have rejected the CBI . . . we gave up the corporate state (*Financial Times*, 9 November 1988).

Corporatism was clearly incompatible with the Thatcherite emphasis on the supremacy of the free market as the only viable means of wealth creation and resource allocation. As such, attempts by governments to regulate or direct economic and industrial activity, in partnership with organized interests such as trade unions, and in pursuit of social objectives, were now deemed by most Conservatives as wrong in principle, and unworkable in practice. Not only were the "social partners" incapable of ensuring that their members adhered to any policies agreed upon with ministers, it was also maintained that corporatist decision-making reflected a naïve and dangerous belief that market forces, and their immutable laws of supply and demand, could be suppressed or circumvented by politicians and the leaders of sectional interests.

Indeed, Conservatives increasingly argued that many of the economic problems which Britain's creeping corporatism purported to address were themselves often caused or exacerbated by the scope and scale of government intervention and interference in the first place, yet the response of post-war Conservative and Labour governments had invariably been to invoke even greater state intervention. The logical conclusion of this process, neo-liberal Conservatives feared, was a form of totalitarianism, whereby all aspects of British economic life would eventually become subject to political control and state direction (Biffen, 1977; Boyson, 1978: 72; Nicholas Budgen, *House of Commons Debates*, 5th series, Vol. 914, cols. 1239–40; Raison, 1979: 13; Shenfield, 1975: 36).

For the Thatcher–Major governments, therefore, the rejection of incomes policies was also integral to their reversal of corporatism, which was itself part of their avowed desire to "roll back the state", thereby permitting the vast bulk of be determined by managers and market forces. As well as dispensing with incomes policies, therefore, the Thatcher–Major governments steadily downgraded and dismantled Britain's corporatist and tripartite institutions, particularly those in which trade unions enjoyed a degree of parity with employers' representatives.

Thus did the NEDC begin to meet less frequently as the 1980s progressed, with Cabinet ministers also increasingly inclined to send their junior ministers or even senior civil servants in their place, claiming that the institution served no useful purpose, and was therefore "a waste of valuable ministerial time" (Lawson, 1992: 713–14; see also Tebbit, 1988: 193). As such, it was somewhat surprising that the NEDC was formally maintained as long as it was, for not until 1992, shortly after John Major's 1992 election victory, was its abolition finally announced, although by this time, many of its sectoral adjuncts – the so-called "Little Neddies" – had already been disbanded.

Vestiges of support for incomes policy in the Conservative party

In spite of the ideological vigour and political determination which the New Right within the Conservative party pursued the above principles and policies, the neo-liberal perspective – and hence the arguments against incomes policies – never went entirely unchecked. A small but dwindling band of older Conservatives continued to hanker after some form of incomes policy – often as part of a wider tripartite forum for economic policy-making throughout Margaret Thatcher's premiership, but their pleas were always treated with disdain or disregarded altogether. Margaret Thatcher's first Employment Secretary, James Prior, "became increasingly worried . . . by the complete rejection of any form of incomes policy", for he "believed that we had to have a policy to encourage voluntary restraint" (Prior, 1986: 109). Another consistent Conservative proponent of incomes policy during the Thatcher years was Ian Gilmour, who maintained that "higher unemployment and/or inflation is surely a far bigger threat to the maintenance of democratic government than an incomes policy". As for the neo-liberal insistence on unleashing market forces and rolling back the state, Gilmour pointed out that: "A Tory should have no objection to interfering with market forces", claiming that throughout the previous one hundred years, Conservative administrations had intervened in the economy in order to regulate or humanize capitalism. Nor was there any "fixed frontier for the activities of the state", Gilmour argued, because "a Tory . . . believes that the economic system has continually to be modified to make it acceptable to the majority of the population". With regard to incomes policy *per se*, Gilmour was convinced that:

> Britain's decentralized system of pay bargaining and the diffusion of power within the unions makes an incomes policy both more necessary than in other countries, and, at the same time, less likely to be successful. But the conclusion should not be that we should never try to have an incomes policy again. That is not feasible . . . The conclusion should be that we should try to avoid the mistakes of the past and go on trying. After all, the argument for an incomes policy is that there is no alternative. Even . . . mass unemployment does not avert the necessity of an incomes policy. (Gilmour, 1983: 178–80)

Like Prior, however, Gilmour recognized that monetarism and deification of the unfettered free market were the order of the day during the 1980s, to the extent that: "Dogma prevented any arrangement for wage bargaining other than ministerial exhortation, ill-treatment of the public sector, and unemployment" (Gilmour, 1992: 82).

The 1980s also heard Francis Pym call – in vain – for "the creation of a partnership between Government, industrial management and unions" (Pym, 1985: 160–2, 182; see, also, Baldry, 1985: 10–11). Further ministerial support for some kind of incomes policy (and tripartite forum) emanated from Chris Patten, who was deeply concerned at the difficulties of pursuing "a fairly explicit public sector pay policy without trying to reach some form of accomodation over pay elsewhere in the economy". As such, Patten suggested that:

> throughout the economy, public and private, we should attempt to replicate what is called "concerted action" in West Germany and other countries . . . bringing together employers, unions, government, the central bank and economic advisers each year to discuss the state of the economy [and the] next wage round. (Patten, 1983: 125, 128)

Such calls were in vain, however, partly because of the conviction and confidence with which the ideological case for neo-liberalism was articulated (buttressed further by the plethora of think-tanks and intellectuals who vigorously canvassed the neo-liberal perspective throughout the 1970s and 1980s. See for example, Cockett, 1994; Denham and Garnett, 1998; Heffernan, 1996: 73–87; Muller, 1996: 88–110), but also because Thatcher's shrewd management of the Cabinet during the 1980s ensured that only those Conservative colleagues who shared her neo-liberal philosophy were allocated the all-important "economic" or non-spending ministries, whilst the "one nation" critics were placed in departments with a social portfolio (such as health or education), or in apparently peripheral ministries (the Welsh, Scottish or Northern Ireland Offices). Alternatively, they were merely dismissed to the backbenches or sent to the House of Lords.

Certainly it was significant that for most of Margaret Thatcher's premiership, Geoffrey Howe, followed by Nigel Lawson, served as Chancellor of the Exchequer, neither of whom displayed the slightest inclination to resort to an incomes policy at any stage (in spite of Howe's former advocacy of an "economic forum" in Opposition). On the contrary, both made clear their belief that monetary policy, entailing rigorous control of the money supply and adjustment of interest rates, was the primary means of controlling inflation, not recourse to incomes policy as many previous post-war Chancellors and Prime Ministers had assumed.

Yet even if there had been greater support in the Conservative party during the 1980s and 1990s for incomes policies, it would have been increasingly difficult to formulate and implement such a policy because of the wider, structural changes taking place in the economy and *inter alia* the labour market, and the manner in which these were impacting upon the trade unions. Whilst many of these changes were actively encouraged by the Thatcher governments, it is also the case that to a significant extent, the trends would have manifested themselves even if another political party had been in Office.

The changing labour market

Since 1979, Britain has experienced a marked contraction of its manufacturing industry, and a concomitant expansion of the service and tertiary sectors of the economy. Although the process of deindustrialization was discernible prior to 1979, it undoubtedly accelerated during the 1980s, not least because the Thatcher governments encouraged such a trend, although as already intimated, much of the process was fuelled by exogenous factors, not least the intensification of globalization and the increasing fluidity and mobility of capital.

Whereas in 1979, 7,107,000 people were employed in manufacturing industries, by 1990 (the year of Thatcher's resignation as Conservative party leader and Prime Minister), only 4,190,000 were similarly employed. Meanwhile, Thatcher–Major governments presided over a slight decline in full-time employment, and a corresponding increase in part-time work, all of which was perfectly in accordance with their constant advocacy of "labour market flexibility" and the end of a "jobs-for-life" culture.

The impact on trade union membership

Economic restructuring and the consequent changes in the labour market naturally had a serious impact on trade union membership during the 1980s and 1990s, virtually halving the number trade unionists in Britain since 1979. Yet even this stark statistic does not reveal the full impact of the changes which occurred.

A significant additional problem for Britain's trade unions is that women and part-time workers – the two categories of employees which have increased during the 1980s and 1990s – have traditionally been less inclined to join trade unions in the first place, so that whereas 38 per cent of all employed men belonged to a trade union in 1993, for example, only 31 per cent of women did so. At the same time, whilst 39 per cent of full-time employees were trade union members, only 21 per cent of part-time workers belonged to a trade union.

To compound these problems for Britain's trade unions, the evidence suggests that trade union membership is lower amongst smaller and/or newer work-place establishments – precisely those which evinced an increase in number during the 1980s and 1990s. For example, in private sector work-place establishments employing less than 50 people, trade union density in 1990 was just 19 per cent, compared to 53 per cent in establishments employing at least 1,000 people (Millward *et al.*, 1992: 64).

With regard to the correlation between trade union membership and the age of a work-place or company, it is significant that whereas union density was 44 per cent in those private sector establishments which had been in existence for more than 20 years, it was only 25 per cent in private sector establishments less than 3 years old in 1990 (Millward *et al.*, 1992: 64).

(De)recognition of trade unions

What also served to reduce trade union membership and density during the 1980s was the increasing number of employers and companies who were refusing to recognize trade unions for collective bargaining purposes. Between 1984 and 1990, for example, the proportion of work-places in Britain which recognized trade unions for the purpose of collective bargaining fell from 66 per cent to 53 per cent. This decline was greatest in the private manufacturing sector, where union recognition declined from 65 per cent of establishments in 1984 to 44 per cent in 1990 (Millward *et al.*, 1992: 71; Hutton, 1995: 93).

The decline of trade union recognition was particularly pronounced in smaller work-places, and also in new enterprises. Indeed many such enterprises "tended to have characteristics associated with low levels of unionization. They were generally smaller, more likely to be in the service sector . . . and had much higher proportions of part-time employees (*Labour Research*, April 1994: 18)

Decline of collective bargaining

Not surprisingly, as a consequence of these changes and trends, the Thatcher–Major governments presided over a marked decline in collective bargaining. Admittedly, many non-trade unionists might still be covered indirectly by collective bargaining, in so far as agreements entered into by trade unions and management will often apply to the whole workforce, but nonetheless, it is undoubtedly the case that collective bargaining diminished throughout the 1980s.

For example, by 1990 less than 50 per cent of employees in Britain had their terms and conditions of employment (including pay) determined via collective bargaining, compared to more than 70 per cent in the 1970s. Furthermore, this diminution impacted upon private and public sectors alike. In 1984, 64 per cent of employees in the private manufacturing sector were covered by collective bargaining, whilst 41 per cent of employees in private services were similarly covered, but by 1990 the figures were 51 per cent and 33 per cent respectively. Meanwhile, in the public sector the proportion of employees covered by collective bargaining declined from 95 per cent in 1984 to 78 per cent in 1990. In short, by the beginning of the 1990s collective bargaining "was present in fewer work-places and affected fewer employees" (Millward *et al.*, 1992: 93, 352).

No scope for incomes policy

All of these wider economic and labour market trends underpinned the Thatcher–Major governments' explicit eschewal of incomes policy. Instead, Conservative ministers sought to treat labour as merely another commodity in a capitalist economy, one whose "natural" price could only be determined by unfettered market forces, operating their immutable laws of supply and demand. Whereas One Nation Tories had maintained, throughout the late 1940s and 1950s, that workers should not be viewed merely as units of production, this was precisely how they were viewed by Thatcherite Conservatives throughout the 1980s and 1990s. Workers were to be "free" to sell their labour power to the highest – or lowest – bidder, without any governmental attempt at promoting social equity or fairness through recourse to an incomes policy.

Furthermore, the rejection of incomes policies, followed by the increasing rejection of collective bargaining from the mid-1980s onwards, reflected the renewed Conservative principle of *individualism* as applied to the sphere of wage determination, as the Thatcher–Major governments recommended that pay bargaining ought, as far as possible, be negotiated with employers by individual employees. This, it was implied, would ensure that workers had to convince their employers that they deserved a pay increase, on the grounds of criteria such as increased productivity and improved efficiency, for example, rather than wages and salaries continuing to be determined for the whole workforce, by the trade unions, according to the "going rate" or "comparability" by trade unions. In this way, of course, the Conservative governments further ensured that the balance of power in industry shifted decisively away from employees and labour back towards management and capital.

The conditions and assumptions which had previously led to the pursuit of incomes policies in post-war Britain, namely governmental commitment to full employment, relatively high trade union membership, extensive collective and national-level pay bargaining, a bipartisan concern to ameliorate the worst excesses and inequalities engendered by "the market", and the assumption that excessive pay increases were the primary cause of inflation, no longer applied or were rejected by the Conservative governments led by Margaret Thatcher and John Major.

Indeed, during the 1980s and 1990s, Conservative ministers could increasingly be heard boasting about the cheapness of British workers compared to their foreign counterparts, a boast which was increasingly made in an attempt to attract inward investment. Indeed, there was something bizarre about Conservative ministers who loudly proclaimed their patriotism, but who then wanted to impoverish millions of British workers in order to make them more profitable for footloose foreign firms and multinational companies. Similarly, ministerial pronouncements about the vital importance of attracting inward investment as the means of facilitating employment seemed somewhat at odds with ministers' proclaimed defence of British sovereignty *vis-à-vis* the European Union. Herein resided one of the increasing contradictions of Conservative party politics since the late 1980s, namely the rhetorical emphasis on defending British nationhood and identity against external (invariably EU) incursion whilst simultaneously embracing and extolling globalization, with all that this implies for the autonomy and sovereignty of the modern nation-state. It is a contradiction which the Conservative party has hardly recognized, yet alone resolved.

8

Towards New Labour, away from incomes policy: The Labour Party, 1979–2001

Aftermath of the "winter of discontent"

Adherence to incomes policies had been a major contributory factor in precipitating the downfall of the Labour government in May 1979, and the issue continued to vex the party during its first term in Opposition for two reasons. First, the inevitable internal "inquest" into the cause of Labour's electoral defeat resulted in considerable attention being focused on the party's various incomes policies, which naturally led to the second reason why incomes policy continued to be an issue for the party during this period, namely the question of what Labour's approach should be in the future with regard to pay determination.

With regard to the role of incomes policies in contributing towards the Callaghan government's defeat in May 1979, some on the left insisted that the Labour government's approach to pay had represented an attack on the living standards of the party's working-class supporters in order to prop up capitalism in one of its periodic crises. In other words, it was intimated, the Labour government had not invoked incomes policies as part of a genuinely socialist strategy to plan the economy and effect a fundamental and irreversible transfer of wealth to ordinary working people but, instead, to restrain wages, and thus suppress living standards. Consequently, Labour's insistence on persevering with incomes policies effectively drove swathes of its hitherto working-class support base into the Conservative camp, where they had been promised a return to free collective bargaining. Ultimately, according to this perspective, it was the Labour leadership, rather than the trade unions, who were the real architects of the Callaghan government's downfall (see, for example, Coates, 1979: 29–30; Hodgson, 1981: 122).

The second account advanced by some within the Labour party was that the principle of pursuing an incomes policy had been correct, but that the government had made errors in the details and execution of such policies. For example, some former Labour ministers acknowledged that the 5 per cent norm sought by the Callaghan government during its final year of office had been unrealistically low, and that a slightly higher figure – albeit still in single figures – would probably have proved more acceptable to the trade unions, and thereby averted the "winter of discontent", and, quite possibly, the defeat of the Labour party at the polls a few months later (Castle, 1993: 507–8; Healey, 1989: 462–3; see also Mitchell, 1983: 19).

Implicit too in this perspective is the notion that electoral defeat might have been avoided if Callaghan had called the general election in the autumn of 1978, rather than deciding to soldier on to the following year. Whilst this account did not exonerate the trade unions entirely, it did apportion much of the blame for Labour's election defeat on the party leadership's rigid adherence to a particularly strict incomes policy.

The third perspective concerning the role of incomes policies in accounting for Labour's defeat in May 1979 lay the blame squarely with the trade unions. To Labour proponents of this view, the trade unions had displayed a flagrant disregard both for the economic problems facing the country and the concomitant political problems facing the Labour government during the latter half of the 1970s; the trade unions were deemed obstinately to have pursued their own short-term and sectional interests over and above the long-term and national interest, and brought about the downfall of the Labour government as a result. Certainly, Joel Barnett, a Treasury Minister during the late 1970s, recalled that "the only give and take in the [social] contract was that the government gave and the unions took" (Barnett, 1982: 49).

What policy for incomes after 1979?

The second reason why the issue of incomes policy continued to vex the Labour party during its first term in Opposition was because of the need to decide whether it would continue to advocate such a policy, or whether its experiences in office, and the Conservative's success in preaching a return to free collective bargaining, would persuade Labour to ditch incomes policies once-and-for-all. Of course, the debate about whether or not the Labour party should persevere with incomes policies in the future closely corresponded to the debate about the extent to which incomes policies were the cause of Labour's downfall in 1979.

As such, the left – who were ascendant within the Labour party during the early 1980s – continued to speak out against incomes policies, unless these were inextricably linked to a socialist strategy for planning the economy and redistributing wealth to ordinary working people. Otherwise, it was alleged, incomes policies were merely a device for holding down workers' wages and living standards in order to protect employers' profits and sustain the capitalist mode of production. According to Tony Benn, the doyen of the Labour Left during this time, "we are never ever going back to the old policies of wage restraint as a means of saving capitalism" (Labour Party Report 1981: 75).

For many on the left, what a future Labour government ought to be committed to was the pursuit of an "alternative economic strategy", entailing the extension of public ownership, selective import controls, more extensive planning agreements, enhanced interventionist powers for the National Enterprise Board, a shorter working week, and a wealth tax (see, for example, Aaronovitch, 1981; Benn, 1980: *passim*; Cripps and Ward, 1982: 22–5; Glyn and Harrison, 1980: 147–64; Hodgson, 1981: 6 and *passim*; Labour Co-ordinating Committee, 1980; Rowthorn, 1981; Sapper, 1981: 19–24). Seeking reflation in a time of recession, rather than more orthodox Treasury-inspired deflation, the *alternative economic strategy* recommended that domestic demand should be increased, and jobs thereby created, by abandoning incomes policy so that wages could increase via the restoration of free collective bargaining. This perspective was made clear by a motion (carried) at the Labour party's 1981 annual conference, moved by the delegate from AUEW-TASS – and supported by the TGWU – which urged that because "increased purchasing power is essential for the Alternative Economic Strategy", the party should declare "its opposition to incomes policy" (Labour Party Report 1981: 68).

However, left-wing advocates of the *alternative economic strategy* also attached considerable importance to import controls, on the grounds that such controls ensure that the higher working-class spending power derived from free collective bargaining did not suck in imports, and thereby plunge Britain's balance of payments (further) into the red, whilst simultaneously contributing to a further contraction of Britain's industrial manufacturing base and concomitant loss of jobs.

This remained a minority view, however, in spite of the advances made by the left in other areas, for the dominant perspective in the Labour party was that some form of agreement was necessary with the trade unions over the issue of pay, as an essential element of economic management. Certainly, as one academic commentator pointed out during this time: "The most fundamental weakness of the entire [alternative economic] strategy is the failure to plan for an incomes policy to cover the interim period whilst the domestic economy expands." Indeed, it was deemed a "fundamentally dishonest argument that Labour can plan the economy and trade without planning incomes"

(Whiteley, 1983: 200–1). This, of course, immediately raised a host of questions about the character of any future incomes policy to be adopted by the Labour party, coupled with the crucial issue of whether trade union agreement could be secured, for without this a Labour government would effectively be left with two unpalatable choices: either it abandoned any pretence at incomes policy (except in the public sector, where a *de facto* incomes policy always operated, via cash limits) and permitted "excessive" wage increases to fuel unemployment and bankruptcies – which was what the Conservative government was doing – or it imposed a statutory incomes policy on the trade unions, in which case, the question of sanctions and penalties would need to be addressed. The latter option, of course, would also enable the Conservatives to warn the electorate of the inevitable industrial conflict and social disruption which would follow the return of a Labour government.

Precisely because these two alternatives were so unpalatable, the dominant perspective within the Labour party during the early 1980s, the opposition of the Bennite Left notwithstanding, remained in favour of a looser, more flexible incomes policy. There was a widespread recognition that: "We cannot have the trade unions initially involved in every aspect of our economic policy except the overall level of earnings." On the contrary, it was emphasized that "to obtain an expansion of the economy which puts our people back to work and pays for the level of social services that we need, there has to be a measure of planning for earnings which is no less effective than the planning of investment, output and exports" (Hattersley, 1983: 5). Hattersley, who was appointed Labour's Shadow Chancellor when Neil Kinnock was elected Party leader in 1983, was adamant that "if we are to have growth without an unacceptable level of inflation, the unions and a Labour government must come to a voluntary agreement about the overall level of money wages" (*The Times*, 9 November 1983).

Indeed, this was a point to which Hattersley devoted considerable atention during the mid-1980s, when he was convinced that free collective bargaining was incompatible with the professed socialist objectives of both the Labour party and the trade union movement, due to the fact that such a mode of pay determination "gives most to the strong and least to the weak". Consequently, Hattersley insisted that "*some* income planning is necessary", although this "should not be an incomes policy of the old model, with its norms, ceilings, and acceptable exceptions". Instead, Hattersley argued that: "A national view on the overall level and general distribution of wages must become a permanent part of both our economic and social strategy", although rather than talk of wage restraint *per se*, he spoke about the planned growth of earnings and the extent to which "wage planning must be directly concerned with relieving the condition of the low-paid" (Hattersley, 1987: 241–3).

Continued trade union antipathy

Yet, as ever, the Labour party was faced by a trade union movement which remained overwhelmingly hostile to incomes policies, suspicious that whatever they were called, and whatever objectives were ascribed to them, they would always be invoked primarily as a means of securing wage restraint. Against such policies, free collective bargaining remained inviolate. As the AUEW delegate had crisply expressed it at the TUC's 1980 conference: "My union stands implacably in favour of free collective bargaining and the right of trade unions to get for their members the rate for the job", it being pointed out that "past wage control agreements have extracted from the workers the full extent of their commitment without anyone being able to extract the same commitment . . . from the employing classes" (TUC Report 1980: 473). This theme was elaborated upon by the AUEW-TASS delegate who explained that all hitherto incomes policies had been:

> based on the misconception that organised workers must be restrained from using their bargaining power to improve their wages and conditions of employment; or worse, that trade unions must be diverted from the ultimate sin of ensuring that the wages of their members keep pace with the cost of living. In honest language, that means accepting cuts in real wages. People do not join trade unions in the expectation that their leaders will conspire with Governments to achieve wage cuts. (TUC Report 1980: 478)

However, the Labour party gleaned some comfort from the fact that the same conference supported – by 5,276,000 votes to 3,628,000 – a composite motion moved by the UCW, which rejected "any wage freeze or incomes policy from the present Government", but then called for the TUC–Labour party Liaison Committee to develop policies for a planned economy in which "wages would not be allowed to fall behind the movement of prices and that anti-inflation measures would not bear merely on pay" (TUC Report 1980: 470). Yet the same conference also endorsed COHSE's motion reaffirming the TUC's "commitment to free collective bargaining and its opposition to incomes policy" (TUC Report 1980: 472).

Not for the first time, therefore, the Labour party was faced by a somewhat schizophrenic trade union movement which apparently wanted both a planned "socialist" economy, in which incomes would also have to be planned, and the maintenance of free collective bargaining. The trade unions themselves did not see any contradiction or inconsistency in these two positions for, they maintained, free collective bargaining was linked with the existence of a capitalist economy in which wages were determined in accordance with market principles and criteria.

However, if and when a Labour government sought to transcend capitalism, the unions implied, then they would no longer need to insist on free collective bargaining as the means of determining wages, because wages could be planned along with all other aspects of the economy, most notably investment, profits and dividends. Furthermore, many trade unions posited a distinction between incomes policies on the one hand, which they associated with wage restraint, and the planned growth of incomes on the other, which was clearly much more acceptable (just as it had been in the mid-1960s).

These nuances were evident at the following year's TUC conference, when delegates approved the motion moved by the AUEW-TASS which "emphatically rejects the view that wage increases are the primary cause of inflation and unemployment" and therefore:

> reaffirms its support for free collective bargaining and is opposed to any pay restraint policies, pay norms, or statutory restraints which would interfere with the rights of unions to determine their own policies and resolve their own negotiating procedures and settlements. To this end, Congress does not agree to any discussions on pay restraint. (TUC Report 1981: 507)

In moving the motion, the AUEW-TASS leader Ken Gill argued that "until a massive shift of wealth and power takes place it is appallingly wrong to give away the right to bargain, the right to extract the best bargain from employers . . . You cannot have a free market for everyone but the worker . . . " (TUC Report 1981: 507). This stance was opposed by NALGO on the grounds that "unfettered free collective bargaining belongs to the Conservative free market economy" and was therefore incompatible with the professed socialist aspirations of the organized labour movement. If the trade unions were seeking the re-election of a Labour government committed to a comprehensive programme of economic planning, then "to exclude wages . . . is idiotic as well as being pure hypocrisy" (TUC Report 1981: 509). These sentiments were echoed by Bill Sirs, leader of the ISTC, who pointed out to delegates the inconsistency of their position, suggesting that those who believed "a Labour government can operate with us and leave wages in isolation . . . are living in cloud-cuckoo-land" (TUC Report 1980: 510).

A National Economic Assessment

Faced with such trade union ambivalence, the Labour party spent the best part of the 1980s trying to avoid explicit references to incomes policy *per se*, preferring instead to advocate a "national economic assessment" which would not only evaluate "the prospects for the growth of the economy, involving such key issues as the use of resources between consumption, investment, public services and the balance of trade", but would also consider "the share of national incomes going to profits, to earnings from employment, to rents, to social benefits and other incomes" (Labour Party, 1981: 17; see also TUC-Labour Party Liaison Committee, 1981: 13; Shore, 1983: 37; Varley, 1983: 74–5).

These debates were rehearsed again at the TUC's 1982 annual conference, when delegates voted once again in favour of a motion extolling the virtues of free collective bargaining, and rejecting the notion that wages could or should be determined on the basis of agreements "with this or any other Government". In endorsing this motion, delegates rejected an amendment moved by Bill Sirs on behalf of ISTC (and seconded by UCW, with further support proferred by Sid Weighell of the NUR, and Frank Chapple of EETPU) which referred to the "problems arising from free collective bargaining" and thereby praised the TUC–Labour party Liaison Committee's policy document *Economic Issues Facing the Next Labour government* "which states that earnings and incomes would be embraced in any national economic assessment carried out jointly by the TUC and a Labour government" (TUC Report 1982: 557).

Once the amendment had been defeated, the motion in support of free collective bargaining was endorsed by 6,187,000 votes to 4,417,000, which indicated that a significant minority of TUC affiliates were not persuaded of the alleged merits of unfetterred free collective bargaining, but recognized, instead, the need for some tentative agreement with the Labour party on a policy for incomes as part of a more comprehensive programme of economic planning.

A few months earlier, in June 1982, the Labour party's own stance had been reiterated via an NEC policy document simply entitled *Labour's Programme 1982*, in which the case was made for:

> a national economic assessment of the prospects for the growth of the economy, inlvolving such key issues as the use of resources between personal consumption, public and private investment, public services, and the balance of trade. Such an assessment, to be comprehensive, has to embrace such issues as the share of the national income going to profits, to earnings from employment, to rents, to social benefits, and to other incomes.

However, *Labour's Programme 1982* also "made clear our opposition to any policies of wage restraint" because these "cannot be maintained for any length of time without putting intolerable strains upon industrial relations and threatening to perpetuate all the anomalies and injustices in the present framework of pay differentials". Yet it was then argued that "the principles of fairness and comparability are central to pay bargaining and cannot be ignored by trade unions, employers or by government" (Labour Party/NEC, 1982: 24–5).

The Labour party's discomfort and dilemma in the face of widespread trade union insistence on free collective bargaining was plain to see; a recognition that government-invoked wage restraint would not work, and that it would exacerbate existing grievances (whilst also generating new ones), yet coupled with an insistence on the need for some agreement over pay as an integral component of economic management.

Electoral considerations

This discomfort was compounded by political and electoral considerations (quite apart from whether or trade unionists themselves would vote for the return of a Labour government pledged to reintroduce incomes policies). The Labour party was faced with the dilemma that if it did not reach a close and coherent agreement with the trade unions over incomes policy, the Conservatives would ruthlessly exploit this glaring gap at the heart of Labour's economic strategy – a policy to plan the economy and control prices and profits but without a corresponding incomes policy with which to control wages and salaries.

On the other hand, if the Labour party were to secure a more forthright and coherent agreement with the TUC in support of incomes policy, this too would gleefully be siezed upon by the Conservatives as evidence of Labour's incestuous links with the trade unions, to the extent that it would be the latter, rather than the Labour government itself, deemed to be "running the country". Furthermore, if the Labour party had enunciated a more explicit incomes policy during the early 1980s, the Conservatives would also have been afforded a further opportunity to woo the skilled working class – the crucial C2s – with pledges to retain free collective bargaining, and thereby restore differentials.

There was one further political problem for the Labour party during the early and mid-1980s which impacted upon the debate over incomes policy, namely the electoral challenge posed by the Social Democratic Party (in "alliance" with the Liberal Party). This new party had been formed in March 1981 by a number of Labour MPs, including four former Cabinet ministers (Roy Jenkins, David Owen, William Rodgers and Shirley Williams), breaking away to form a new centrist party in response to Labour's apparent "capture" by the Bennite Left and the role ascribed to the trade unions in the election of the Party leader via the new electoral college. The Social Democratic Party purported to favour many of the "moderate" policies which it believed the left-dominated Labour party had effectively abandoned, and thus sought to offer the electorate a "middle way" between Bennite Socialism and Thatcherite Conservatism.

In particular, the Social Democratic Party emphasized the continued need for an incomes policy, albeit one which reflected the need for "a more flexible, decentralized approach" on the grounds that a major failing of previous incomes policies had been "excessive centralization" (Owen, 1981: 105; Rodgers, 1982: 116). This perspective seemed to be shared by Shirley Williams, who believed that previous incomes policies had disintegrated in large part due to a backlash from ordinary trade union members and their shop stewards (Williams, 1981: 131).

However, whilst Williams (and David Owen) might have seen this backlash as a consequence of the over-centralization of previous incomes policies, it did beg the question of whether a more decentralized incomes policy along the lines urged by the Social Democratic party would merely enhance even further the power of local-level trade union officials and shop stewards, to the extent that any nationally-recommended "pay norm" was rendered meaningless. Such ambiguity was not ameliorated by such vacuous platitudes as: "A successful incomes policy requires to sustain it political skills of a high order with difficult decisions coolly taken" (Rodgers, 1982: 117).

Unfortunately, the Social Democratic Party's espousal of such principles as decentralization and flexibility – along with David Owen's predilection for alliterative polarities such as "tough but tender" or "competition and compassion" – was symptomatic of its vagueness and vacillation on a range of key issues. For example, there seemed to be a difference of opinion among the leaders of the Social Democratic Party over whether or not an incomes policy should be linked to the principle of egalitarianism, for whilst William Rodgers argued that such a policy, particularly if pursued on a long-term basis, "must have redistributive goals" and "promote greater social justice" (Rodgers, 1982: 122), David Owen was equally insistent that any wealth redistribution should be sought through the tax and social security system, rather than through incomes policies (Owen, 1981: 105).

Yet such ambiguities did not prevent the Social Democratic party from posing a serious electoral threat to the Labour party during the first half of the 1980s, to the extent that there was a widespread expectation that the new party might replace Labour as the main Opposition and alternative to the Conservatives. With regard to Labour's own deliberations over incomes policy, the party could not ignore the fact that during the Social Democrat's fledgling years, it appeared to enjoy as much support amongst trade unionists as the Labour party itself. It was in this context, with the Conservative Government – and many trade unions – rejecting incomes policies outright (public sector cash limits notwithstanding) and the new Social Democratic Party espousing a more decentralized and flexible incomes policy, that the Labour party anguished over determining its own policy on incomes during the early 1980s.

Neil Kinnock and the loosening of Labour's links with the unions

The crushing general election defeat in June 1983 provided a new impetus for reconsidering the Labour party's stance on the related issues of industrial relations, trade unionism and incomes policy, particularly once Neil Kinnock had replaced Michael Foot as party leader. Indeed, from this time onwards, the Labour party's deliberations over incomes policy became inextricably linked to attempts by the party leadership to start loosening Labour's links with the trade unions. This strategy became more explicit and extensive after a third successive election defeat in 1987, by which time, a number of senior figures in the party were convinced that Labour's organizational and financial links with the trade unions, coupled with its hitherto opposition to the Conservative governments anti-trade union legislation, were alienating millions of former or potential voters, including many trade union members themselves.

Thus it was that Neil Kinnock's period of leadership, from 1983 to 1992, was characterized by a loosening – slow at first, but accelerating after the 1987 election defeat – of the Labour party's relationship with the trade unions, which, in conjunction with the party's gradual embracing of "the market", had profound implications for Labour's stance on incomes policy.

Even back in 1984, Neil Kinnock had sought the adoption by constituency parties of One-Member One-Vote (OMOV) for the selection of Labour's parliamentary candidates. This proposal, however, was rejected by Labour's annual conference, at which the trade unions commanded virtually 90 per cent of the vote. Yet such an initiative provided a clear indication of the direction in which Kinnock wanted to move the Labour party, as was his explicit acceptance, by 1985, of Conservative legislation obliging trade unions to ballot their members prior to embarking on strike action. With regard to wage determination in particular, the emphasis on a National Economic Assessment was accompanied by an insistence, via the 1985 TUC–Labour party Liaison Committee's policy document *A New Partnership: A New Britain* that "statutory norms and government imposed wage restraint offer no solutions".

The following year witnessed the publication of a policy document, *People at Work: New Rights and Responsibilities*, the title itself being particularly significant, for the emphasis in this document was not on the repeal of Conservative trade union legislation and concomitant restoration of trade union immunities, but on the rights of employees to be consulted and informed by management of matters pertaining to the enterprise in which they were employed. This neatly fitted in with the Labour leadership's new emphasis on characterizing industrial relations not as an arena of (class) conflict between employers and employees, but as a sphere in which partnership between the two sides of industry – rather than between trade unions and the state – was the key to economic success.

A further indication that Neil Kinnock and many of his senior colleagues in the parliamentary Labour party wished to loosen the links with the trade union was the down-grading of the Labour party–TUC Liaison Committee, which had been established in 1971 to provide the unions with a significant input into economic and industrial policy-making. Indeed, the Liaison Committee had fallen entirely into abeyance by the end of the decade, its role increasingly undertaken by a less formal Contact Group whose membership was fluid, but still comprised senior Labour party figures and trade union leaders (Minkin 1991: 469). Meanwhile, the Labour party's 1987 general election manifesto made only scant reference to a partnership with the trade unions, blandly observing instead that "rights and responsibilities" would provide the basis of "good industrial relations".

The biggest impetus for a review of Labour's trade union links, however, was the party's emphatic defeat (its third in succession) in the 1987 general election. This appeared to provide Kinnock with a two-fold justification for a process of modernization, a process which would entail, among other things, a looser relationship between the Labour party and the trade unions, and even less emphasis on incomes policy. First, the fact that Labour had once again lost an election so heavily (the Conservatives won in 1987 with a 101 seat majority) emboldened those in the party who insisted on the need to modernize and moderate its policies generally, and reconsider its relationship with the trade unions in particular.

Secondly, the "modernizers" could point to the fact that Labour had regained at least some of the electoral support lost in 1983, and reduced the Conservatives majority, which seemed to indicate that the party was moving in the right (sic) direction. On both counts, therefore, the 1987 election defeat provided Kinnock and his closest colleagues with both the justification and the confidence to embark on a fundamental reappraisal of Labour's principles and policies, through a formal Policy Review. This in turn was to have important implications for Labour's approach to the trade unions and *inter alia* the party's stance on incomes policy.

The Policy Review

The Policy Review launched by Neil Kinnock in the wake of the 1987 election defeat clearly intimated, at both a general and a specific level, that the Labour party's approach to the trade unions was changing. Indeed, having formerly been a Tribunite on the Left of the Labour party, Kinnock steadily moved to the Right during his time as leader, to the extent that in 1989, his aide, Peter Mandelson, is alleged to have claimed that "Neil is to the right of Margaret Thatcher on the unions" (quoted in Heffernan and Marqusee 1992: 147).

At a general level, the Policy Review clearly signified the Labour party's partial acceptance of Thatcherism, most notably with regard to the role of the market economy, along with the importance of individualism. It also signalled the prioritization of consumer interests, rather than those of producers. Embracing such aspects of the Thatcherite agenda clearly implied that a Labour government would ascribe the trade unions less importance and influence than hitherto.

This implication was confirmed at a more specific level, namely the Policy Review's stance on industrial relations, which focused on individuals and employees within the work-place, rather than on the trade unions *qua* institutions. Of the seven groups established by Kinnock under the Policy Review, it was the People at Work group which most directly addressed the Labour party's future approach to trade unionism. Indeed, the People at Work group was at considerable pains to shift debate away from emphases on the rights of trade unions as corporate bodies, along with talk about the restoration of legal "rights" pertaining to strikes and picketing. Such a discourse was felt to be too negative, whilst also enabling the Conservative party to continue portraying Labour as the party of industrial conflict and trade union militancy: "the striker's friend".

Instead, the People at Work group placed much stronger emphasis on enhancing the rights of individuals as employees, rather than as trade unionists. There was also considerable emphasis on partnership in the work-place, this further reflecting the group's concern to move away from the notion of industrial relations as inherently conflictual. Indeed, when the outcome of the Policy Review was presented in the 1989 document *Meet the Challenge, Make the Change*, it was emphasized that: "Economic success depends on good working relationships and partnership in industry" (Labour Party, 1989: 25).

The Labour party was thus seeking to present the case for employees' rights and partnership in the work-place not so much on the grounds of social justice or industrial democracy, but economic efficiency and international competitiveness. Employment rights were presented not as a counterweight to the operation of a market economy, but as an adjunct to it. *Meet the Challenge, Make the Change* emphasized Labour's commitment to the rights of employees (to be enshrined in a new Charter for Employees), in the form of basic contracts of employment, equal opportunities, health and safety, a minimum wage, trade union membership, and protection against unfair dismissal, but was more opaque in its pledges concerning the rights and powers of the trade unions themselves. It was also equivocal on such issues as how a Labour government would deal with industrial disputes, and to what extent secondary industrial action would be permitted, even though it was deemed unfair "that all forms of sympathetic action by other employees, following a majority vote, should be unlawful" (Labour Party, 1989: 17–27).

Some clarification was provided when *Looking to the Future* was published the following year, reflecting the refinement of some of the proposals enshrined in *Meet the Challenge, Make the Change*. For example, in addition to reiterating Labour's commitment to the rights of employees and promoting partnership in the work-place, *Looking to the Future* asserted that a Labour government would establish an industrial court which could adjudicate in major disputes. With regard to secondary or sympathy industrial action, *Looking to the Future* declared that such action would be permissible in circumstances where there existed shared occupational or professional interests, or when one employer was directly helping another in order to undermine a legitimate industrial dispute (Labour Party, 1990: 32–5).

By the time that the Policy Review had been completed, though, the National Economic Assessment had been downgraded by the Labour leadership, thereby reflecting the party's continued drift away from incomes policy (Shaw, 1994: 44, 95–6). Thus did John Smith, having succeeded Roy Hattersley as Labour's Shadow Chancellor, inform delegates at the TUC's 1990 conference that: "There will be no return to 5 per cent, 8 per cent or 10 per cent norms under Labour", for "that way lies disaster". Yet as Shaw observes, in downgrading and quietly abandoning the notion of a National Economic Assessment – which had always "rested on brittle foundations" due to the trade unions' organizational and ideological inability "too justify and enforce the subordination of sectional concerns to wider societal ones" – the Labour party's "lack of a credible anti-inflation strategy was a problem which it never resolved" during the early 1990s (Shaw, 1994: 11).

Paradoxically, perhaps, although the Labour leadership was seeking to distance itself from the trade unions, the party's drift away from incomes policy was actually bringing it in line with the stance of most trade unions on this particular issue. Admittedly, some trade union leaders, most notably John Edmonds of the GMB and Alan Tuffin of the UWC, did propose some form of "synchronized pay bargaining", but the less than enthusiastic response with which this was greeted by several other trade unions effectively vindicated the Labour leadership's continued drift away from an incomes policy (see, for example, *The Guardian*, 7 May 1991 and 12 June 1991).

Besides, the Thatcher governments' attack on *national* pay bargaining during the second half of the 1980s served partly to deflect trade union attention away from the issue of incomes policy; their preoccupation was increasingly about defending free collective bargaining at national level in the face of the Conservative's avowed objective of eradicating such wage determination in favour of individual, local or plant-level pay determination (which was clearly intended to tilt the balance of power in the work-place even further in favour of employers and management). It was this issue, for example, which superseded arguments about incomes policies at the TUC's 1987 annual conference (TUC Report 1988: 519–21). This, in turn, made it easier for the Labour party leadership to continue downgrading its own increasingly nebulous commitment to incomes policy.

Reforming the Labour–trade union links under John Smith

Whereas Neil Kinnock had been primarily concerned to modernize Labour party policies with regard to trade union law and industrial relations – effectively accepting many of the Thatcher governments' legislative reforms – his successor, John Smith, devoted much of his attention from July 1992 until his untimely death in May 1994 to reforming the organizational relationship between Labour and the trade unions, although it has been claimed that the considerable trade union support which Smith received in Labour's 1992 leadership contest was partly derived from an understanding that "he had no interest in diminishing the union role in party affairs" (Fielding, 1995: 87).

Such an assumption was to prove unwarranted, however, for Smith was particularly determined to loosen the ties between the Labour and the trade unions, a determination which was underpinned by the widely-held belief in senior Labour circles that the party's close ties with the unions had contributed to the 1992 election defeat. Whilst it was not suggested that this had been the *main* reason for Labour's fourth consecutive election defeat – it was universally acknowledged that the most important factors had been the party's susceptibility to Conservative propaganda and scaremongering (slavishly endorsed by most of the tabloid press) about its taxation policies and allegations of economic incompetence – there was nonetheless a firmly held view amongst much of the Labour leadership that the party's organizational and financial relationship with the trade unions had cost it many votes. The

Conservatives had once again sought to remind voters of the 1978–9 "winter of discontent", strongly implying that the return of a Labour government would also herald the return of industrial conflict and trade unions "running the country".

The view that the Labour party had suffered by virtue of its links with the trade unions was endorsed a few weeks after the 1992 election defeat, when Labour's Shadow Communications Agency presented the National Executive Committee with the results of its own surveys, which revealed that many voters were still deterred from supporting the party because of its cloth-cap, trade union-dominated image, even though they were otherwise attracted by its stance on most social issues.

A few within, or sympathetic to, the labour movement even recommended a "divorce" between the Labour party and the trade unions, so that each was independent of the other. Advocates of this strategy insisted that Labour "cannot hope to convince the electorate that it will pursue the public interest when it is tied to sectional pressure groups". It was suggested that by virtue of its links with the trade unions, Labour was widely seen as a party concerned primarily with the interests of trade union members in particular rather than workers generally (a crucial distinction given that significantly less than half of the labour force in Britain now belongs to a trade union), and with the interests of producers rather than consumers. Indeed, it was claimed that as many as "one-third of voters who were once Labour supporters do not vote Labour because of the union link", whilst trade union "domination makes the task of winning over floating Liberal Democrats immeasurably harder" (Walsh and Tindale, 1992: 10).

Proponents of this perspective therefore claimed that the Labour party ought to sever its ties with the trade unions, and thereafter treat them as just one of any number of organized interests in society who would be consulted from time to time. It was claimed that: "The only way that the [Labour] Party can modernize itself is to start from a clean sheet . . . it is time to break the link." By making this break, it was alleged that the Labour party could broaden its electoral appeal so as to win support from non-trade unionists, sections of the middle class and consumers. Freed of its financial and organizational ties to the trade unions, the Labour party could "champion the cause not just of organized labour, but of all labour" (Dewdney, 1992: 4, 11). In short: "The separation of unions from formal party politics is now an imperative" (MacShane, 1993: vii).

However, what the Labour party actually sought was not a "divorce", but a more "open marriage" with the trade unions. It was widely acknowledged in the party that Labour's links with the trade unions were disliked and distrusted by much of the electorate, but the solution was not deemed to be a complete break or separation. To this end,

Labour's National Executive Committee established a review group to examine the party's links with the trade unions, this subsequently making a number of recommendations for reforming the relationship between the industrial and political wings of the labour movement. Indeed, several of these proposals were subsequently endorsed at Labour's 1993 annual conference.

First, there was reform of the trade unions' block vote, for at the beginning of the 1990s this constituted about 90 per cent of votes cast at Labour's annual conference, with the four largest trade unions alone enjoying over 50 per cent of conference votes. Furthermore, the vote of the TGWU alone was almost double that of the constituency Labour parties (Minkin, 1991: 663). John Smith's response was to seek a reduction in the size of the trade unions' vote at Labour's annual conference, from 90 per cent to 70 per cent in the first instance. He also proposed that dependent on an increase in Labour party membership – to be achieved through a recruitment drive – the unions' share of the vote should ultimately be reduced to 50 per cent, whereupon Labour's critics could less plausibly claim that the trade unions *dominated* annual conference and *inter alia* party policy-making.

It was not just the size of the block vote which was to be reduced, however. A further reform endorsed at the Labour party's 1993 conference was that the votes cast by delegates on behalf of affiliated trade unions would henceforth be "split" so as to reflect opinion within each union. No longer would *all* of a trade union's votes be cast for or against a particular policy *en bloc*. Instead, the splitting of each union's votes would ensure that the views of its members were more accurately reflected.

The 1993 Labour conference also endorsed reform of the electoral college, which had been established in 1981, and had allocated the trade unions 40 per cent of the votes, compared to 30 per cent each for the parliamentary Labour party and the constituency Labour parties. This was changed in 1993 to 33.3 per cent for each of the three bodies. Furthermore, as with the block vote, each trade union's votes in the electoral college would have to be "split", thereby reflecting the preferences of individual members within each union.

Another significant reform which was endorsed – just – at the 1993 Labour party conference was the "one member, one vote" (OMOV) for the selection of parliamentary candidates. Two of the biggest trade unions – TGWU and GMB – expressed opposition to this reform, and it was only after a passionate speech in support of John Smith by John Prescott – "He has put his head on the block . . . let us vote to support him" – coupled with a last-minute decision to abstain by MSF, that the reform was approved by the narrowest of margins: 48.645 per cent – 48.454 per cent. What also partly persuaded some trade unions to support OMOV was the accompanying "levy plus" scheme, whereby individual trade unionists could choose to become members of the Labour party for an additional £3 fee. The Labour leadership clearly hoped that: "The prospect of more trade unionists active in individual CLPs [constituency Labour parties] would . . . help to reconcile the unions to their exclusion from the candidate selection process" (Alderman and Carter, 1995 :331). An additional advantage envisaged by the Labour leadership was that by increasing party membership, the "levy plus" scheme would hasten the proposed reduction – to 50 per cent – of the trade unions' block vote at Labour's annual conference.

Tony Blair and the final eschewal of incomes policy

Tony Blair's election as Labour party leader in July 1994 heralded an acceleration of Labour's modernization programme, with Blair even more determined than his two predecessors to loosen further the organizational and financial links between Labour and the trade unions, whilst also reducing the unions' role in policy-making. Lest he needed any encouragement in this respect, the party's own pollsters informed Blair in 1995 that "New Labour is defined for most voters by Tony Blair's willingness to take on and master the unions . . . In focus groups, the switchers spoke of little else" (Gould, 1998: 257–8).

Blair also made clear his increasing commitment to neo-liberal economic orthodoxy, entailing a preoccupation with "macroeconomic conservatism and fiscal stability", coupled with a strong emphasis on such criteria as competitiveness, flexibility and deregulation. In other words, throughout the 1990s, but particularly after Blair's election as party leader in July 1994, "the general trajectory of Labour's [economic] reforms" has been that of "convergence on an agenda increasingly circumscribed by the tenets of neo-liberal economics", the consequences of which "are surely to reaffirm and consolidate an emergent bipartisan consensus on economic, industrial and competition policy which will, for the foreseeable future, remain couched within, and circumscribed by, the now dominant neo-liberal paradigm" (Hay and Watson, 1999: 156–7; see also: Hay, 1999, 123–30 and *passim*; Heffernan, 2001: *passim*; Hutton, 1999: 261–6; Thompson, 1996: 37–54; Wickham-Jones, 1995: 465–94).

At a general level, Blair embraced even more enthusiastically than Kinnock or Smith some of the key tenets of the Thatcherite agenda, most notably the alleged virtues of the market economy and competition. Indeed, Blair has spoken in glowing terms about some of Thatcher's achievements during her eleven years as Prime Minister, declaring, for example, that "Thatcher's emphasis on enterprise was right" (*The*

Sunday Times, 23 April 1995). Meanwhile, the year after Blair became Labour leader, the party published a policy document which emphasized the economic priority of achieving "a robust and stable framework of monetary and fiscal discipline" (Labour Party, 1995), whilst 1995 also witnessed Tony Blair deliver the Mais lecture in which he reiterated the Party's primary commitment to low inflation and taxation, strict control of public expenditure, and supply-side reforms as the basis both of economic stability and longer-term investment upon which non-inflationary growth and employment creation ultimately depended. Nowhere was there the slightest indication of any desire for an incomes policy, to the extent that towards the end of the Blair government's first term of office, the issue of wage bargaining continued to constitute a "glaring absence" from Tony Blair's and Gordon Brown's approach to economic management and the primary objective of maintaining low inflation (Glyn and Wood, 2001: 56).

Consequently, through the revision of Clause IV of Labour's constitution, along with a various speeches and policy pronouncements, Blair and his modernizing colleagues completely abandoned nationalization, opting instead to accept both the primacy and the permanence of a market economy. This entailed a further downgrading of the role of the trade unions, for the logic of embracing such principles as competition, management's right to manage and market forces, led ineluctably to the continued marginalization of the trade unions in economic affairs and policy-making. Blair confirmed this last point by declaring on numerous occasions that the trade unions would not be granted special status or preferential treatment under a Labour government, but, instead, in true pluralist style, would merely be but one of many groups and organized interests seeking to influence ministers: "I reject . . . as out of date and impractical, the re-creation or importation of a model of the corporate state popular a generation ago" (Blair, 1996: 109; see also Mandelson and Liddle, 1996: 25). Indeed, on his first full day as party leader, Blair declared that under a future Labour government: "Trade unions will have no special and privileged place. They will have the same access as the other side of industry". Blair reiterated this point at the TUC's 1995 annual conference, when he informed delegates that: "We have an obligation to listen, as we do to the employers. You have the right to persuade, as they do. The decisions, however, rest with us . . . we will govern for the whole nation, not any interest within it." Yet in a capitalist liberal democracy, what is defined as the national interest is almost always interchangeable with the interests of the business community and the City

The Labour party's endorsement of the market, and the concomitant marginalization of the trade unions, was both reflected and reinforced by the Party leadership's consistent repudiation of incomes policy as a mechanism for determining wages. References to a National Economic Assessment disappeared entirely under Blair's leadership, with the dominant discourse having become that of "responsible" pay bargaining between employers and employees, "responsible" in this context clearly referring to criteria such as competitiveness, productivity, profitability, etc., whilst the Blair government – or, rather, the independent Bank of England, via its monetary policy committee – seeks to control inflation primarily through the adjustment of interest rates.

The character of the labour market in the 1990s

Although Blair's repudiation of incomes policy is entirely explicable in terms of embracing of "the market", along with the distancing of the Labour party from the trade unions, this is not the sole explanation. Also important is the acknowledgement by Blair and his fellow Labour modernizers (and by some trade unions also) of the extent to which the economic structure and the concomitant character of the labour market have altered since the 1970s, when the Labour party was last in Office. As we noted in chapter 7, large-scale Fordist industry has contracted, along with trade union membership, whilst the service sector has expanded, as have the number of small or medium-sized firms. In both of these areas, trade union membership tends to be much lower than in the older manufacturing or "extraction" industries. Similarly, trade union membership tends to be lower in the private sector, a point which assumes particular significance in the context of the Conservatives' privatization programme during the 1980s and 1990s, and the contracting-out of many services previously provided by local authorities and the public sector.

Furthermore, incomes policies in the past implied the existence of a *national* economy to which such policies could be applied; in the era of globalization and multinational corporations, the notion of a *national* economy is highly questionable, and thus renders even more problematic the pursuit of incomes polices.

The Labour party's repudiation of incomes policy is also a consequence of the trend towards decentralization of pay bargaining through such phenomena as "cost centres" at local level, or the breaking up of public services into smaller units, such as NHS Trusts or the "agencification" of the civil service. Coupled with the shift towards individual contracts and performance-related pay in many industries and professions, such fragmentation further militates against the adoption of an incomes policy by the Blair Government.

Some trade union leaders themselves have cited such economic restructuring as an argument against incomes policy, with Ron Todd in particular observing that collective bargaining had become "too decentralized, too close to the point of production, too democratic in the broadest sense of the term, to be amenable to the sort of simple wage restraint arithmetic which had been the traditional basis of incomes policies in this country" (quoted in Minkin, 1991: 430).

In the context of these economic changes, New Labour deemed it futile to seek to determine pay via discussions between ministers, trade union leaders and employers' representatives. The labour market changes referred to previously underpinned New Labour's conviction that: "Centralized incomes policies are no longer appropriate . . . ". Indeed, it was suggested that "New Labour should promote increased flexibility in the setting of employee rewards that genuinely relate pay to performance" (Mandelson and Liddle, 1996: 80, 81).

The need to establish Labour's statecraft

One final, but vitally important, reason why "New Labour" has echoed the Conservative's repudiation of incomes policy as a means of wage determination concerns the notions of statecraft and political authority. The Labour party now accepts that for government to seek to determine wage levels and pay rises is almost inevitably to embroil government and the state in damaging confrontations with organized interests. Not only would recourse to incomes policy necessitate ministers expending valuable time and energy seeking to reach an agreement with trade unions over an appropriate figure for wage settlements each year, it would also yield problems of implementation and enforcement.

Drawing upon the lessons of previous Labour governments, "New Labour" acknowledges that incomes policies invariably damage the authority of government and the state, for either such policies are undermined by rank-and-file resistance and defiance, and subsequently abandoned, or the government is drawn into a confrontation with the trade unions in an attempt at imposing an incomes policy, possibly by invoking legislation, which in turn raises the question of penalties and sanctions against recalcitrant unions or employers. In either case, New Labour recognized that the authority of the government and the state were likely to be undermined, possibly resulting in a crisis of political legitimacy.

Furthermore, in either scenario, a Labour government is vulnerable to the suggestion that it is unable or unwilling "to stand up to" the trade unions, and can only govern with their consent and cooperation. Repudiation of incomes policy by "New Labour" is thus intended to ensure that having been elected to Office, it avoided becoming directly embroiled in conflict with the trade unions over matters pertaining to pay levels and wage determination. This, in turn, is further intended to persuade "Middle England" of the Labour party's new-found competence and fitness to govern, and worthiness to be re-elected in the 2001 general election.

The minimum wage

There have, of course, been two important exceptions to this non-interventionist stance *vis-à-vis* pay determination, namely the statutory minimum wage, and Gordon Brown's determination to control public expenditure, which has meant, in turn, strict curbs on public sector pay.

Whilst John Smith was leader, the Labour party had committed itself to a statutory minimum wage which would initially be set at half average male earnings, thereafter increasing to two-thirds. However, when Tony Blair became Labour leader, this "target" became more controversial, thereby serving to remind the party leadership of the problems engendered by the political determination of pay, even with regard to an ostensibly popular measure like a minimum wage.

Many of Britain's key trade unions, such as the GMB, TGWU and UNISON, demanded a minimum wage of at least £4 per hour, with some unions insisting on an hourly rate of £4.15. However, this conflicted with the Labour leadership's insistence that the precise figure would only be determined after a Labour government had established – and received the recommendations of – a Low Pay Commission, whilst Blair himself insisted that any minimum wage had to be introduced in a "sensible" and "flexible" manner (thereby causing anxiety amongst many trade unions that the Labour party's commitment to a minimum wage was being watered down).

This divergence led the TUC General Secretary, John Monks, to warn the trade unions of the damage which might be done (both to their relationship with the Labour party, and Labour's election prospects) if they formally endorsed the figure of £4.15. Consequently, a compromise was secured at the TUC's annual 1995 conference, where delegates endorsed a minimum wage based on half of median male earnings (yielding a figure in the range £3.60–£4.15), a decision which Blair hailed as "evidence of a far more mature relationship between trade unions and the Labour party".

Yet this compromise failed to assuage trade union suspicions that the Low Pay Commission insisted upon by the Labour leadership would result in both a lower figure than they wanted, and a delay in implementation of a minimum wage. Nor did this compromise over the precise figure prevent the engineering union, the AEEU, from warning that it would seek to reverse any reduction in differentials which its members experienced as a consequence of a Labour government implementing a statutory minimum wage (*The Guardian*, 11 September 1995).

The debates over the precise amount at which a minimum wage should be established were accompanied by disagreements concerning exemptions for employees less than 21 years of age. Many trade unions were deeply concerned that such exemptions would undermine the principle of a minimum wage, and suspected that this was precisely why the CBI was so keen on exempting certain categories of workers, particularly as the CBI's arguments were received sympathetically by Labour ministers committed to a marked reduction in youth unemployment.

Consequently, when the details of the minimum wage were finally announced in May 1998, the influence of the CBI was evident with regard both to the level at which the minimum wage was to be set, and its scope. The minimum wage was established at £3.60 per hour (only marginally above the £3.50 which the CBI had urged, but considerably less than the £4.15 which a number of trade unions had sought) whilst employees aged 18 to 21 were to receive only £3.20 per hour. Those in the 16–18 age group were exempted from any statutory entitlement to the minimum wage altogether. One further disappointment for the trade unions was the Blair government's insistence that the minimum wage would not automatically be uprated every year.

However, the Chancellor, Gordon Brown, was keen to place the minimum wage in a wider context, namely New Labour's commitment to reform of the tax and social security system which, it was claimed, would provide the low-paid with a combination of "top-up" benefits, assistance towards the cost of child-care, and higher levels of child benefit, as well as the promised introduction of a 10 per cent tax band. All of these measures, Gordon Brown and Tony Blair insisted, were of signal importance in eradicating poverty and assisting the low paid, but without requiring recourse either to inflationary or job-destroying wage increases, the imposition of punitive levels of income tax on the better-off, or improved welfare benefits for the unemployed which would otherwise reduce the incentive to find work. Such measures have further obviated the need for an incomes policy.

Public sector pay

As with its Conservative predecessors, New Labour's eschewal of incomes policy has not prevented it from seeking to exert rigorous controls on pay in what remains of the public sector. On the contrary, the Blair government's determination to establish a reputation for economic competence, in which control of inflation and public expenditure are *the* primary economic objectives, coupled with a strong commitment *not* to raise incomes tax, led Gordon Brown – fully supported by Tony Blair – to adhere to the outgoing Conservative administration's public expenditure plans for the first two years in Office, and subsequently beyond. This meant that during the first two years of the Blair government, public sector pay was increased only in line with inflation, which effectively constituted a *de facto* pay freeze. In so doing, "New Labour" sought to refute the traditional charge that the Labour party is beholden to the public sector and service providers (as opposed to the private sector and service users).

Indeed, it was made clear by Gordon Brown during the latter half of 1998 that the public sector would continue to be subject to strict cash limits right through the remainder of Labour's term of Office, with any increases in pay having to derive from increased productivity. Furthermore, when the government announced the public sector pay increases to be introduced in April 1999, it was emphasized that in subsequent years there would be an increasing emphasis on performance-related pay (linked to further reform of the public sector), which in turn would entail greater differentials.

Halfway through the Blair Government's first term of office, therefore, it had become clear that apart from the provision of a minimal minimum wage, egalitarianism and social justice were no longer appropriate criteria for the determination of pay. Instead, the implication was that inequalities of incomes were entirely acceptable if they genuinely derived from increased productivity, improved performance, and the undertaking of greater responsibilities. Here was New Labour's vision of a truly meritocratic Britain for the new Millennium; a floor below which no one should be permitted to fall, but no ceiling to limit how far anyone could rise.

The European dimension

New Labour's eschewal of incomes policy cannot be viewed in isolation from the party's generally more positive stance towards the European Union, for by the very end of the 1980s there was a growing belief in senior Labour circles that: "On inflation, we could solve a large number of our problems at a stroke by declaring that it is our intention to join the EMS [Economic and Monetary System] . . . it would transform the perception of how serious our economic policy really is" (quoted in Shaw, 1994: 97). With regard to the eschewal of incomes policy in particular, the view became established amongst much of the Labour leadership that locking Britain into the Exchange Rate Mechanism

(ERM) would prove a far more effective counterweight to inflationary pressures in the British economy than seeking trade union support for – and adherence to – an incomes policy (see, for example, George and Rosamond 1992 :181–2).

That the Major government, in September 1992, was obliged to terminate Britain's membership of the Exchange Rate Mechanism did not diminish New Labour's conviction that European economic and monetary union offered the best prospect – in conjunction with continued prudent domestic fiscal policy and control of public expenditure – of securing low inflation and, therefore, sustainable economic growth. Indeed, Gordon Brown's statement to the House of Commons in October 1997 emphasized the extent to which control of both public expenditure *and* inflation were among the prerequisites of eventual British membership of a single European currency.

No U-turn likely

Whereas previous post-war Labour governments entered office eschewing incomes policies (as opposed to a planned growth of wages) as a major means of curbing inflation, only to resort to such policies once in Office in the context of mounting economic problems, the Blair Government had, by the autumn of 1999, presided over a remarkably benign economic situation, with a recession predicted earlier in the year failing to materialize. Instead, unemployment had fallen to 4.3 per cent, its lowest level for more than twenty years, whilst the underlying rate of inflation in August had fallen to 2.1 per cent, with the headline figure for the twelve months to August 1999 a mere 1.1 per cent, the lowest since July 1963 (Hindmoor, 2000: 269). Indeed, by early 2001 – less than five months before the anticipated general election – the headline inflation rate had fallen further, to just 1.8 per cent, thereby ensuring that the underlying rate had been below the Blair government's 2.5 per cent target for 22 consecutive months. At the same time, unemployment continued to fall during this period, to its lowest level for 25 years (*The Guardian*, 14 February 2001). Thus could Labour ministers reflect that they had achieved both low inflation and virtual full employment without recourse to incomes policy.

The second half of 1998 and the first half of 1999 witnessed a correspondingly gentle downward drift in most pay awards, to the extent that by the summer of 1999 most were hovering between 2.5 and 3 per cent (the government's own overall inflation target being 2.5 per cent). With inflation at such low levels, of course, even these modest pay awards enabled most employees to obtain real increases in take-home pay without causing ministers or the Bank of England undue concern (unless one includes the escalation in house prices which occurred during the summer of 1999 due to these increases in net pay combined with interest rates of just 5–6%). Furthermore, some commentators have ventured to suggest that following the severe economic problems of the 1970s and 1980s, Britain might be entering a new era in which "economic cycles are shallow and prolonged", with the world quite possibly "on the cusp of a long boom" (Elliott, 1999: 13), although by the end of 2000, commentators were beginning to express concern about a downturn in the American economy, and speculating on how this would impact on European economies.

In the meantime, the trade unions themselves have remained hostile to incomes policies, whilst also recognizing that the changes in the labour market during the 1980s and 1990s make an incomes policy impracticable. As John Monks, the TUC's General Secretary, has explained: "We have a largely decentralized labour market . . . It is no longer feasible for the nation's pay to be set in talks between the government, the TUC and the CBI in smoke-filled rooms, over beer and sandwiches" (Monks, 1998: 124). Furthermore, many trade unions became (more) concerned about a range of other issues during the 1990s, most notably the increase in working hours, stress and job insecurity which millions of workers have suffered, as well as recruitment and recognition campaigns. Whilst pay bargaining still remains vitally important to the trade unions, their increased focus on these other problems is likely to reinforce their marked lack of interest in seeking a return to incomes policy.

Meanwhile, not only is Tony Blair determined to avoid the entanglements with the trade unions which an incomes policy would almost inevitably entail, he is also determined to illustrate that "New Labour" in Office is qualitatively" different to "Old Labour", which means unequivocally rejecting a number of policies and priorities which characterized previous Labour governments, such as public ownership, economic planning, wealth redistribution via higher income taxes imposed on the better-off, and expansion of the welfare state. Incomes policies can now also be added to Old Labour policies which have been abandoned by New Labour. Having been killed off by the 1979–97 Conservative governments, incomes policies have not been resurrected by New Labour and the Blair Government. As Ludlam has recently emphasized, previous sources of tension and conflict between Labour governments and the trade unions, most notably tripartite planning and incomes policies, "are off the agenda" (Ludlam, 2001: 128). Indeed, it is now extremely difficult to imagine incomes policies ever being placed back on the agenda, irrespective of which political party is in Office.

9

The rise and fall of incomes policy in Britain since 1945

In the context of a combined commitment to full employment, price stability, and non-inflationary economic growth, measures to secure wage restraint were a major preoccupation of virtually all governments from 1945 to 1979, whilst from 1979 onwards, higher unemployment itself became a tool intended to restrain wages instead of incomes policy, coupled with much more rigorous control of the money supply as the primary means of controlling inflation.

The pre-1979 preoccupation with securing pay restraint meant that most post-war governments sought recourse to an incomes policy of one variety or another, the only exceptions being the Conservative administrations of the 1950s, which nonetheless sought wage moderation and "responsibility" through exhortation and "education" of the trade unions, before finally becoming convinced of the need for a long-term incomes policy during the early 1960s.

The 1950s' Conservative administrations aside, governments between 1945 and 1979 invariably entered office pledging *not* to introduce incomes policies (at least, not as a means of securing pay restraint in order to tackle inflation, as opposed to the first Wilson Government's incomes policy for achieving a 'planned growth of incomes'), but instead, committed themselves to upholding free collective bargaining, albeit conducted "responsibly", by the trade unions.

Sooner or later, in the context of rapidly rising inflation and/or increases in unemployment, coupled with balance of payments crises or a loss of confidence amongst the financial community, these governments would resort to an incomes policy, ostensibly on a temporary basis in lieu of a return to free collective bargaining, though often coming to the conclusion that a more permanent system of pay policies was needed as an integral component of economic management.

Yet the continuation of these incomes policies beyond a couple of years, coupled with allusions to making them more permanent or long term, alienated the trade unions, whereupon the pay policy was terminated either by increasing union non-compliance or a general election, and in some instances, both of these.

The trade unions, meanwhile, would tend initially to offer varying degrees of acquiescence – more particularly when an incomes policy was introduced by a Labour government – on the assumption that the policy was indeed a temporary expedient prompted by particularly serious economic circumstances, pending the resumption of "normal service", namely a return to free collective bargaining. Then, when it became apparent that ministers might pursue an incomes policy indefinitely or even permanently, the trade unions' initial support would dissipate, particularly as by this stage their members were evincing increasing frustration and resentment against the existing policy of wage restraint.

Furthermore, the termination of an incomes policy often yielded a "pay explosion" due to trade unions and their members viewing the return to free collective bargaining as a prime opportunity to recover the increases foregone or prevented during the pay policy. This, in turn, refuelled ministerial concerns about inflation – as well as alarming the City and the international financial community, of course – whereupon the increasingly desperate exhortations to the trade unions to exercise responsibility and moderation would invariably be followed by recourse to a new incomes policy. The whole cycle then repeated itself.

Post-war incomes policies thus served to highlight a number of issues and problems of interest to political scientists and policy analyists, most notably the objectives and rationale attributed to any particular pay policy, their scope in application and flexibility in implementation, the institutional framework devised to administer them, and the problems of compliance and enforceability. These aspects are considered below, as are the various factors underpinning trade union antipathy towards incomes policies, and the links between political philosophy, ideology and incomes policy in Britain.

Objectives and rationale

Undoubtedly the primary objective attributed to incomes policies by politicians in post-war Britain until 1979 was the reduction of inflation. Incomes policies reflected a long-standing cost-push (or wage-push) theory of inflation, whereby rising prices were deemed a consequence of higher wages, unmatched by corresponding increases in productivity. As the 1976 White Paper *The Attack on Inflation* emphasized, "if pay increases do not slow down, there can never be a slow-down in price increases" (Treasury, 1976: 8).

Successive post-war governments were thus confronted with a vicious circle, whereby employers sought to recoup higher labour costs and maintain profitability by raising prices, and the trade unions, in response, sought compensatory wage increases to cover the increased cost of living subsequently experienced by their members. Although there were sporadic, and somewhat half-hearted, attempts by governments to curb price increases in the hope this would facilitate a corresponding slow down in pay increases, it was usually wages themselves which became the target of ministers seeking to curb inflation, and which thus prompted repeated recourse to incomes policies.

On numerous occasions, however, incomes policies have also been portrayed as a means of improving industrial productivity and *inter alia* labour market efficiency. It is surely no coincidence that incomes policies became an almost permanent feature of macro-economic policy and industrial relations during the 1960s, the decade in which it was also recognized that Britain's economic performance was being superseded by a number of other industrialized nations (most notably France, Italy, Japan, United States and West Germany), with low industrial productivity being identified as a particularly important problem, along with overmanning, and restrictive practices perpetuated by trade unions. Thus it was that incomes policies usually incorporated productivity "clauses", whereby pay increases were at least partly dependent upon higher industrial output or/and greater efficiency.

A third objective sometimes ascribed to incomes policies in Britain – mainly, but not solely, under Labour governments – was the amelioration of poverty and a reduction in inequality. In this respect, Labour ministers variously sought to depict incomes policies as "redistributional" in character, a means of establishing a fairer, somewhat more equal, society (in conjunction with progressive taxation and welfare provision via the social wage). A redistributional dimension was usually enshrined in an incomes policy in one of three ways.

First, by stipulating a cash-based increase, which is clearly of greater benefit to the low-paid, as evinced by the £6 incomes policy invoked by the Labour Government during 1975–6. Secondly, by providing for percentage increases, but with an additional sum – usually cash-based – for the low-paid. This was the case with "stages" two and three of Heath's statutory incomes policy in 1973. Thirdly, by invoking a percentage increase which is not payable to those earning above a specified amount, as was the case with Labour's 1975–6 incomes policy cited above, when those earning more than £8,500 per annum were denied the £6 per week (maximum) increase that lower-paid employees were entitled to.

As we will note more fully below, however, incomes policies which incorporate a redistributional dimension are unlikely to last longer than a couple of years, due to the inevitable resentment which accrues amongst those on higher incomes concerned at the erosion of differentials. Furthermore, some of the low-paid themselves may decide that the redistributional element is insufficient or inadequate, thereby fostering the view that a return to free collective bargaining will yield more substantial wage increases. Thus it was that by the end of 1978, some of the most trenchant critics of the Callaghan government's incomes policies were trade unions representing low-paid workers in the public sector, who were convinced that their members' living standards were being eroded as a consequence of continued pay restraint, irrespective of any redistributional elements enshrined within the pay formulae. It was primarily these workers who were most intimately involved in the industrial action which constituted the "winter of discontent".

Whatever the objectives ascribed to, or enshrined in, incomes policies, it is important to recognize the extent to which a number of them have been invoked in response to pressure from the City and the international financial community, in order to allay concerns about the government's economic competence and strategy. This has been especially true of various incomes policies pursued by Labour governments since 1945, leading Panitch to assert that Cripps' 1948 wage freeze, and the Wilson governments' recourse to statutory incomes policies during the mid-1960s were ultimately concerned to assauge "the CBI, the City and Britain's foreign creditors" in the context of devaluation (Panitch, 1976: 243).

Scope and flexibility

Even when governments have been clear – at least in their own minds – as to their primary objective in pursuing an incomes policy, they have had to grapple with a range of other problems pertaining to the precise format of such policies, their scope, and the criteria or rationale for any exemptions.

With regard to the format, ministers have invariably oscillated between the adoption of a percentage norm and a cash-based sum. Flat-rate increases are clearly of more benefit to the lower-paid, but for that very reason, as noted above, have proved less acceptable to those on higher wages and salaries concerned at the erosion of differentials (and possibly the concomitant loss of status *vis-à-vis* the lower paid). Yet conversely, an incomes policy whose format is based on a percentage "norm" will be most beneficial to those with higher incomes, and thus likely to alienate the low paid. Thus it was that both Conservative and Labour governments in the 1970s sometimes fashioned a hybrid incomes policy, whereby a percentage "norm" was accompanied by an additional lump-sum cash increase to workers defined as being low paid.

A second problem which bedevilled various incomes policies in post-war Britain concerned the distinction between wages and earnings. Whilst ministers invariably sought to specify a "norm" or limit for wage increases when formulating an incomes policy, they frequently experienced exasperation due to the fact that actual earnings often increased at a faster or higher rate. This was because many employees were able to secure other increases in their incomes, usually through overtime, bonuses, and a plethora of perks and fringe benefits, even if their basic hourly rate of pay only increased in accordance with the government's stipulated pay "norm" or limit. Thus it was that many incomes policies were undermined by the phenomenon of wage drift, with actual earnings and local or plant-level pay deals proving to be in excess of the government's own specified target or limit.

Yet for ministers to have sought more detailed and prescriptive controls over earnings – beyond specifying a pay "norm" or limit – would invariably have embroiled them in even more conflicts with the trade unions and their members on the factory-floor, who would resent and repel what they perceived to be unwarranted political interference in their affairs.

Furthermore, it was often ministers themselves who sought to include productivity deals and efficiency bonuses when devising their incomes policies, which effectively meant that to a certain extent, they themselves were encouraging an increase in overall earnings in excess their own pay "norms". Yet ministers also recognized that without some scope for exemptions based on increased productivity, incomes policies would lack sufficient flexibility, thereby rendering them even less acceptable to the trade unions.

A third problem experienced by post-war governments (up until 1979) concerning the scope of their incomes policies was the extent to which they should be applied to the private sector as well as the public sector, or applied solely to the public sector in the expectation that "if the Government set an example in the public sphere, the private sector would automatically follow" (Jones, 1973: 126).

Obviously, it is easier for any government to impose an incomes policy on its own employees in the public sector, particularly through the application of "cash limits", whereas, short of statutory measures or compulsion, an incomes policy applied to the private sector needs to be based on consultation and consent. Yet this immediately raised the question of what sanctions a government could impose on recalcitrant private sector workers or employers who breached a specified pay limit or "norm". On the other hand, if an incomes policy applied solely to the public sector, and the private sector failed to match this with voluntary pay restraint, then hostility and resentment amongst public sector employees and their unions would inevitably increase as the disparities between public and private sector pay widened yet further. This might well result in a damaging, even mutually destructive, confrontation between government and its own employees, as symbolized by the "winter of discontent". This has proved particularly problematic given that many public sector employees have traditionally been amongst the lowest paid workers in Britain.

Furthermore, the various productivity deals enshrined in many incomes policies have been less applicable or appropriate to the public sector. In fact, there have been two problems here. First, to what extent could public sector employees such as nurses, social workers and teachers genuinely increase productivity, and secondly, even if some quantifiable criteria were stipulated – such as treating more patients, tackling more instances of child abuse, or improving literacy rates, for example – how would these themselves actually generate increased revenue with which to finance productivity bonuses?

However, during the 1980s and 1990s, a number of ministers asserted that the earnings gap between the public and private sectors was not a significant problem, because pursuing a public service profession such as teaching or nursing was an end in itself, and should not therefore be viewed primarily in terms of higher financial remuneration or economic reward. Indeed, Tony Blair himself made just such a claim early in 1999 (the first of several disparaging remarks about the public sector made by him that year).

With regard to public sector pay, Tony Blair's much-vaunted "third way" seems to comprise further exhortations to secure greater flexibility and productivity, coupled with proposals for accelerated promotion and higher salaries for a cadre of "super-teachers" and "super-nurses". It was envisaged that not only would this provide greater incentives in parts of the public sector, but also enable at least some public sector employees to bridge the earnings gap with their private sector counterparts, which, in turn, might help to alleviate the recruitment problems which have predictably arisen after nearly a decade of pay freezes, diminished status and an ever-widening chasm between the public and private sectors with regard to pay.

On the other hand, such differentials and distinctions – coupled with the increased advocacy of payment-by-results in the public sector (particularly in the teaching profession) – might well breed further discontent and frustration, and thereby compound the problems of recruitment and low morale.

Institutional innovations

In order to supervise the implementation (and evaluate the success) of incomes policies, post-war governments often sought to create institutions whose primary function was to monitor pay increases, and consider whether these were compatible with the government's policy, or affordable in terms of the overall economic situation at any specific juncture.

In creating such institutions, governments had to determine not only the precise remit of the pay body concerned, but also two other aspects. First, whether these bodies should examine pay claims before any award was made (and thereby be able to challenge or even forbid the award), or whether they ought merely to be retrospective, considering the merits or otherwise of a pay award after it had been made. Secondly, governments had to consider whether such institutions should be vested with statutory powers, thereby rendering their judgements legally binding on trade unions and/or employers, in which case the question of enforceability (including penalties and sanctions for non-compliance) would inevitably arise.

The first institutional innovation concerned with pay awards in post-war Britain was the Council on Prices, Productivity and Incomes (more commonly known as the Cohen Council) established in 1957, although the Macmillan government which launched this body was not actually pursuing a formal incomes policy at the time. Instead, it was relying upon increasingly urgent exhortation of the trade unions to restrain wage increases, but shied away from invoking an incomes policy *per se*. In this respect, the Cohen Council was ascribed an educative function, both on public opinion in general and on trade unions in particular, by virtue of publishing periodic reports on pay increases, and placing them in the context of the wider economy, with a view to indicating their likely impact on inflation and employment.

The next institutional innovation came in 1962, with the establishment of the National Incomes Commission (NIC). By this time, several senior Conservative ministers had become convinced of the need for incomes policies, not just as a short-term response to urgent economic exigencies, but as a permanent tool of macro-economic management. However, like the Cohen Council, the NIC had no effective power, with the Macmillan government continuing to seek cordial relations with the trade unions, and hoping that education and exhortation would be sufficient to yield moderation *vis-à-vis* wage determination. Meanwhile, the other institutional innovation of the early 1960s, the National Economic Development Council (NEDC) was not formally concerned with incomes policies as such, although it was envisaged that its discussions and pronouncements on the overall economic situation would exert an indirect influence on trade union behaviour with regard to pay claims.

The NIC was then replaced, in April 1965, by the National Board of Prices and Incomes (NBPI), established by the recently elected Labour Government. The NBPI differed from its institutional predecessors in two main respects. First, prices were now explicitly included in its remit, alongside wages, thus reflecting the shift towards prices *and* incomes policies during the latter half of the 1960s. Secondly, during the year following its inception, the NBPI was vested with certain statutory powers, most notably to compel the submission of "evidence" in connection with pay claims and awards. However, in the cause of good industrial relations, it declined ever to invoke these powers, preferring instead to rely upon the voluntary compliance and cooperation of trade unions and employers.

Furthermore, the NBPI lacked the power to enforce its conclusions when publishing reports on particular increases in prices or incomes. Ultimately, "the burden of pay and price control largely remained with government departments through the successive phases of [prices and incomes] policy" (Towers, 1978: 14).

Even more ambitious were the institutional innovations which, in 1972, replaced the NBPI, namely the Pay Board and its counterpart, the Price Commission. These twin bodies were an integral part of the statutory prices and incomes policies invoked by the Heath government from 1972 to 1974 (Heath's protracted discussions with the TUC between March and November 1972 having failed to yield agreement on a voluntary prices and incomes policy). The Pay Board was charged with legal responsibility for administering – with the assistance of the Department of Employment – the pay controls enshrined in the Counter Inflation legislation, whilst the Price Commission was responsible for ensuring that price increases only corresponded to genuine increases in costs. The Pay Board was then abolished by the Labour Government elected in February 1974, whilst the Price Commission was scrapped when the Conservatives were returned to office in 1979.

The history of wage determination in post-war Britain has also been characterized by numerous proposals for institutions which failed to materialize due to insufficient ministerial or trade union support. For example, the Central Arbitration Tribunal proposed by Stafford Cripps in 1947 never saw the light of day due to lack of Cabinet support, with the same fate befalling the Wages Advisory Council when it was recommended by the Cabinet's committee on economic policy in 1950 (although such bodies were also opposed by the trade unions).

In 1967, Harold Wilson briefly flirted with the idea of establishing a National Dividend, whereby ministers, trade union leaders and employers' representatives would meet to determine what the economy could afford each year with regard to wages and salaries. However, like its predecessors, this idea never materialized, partly due to lack of support, and partly because Wilson's government was compelled, due to the urgency of circumstances and events, to take immediate action *vis-à-vis* prices and incomes. In any case, it was difficult to discern how the National Dividend would differ significantly from the existing National Economic Development Council; a duplication of functions, and a conflict of authority, would probably have proved inevitable.

A few years later, Anthony Barber and Maurice Macmillan, Chancellor of the Exchequer and Secretary of State for Employment respectively in Edward Heath's Conservative administration, briefly suggested the creation of a new conciliation agency alongside the establishment of "a completely new, independent fact-finding agency" (Heath, 1998: 406), whilst other senior Conservatives, as noted in chapter 7, subsequently floated the idea of an "industrial parliament" or "economic forum" to discuss economic affairs, including pay settlements, although obviously these ideas received short shrift from Margaret Thatcher. Finally, in Opposition during the 1980s and the early 1990s, the Labour party appeared favourably disposed towards establishing a National Economic Assessment, although when Tony Blair became the party's leader, nothing more was heard of this innovation.

One other idea which was occasionally mooted, but never pursued in practice, was to harmonize or synchronize pay awards so that all wage and salary increases were awarded at the same time every year. Whilst this might not constitute an incomes policy *per se*, it was nonetheless sporadically discussed by ministers in the context of their search for a policy on incomes, with an annual pay settlement date proposed as a means of contributing towards greater stability and order in the sphere of wage determination, whilst also overcoming the constant problem of "leap-frogging" caused by different trade unions negotiating pay deals at different times of the year. Yet insufficient support, and problems pertaining to implementation and enforcement, meant that such synchronized pay deals were never actively pursued.

One major reason for the plethora of institutional innovations proposed or introduced with regard to incomes policies in Britain concerned the organizational weakness of the TUC and the CBI themselves (quite apart from their stance *vis-à-vis* any specific incomes policy). It has been widely noted that the federal structure of both the TUC and the CBI rendered them incapable of effectively administering a prices and incomes policy, due to their inability to enforce compliance on affiliated organizations, and their unwillingness even to attempt such enforcement.

The power of the CBI and TUC – such as it is – over their constituent members depends predominantly on their ability to persuade, and this clearly places significant limits on their efficacy in helping governments to administer any prices and incomes policy. Indeed, the leaderships of the CBI and TUC have often been obliged to acknowledge that if they appeared too willing or eager to assist governments in securing restraint, they were likely to forfeit the trust and loyalty of their affiliates, and thereby weaken their moral authority. As one commentator has observed, the CBI "has tended . . . to be an unwieldy, conservative body unable and unwilling to exert any great central co-ordination over its members", whilst the TUC itself is "splintered . . . made up of an enormous number of individual unions organized on an occupational basis", the combined effect of which was seriously to reduce "the chances of any centrally imposed incomes policy working" (Jones, 1987: 140–1). In similar vein, Lovell and Roberts once declared that: "The untidy structure . . . of the trade unions in Britain has long been recognized as a major handicap to the development and the carrying out of an effective central policy" (Lovell and Roberts, 1968: 178).

Furthermore, the lack of power exercised by the TUC over affiliated trade unions has been reflected, and to a significant extent reinforced, by the gulf which incomes policies inadvertently fostered between national-level trade union leaders and their rank-and-file members at local or plant level. This schism was partly the result of the growing scale of British industry, whereby the expansion, amalgamations and mergers of many companies and enterprises in the post-war period ensured that the British economy was increasingly dominated by "national" companies, with their headquarters invariably based in London. Furthermore, such expansion was accompanied by increasing bureaucratization within companies and industries, thereby ensuring that the senior management was ever more distant from those it employed. This "nationalization" and bureaucratization was mirrored within the trade unions themselves, thereby ensuring that trade union leaders became increasingly remote from those they sought to represent.

Yet at the same time, this growing gulf between employers and trade union leaders on the one hand, and employees and trade union members on the other, was actually reinforced by the development of incomes policies, for both employers and trade union leaders were drawn even more closely into national level pay agreements with politicians and senior civil servants, whereupon they appeared even more distant to those they officially represented in the work-places throughout the country. This facilitated a widening gulf and power vacuum inside many trade unions, into which local level trade union officials and shop stewards stepped, often securing the loyalty of union members at local level not only by virtue of their proximity and visibility, but even more importantly, by their regular success in securing pay increases greater than those negotiated by the national union leadership in London.

In this respect, governmental attempts at restraining wages through the incorporation of national-level trade union leaders actually exacerbated the problem of wage drift, particularly when local union officials and shop stewards were better placed to negotiate productivity deals and bonuses at plant level.

Indeed, as previously intimated, initial support for an incomes policy by national-level trade union leaders invariably dissipated after a couple of years precisely because they became aware of their diminishing authority and legitimacy *vis-à-vis* their members, and their inability to "carry" the grass-roots union membership with them if they continually acceded to ministerial requests for wage restraint.

Implementation and enforceability

There is thus no doubt that a major problem for post-war governments pursuing incomes policies was how to respond when trade unions or employers defied the stipulated pay limit or "norm". The credibility of both incomes policy and government itself has sometimes depended in large part upon this issue.

Most governments resorting to incomes policy have initially sought to secure a voluntary agreement with the trade unions concerning the permissible level of wage increases – if any – during the existing or forthcoming "pay round". This preference for *voluntary* incomes policies clearly reflected the widespread belief during the 1960s and 1970s that such policies would be more likely to command the support of the trade unions, and therefore more likely to be adhered to. Without such support, it was recognized that an incomes policy was unlikely to enjoy legitimacy amongst trade unions and their members, which, in turn, would almost inevitably condemn the policy to failure.

However, both Labour and Conservative governments resorted to statutory or compulsory incomes policies when they were unable to secure trade union support for a voluntary policy, and when economic circumstances appeared serious enough to warrant the legislative restraint of incomes. It was on such occasions, however, that the question of sanctions was raised. Ministers needed to determine what action – if any – they would take if a trade union insisted upon pursuing an excessive pay increase and/or an employer offered a wage increase in excess of the government's pay "norm" or limit.

The most draconian option, imprisonment of the trade union officials concerned, has invariably been rejected, largely on the grounds that the severity of such a measure would almost certainly provoke a display of trade union solidarity and defiance against the government of the day, whilst also causing irreparable damage to industrial relations in general.

There was also concern that public opinion might actually prove rather fickle, so that initial support for such an approach would rapidly dissipate if several trade unionists were actually imprisoned and the media published graphic accounts of the consequent plight of families deprived of their breadwinner, and thus plunged into financial hardship or dependency on the state.

Somewhat less draconian was the occasional suggestion that trade unions acting in defiance of an incomes policy should be subject to financial penalties, such as fines or partial sequestration of their funds. Again, however, during the 1960s and 1970s, ministers tended to shy away from such sanctions, fearing that this too would provoke a dangerous backlash from the trade union movement, with even union moderates likely to rally against such blatant political interference in the trade unions' internal affairs.

One other option which was occasionally favoured by some ministers was to impose financial penalties on employers who awarded pay increases which transgressed the government's incomes policy. Not only was this seen as a means of avoiding a damaging confrontation with the trade unions themselves, it was also hoped that it would effectively provide employers with a financial incentive to stand firm when faced with an "excessive" pay claim. Certainly, during the latter half of the 1950s, a number of Conservative ministers mooted the idea of imposing a "payroll tax" on companies which awarded "excessive" pay increases, this being viewed as a more viable alternative to invoking financial penalties against trade unions who pursued such pay increases. Meanwhile, as noted in chapter 4, Tony Benn proposed a similar kind of tax during the late 1960s.

Two decades later, towards the end of the 1970s, James Callaghan's Labour government sought to invoke sanctions against companies which awarded pay rises in excess of the government's own specified limit or "norm", including the withdrawal or withholding of government contracts. Yet it became apparent that if the government did not have any or many contracts with the company concerned, then the sanctions would be ineffectual. On the other hand, if it did have a number of contracts, and carried out its threat to cancel them, the government might well be contributing to a further loss of jobs in a period of already increasing unemployment.

Trade union antipathy to incomes policies

Trade unions are organizations concerned primarily to protect and promote the economic interests of their members. In particular, they exist to defend or improve the terms and conditions of their members' employment, particularly with regard to wages. As the Webbs explained as long ago as the final decade of the nineteenth century, a trade union is "a continuous association of wage-earners for the purpose of maintaining or improving the conditions of their working lives" (Webb and Webb, 1894: 1), whilst the Advisory, Conciliation & Arbitration Service (ACAS) much more recently asserted that "trade unions are organizations of workers set up to improve the status, pay and conditions of employment of their members" (ACAS, 1980: 39). The chief mechanism by which trade unions have traditionally sought to fulfil their primary function is that of *free collective bargaining*.

The TUC once declared that: "Collective bargaining is the most important trade union method. It is in fact more than a method, it is the central feature of trade unionism" (TUC 1966: 47), an assertion supported by Hawkins' observation that: "Collective bargaining has long been regarded as the principal activity, indeed the *raison d'être* of trade unions in Britain" (Hawkins, 1981: 173). This view was further endorsed by Fishbein's claim that "the British trade union movement views its mission as being that of advancing the living standards of its members through free collective bargaining" (Fishbein, 1984: 11), whilst Farnham and Pimlott believe collective bargaining to be "the major institutional feature of British industrial relations" (Farnham and Pimlott, 1986: 142). As such, trade unions have tended to view incomes policies as a serious infringement of their right and their ability to pursue *free* collective bargaining.

A second reason why a number of trade unions so often proved antipathetic to incomes policy derives from the mildly egalitarian or redistributive features which such policies sometimes enshrined. As we have already noted, a number of post-war governments viewed incomes policies as a means of tackling poverty and low-pay, and therefore permitted larger and/or cash-based increases for employees on the lowest incomes. Yet sooner or later, such policies encountered the antipathy of those trade unions and their members resenting the narrowing of the gap between themselves and lower-paid workers. It has invariably been Britain's "labour aristocracy", sections of the skilled working class, who have been most antipathetic to the erosion of differentials engendered by egalitarian or redistributive incomes policies, for their skills and "market position" have enabled them to command the highest wages amongst the working class. Such workers, therefore, have invariably been hostile to the pursuit of greater equality when it meant that low-paid workers start to "catch-up" with them.

However, the less than fraternal attitude of skilled workers towards their unskilled, lower-paid counterparts is not an entirely new or recent phenomenon. After all, much of the impetus for the early development of trade unions in Britain emanated from skilled workers and artisans concerned that their privileged position in the labour market was threatened by the increasing number of unskilled or semi-skilled workers who, it was feared, might be used by employers to undercut the wages and undermine the position of the skilled working class once factory production became more widespread (Musson, 1972: 16–19; Pelling, 1963: 24; Stevenson, 1982: 11–37). Much more recently, of course, it was the skilled working class – the C2s in contemporary political discourse – who proved most responsive, in May 1979, to Margaret Thatcher's pledge to abandon incomes policy, return to free collective bargaining, and thereby encourage the restoration of differentials.

In this context, there has often been a marked disjuncture between the socialist rhetoric espoused by trade union leaders at rallies and conferences, and their day-to-day activities and objectives. Indeed, most trade unions have invariably acted as creatures of the very capitalist system that they publicly denounce, for as Rosa Luxemburg once observed:

> The scope of trade unions is limited essentially to a struggle for an increase of wages and the reduction of labour time, that is to say, to efforts at regulating capitalist exploitation . . . Trade unions are nothing more than the organized defence of labour power against the attack of profit. (Luxemburg, 1900: 50, 71. Italics in original)

In similar vein, Gramsci argued that trade unions are "a type of proletarian organization specific to the period when Capital dominates history . . . an integral part of capitalist society, whose function is inherent in the regime of private property" (quoted in Anderson, 1967: 334). Or as Anderson himself elaborates:

> As institutions, trade unions do not challenge the existence of society based on a division of classes, they merely express it. Thus trade unions can never be vehicles of advance towards socialism themselves; by their nature, they are tied to capitalism. They can bargain within the society, but not transform it. Trade unions are a de facto representation of the working class at its work-place. (Anderson, 1967: 264–65)

Although these are observations associated first and foremost with Marxist critiques of trade unionism, similar conclusions about the ultimately capitalist character of Britain's trade unions have been drawn by various non-Marxist commentators, most notably Alan Fox, who declared that:

> Their aspirations are for marginal improvements in their lot, not for eliminating private property, hierarchy, extreme division of labour, and the principles and conventions which support great inequalities of wealth, income, and opportunities for personal fulfilment. (Fox, 1974: 278)

Even Harold Macmillan, as noted in chapter 3, observed the

essentially capitalist behaviour of the trade unions, in sharp contrast to those of his Conservative colleagues who invariably viewed trade union pay claims as evidence of their left-wing motivations and anti-capitalist machinations.

Consequently, Britain's trade unions have evinced a significant degree of sectionalism and short-termism, seeking to obtain the best and most immediate material improvements and deals for their members. This reflects the fact that: "Trade union officials are paid to look after their own; they are not watchdogs of the working class as a whole or immediately concerned with national welfare" (Donaldson, 1965: 203). Indeed, just as the character of British capitalism compels short-term profit-maximization among private companies in order to yield almost immediate dividends to shareholders, so too have trade unions invariably felt obliged to pursue short-term, material objectives (i.e., pay increases) on behalf of their members, irrespective of longer-term political goals, the "national interest", or the objective interests of the working class as a whole.

This, in turn, has invariably conflicted with the governmental pursuit of incomes policies, for these invariably required wage restraint in the short-term in lieu of higher wages in the longer-term. Herein lies another reason, therefore, for the repeated disintegration and discontinuity of incomes policies in post-war Britain.

Political and ideological perspectives

A final problem engendered by incomes policies in post-war Britain concerns the dissent and disagreements which such policies have occasioned both between and within the Conservative and Labour parties, these divisions frequently corresponding to traditional ideological lines.

In the Conservative party, attitudes towards incomes policies have invariably reflected divisions between *dirigiste* "one nation" Conservatives on the left of the party, and neo-liberal proponents of the free market on the right. The former have generally been in favour of incomes policies, believing that deflationary measures to curb inflation and the resultant high levels of unemployment would serve to exacerbate poor industrial relations, whilst also threatening to undermine social stability and political legitimacy.

The "one nation" Conservatives' emphasis on abating class conflict and keeping socio-economic inequalities within bounds (whilst firmly rejecting egalitarianism) has strongly endeared them to seeking partnership with the trade unions (and employers' representatives), whereupon agreement can be sought on economic objectives and priorities. This has invariably led One Nation Conservatives to seek an incomes policy of one kind or another. Nor were One Nation Conservatives deterred by the problems – most notably trade union opposition – engendered by the various incomes policies pursued during the 1960s and 1970s. On the contrary, they remained convinced that governments ought to redouble their efforts at constructing an effective and acceptable (to the trade unions) incomes policies, insisting that the problems this would entail would not be nearly as great as the social, political and economic problems likely to arise from tolerating high inflation and unemployment.

In spite of the serious difficulties which he personally encountered in the 1970s, Edward Heath still believes that Conservative advocates of incomes policy have been "concerned with the practical questions of running the economy and choosing the 'least worst' of the options before us", before reiterating his view that "policies which allow unemployment to rise to levels of 3 million or more, and which in effect marginalize the trades unions" are hardly likely "to promote long-term economic, social or political stability" (Heath, 1998: 571, 731).

Until the 1970s, it was this "one nation" perspective which prevailed overall within the Conservative party, and which was thus instrumental in the refusal of many senior Conservatives to countenance higher unemployment as a means of curbing inflation or weakening the trade unions. Instead, the emphasis was on consultation and cooperation, education and exhortation, reflecting a conviction that sooner or later, once they had been appraised of the economic facts of life, trade unions and their members would finally evince greater moderation and responsibility in pay bargaining.

The prevalence of One Nation Conservatism during much of the post-war era until the 1970s was also, in part, generational, for many senior Conservatives – Harold Macmillan especially – had recollections of the misery caused by the mass unemployment of the 1930s, and were determined to avoid any revival of the economic depression and social deprivation which so clearly characterized the inter-war years.

From the 1970s onwards, however, there was a generational and ideological change in the Conservative Party, with the older "one nation" paternalists increasingly replaced in the House of Commons by a younger cohort of MPs. These newer Conservative were too young to have witnessed the mass unemployment and concomitant misery of the inter-war years, and believed that many of their older colleagues were afflicted with a guilt complex about the 1930s which had inhibited them from taking tough, but necessary, economic decisions. Indeed, many younger Conservative MPs believed that the consensual, conciliatory approach to the organized working class which their more senior "one nation" colleagues had pursued constituted little more than craven cowardice and abject appeasement *vis-à-vis* the trade unions.

This new generation of Conservative MPs, entering Parliament from the late 1950s onwards, and ascending through the party's ranks to senior positions by the 1970s, also subscribed to a different ideological perspective, believing not only that the Conservative party ought to campaign much more vigorously for capitalism and the free market, but that the preoccupation with maintaining full employment ought to be replaced by the priority of curbing inflation, even though this would entail much higher levels of unemployment (at least, in the short term).

Furthermore, in insisting that the underlying cause of inflation was an excessive increase in the money supply, rather than pay increases *per se*, this newer generation of Conservatives rejected the deployment of incomes policy as a counter-inflationary measure. Instead, their advocacy of a return to free collective bargaining was accompanied by an insistence that whilst higher wages were not the primary cause of inflation, they were a cause of higher unemployment as workers priced themselves out of work. Ultimately, therefore, a new (or, perhaps, the revival of a pre-war) economic orthodoxy became established in the Conservative party from the late 1970s onwards, whereby "the market" and the fear of unemployment would act as a far more effective means of securing wage restraint than any formal incomes policy, albeit buttressed by a highly restrictive framework of trade union and industrial relations legislation, as well as the strict application of cash limits to the public sector.

One of the reasons why the 1970s witnessed so much anguish and ambiguity in the Conservative party over the issue of incomes policy was that the newer, neo-liberals had not yet quite eclipsed the older "one nation" Conservatives, and hence the leadership initially found itself having to equivocate over the Party's stance on incomes policy in order to maintain a semblance of unity.

From 1979 onwards, however, the Conservative neo-liberals were clearly in the ascendant, as evinced by their appointment to key ministerial posts (particularly the economic ministries), and strident advocacy of Thatcherite policies. The older "one nation" generation of Conservatives were brusquely swept aside, many of them removed to the House of Lords, with some making futile attempts at stalling the march of neo-liberalism through "coded" speeches urging reflation, industrial partnership (which implied recourse to an incomes policy), and a continued call for consensus.

Whereas the acolytes of Margaret Thatcher believed that a weakened trade union movement rendered an incomes policy unnecessary (quite apart from their intellectual conviction that strict control of the money supply was the key to curbing inflation), the "one nation" Conservatives believed that it was precisely because they had been so chastened that the unions would henceforth be more amenable to reviving incomes policies. Needless to say, it was the former perspective which prevailed in the Conservative party throughout the 1980s and 1990s.

Meanwhile, the issue of incomes policy has also proved damaging and divisive for the Labour party during much of the post-war era. The right or "revisionist" wing of the Labour party has tended to view incomes policies as a vital means of economic management, particularly in the context of a commitment to maintaining full employment, whilst also inclined to see incomes policies as a means of creating a slightly more equal (or less unequal) society, in which poverty and low-pay are ameliorated without counter-productive attacks on "wealth-creators" and high earners. Yet at the same time, the revisionists have also veered towards incomes policies in order to assuage the concerns of the City and the international financial community with regard to Labour's economic probity and fiscal rectitude.

The left of the Labour Party, by contrast, was generally critical of incomes policies on the grounds that they were invariably invoked in order to secure wage restraint by ordinary working people, many of whom were already amongst the lowest paid in British society. As noted in chapter 4, the Labour Left frequently argued that it would only be inclined to support an incomes policy if it was linked to comprehensive planning of industry and the economy, and thus formed part of a genuine socialist programme for transferring wealth and economic power to the working class. It would also, in order to render it acceptable to Labours' Left, needed to have enshrined controls on all other incomes, namely prices, profits and dividends. According to the Labour Left:

> People are willing to see an element of wage planning as part of a planned economy, but what is not acceptable is that wages should be planned, but the salaries of professional people, people who live on dividends, and those who are living on incomes which cannot be easily measured should be exempted, and that prices should be exempted and that foreign trade or capital movements should be exempted from parallel developments in planning. (Benn, 1980: 155)

The main problem with most incomes policies pursued by Labour governments, however, according to those on the left of the party, was that they were introduced primarily to stabilize, not transcend, capitalism, by imposing wage restraint on working people precisely in order to restore profitability and appease business opinion. In other words, the Labour Left argued that it was not incomes policies *per se* which they were opposed to, but the type of incomes policies which Labour (and Conservative) governments invariably pursued in practice, and the reasons for which these particular policies were introduced.

Furthermore, whereas Labour's Left tended to view a socialist incomes policy as part of a long-term strategy, the party's revisionists usually resorted to incomes policy as a short-term, reactive and temporary measure in response to serious economic problems. Then, having resorted to incomes policies as a form of crisis management, some of Labour's revisionists became persuaded of the merits of a longer-term incomes policy as an integral part of securing non-inflationary economic growth in a predominantly capitalist economy.

However, this left–right division within the Labour party with regard to incomes policy was often complicated by the existence of a relatively large number of MPs sponsored by the trade unions, for irrespective of ideological orientation, they too tended to be antipathetic towards such policies, reflecting and seeking to uphold the trade unions' commitment to free collective bargaining. This was certainly the case during the latter half of the 1960s when Harold Wilson found his government's incomes policies increasingly criticized not just by the left (particularly by MPs associated with the Tribune Group), but also by trade union-sponsored Labour MPs, regardless of their ideological position in the party.

Such divisions and tensions seem unlikely to occur today. The intellectual and political landscape has changed beyond all recognition compared to the 1960s and 1970s. The emphasis has switched to supply-side economics rather than Keynesian demand management, with inflation – rather than unemployment – considered the greater economic and social evil, and with control of the money supply, in conjunction with adjustment of interest rates, widely deemed the only effective means of securing non-inflationary growth and stability. There is now a remarkable political consensus that monetary policy, not incomes policy, is the most effective means of curbing inflation.

This change in the intellectual climate has been reflected and reinforced by changes within the two main political parties themselves. In the Conservative party, the generation of "one nation" Conservatives have increasingly disappeared or been marginalized (Dorey, 1996), to the extent that by the 1990s, very few Conservative politicians were publicly hankering for a return to incomes policy. Indeed, with the possible exceptions of Edward Heath and Ian Gilmour, it is virtually impossible to imagine a Conservative today calling for a tripartite agreement between government, trade unions and the CBI with regard to determining prices and incomes.

Yet it is also increasingly difficult to imagine such a call being made by the apostles of New Labour, whose new-found commitment to the market has been matched by their determination to adopt a much more arms-length relationship with the trade unions, thereby precluding any institutional or policy innovations which might even remotely be construed as a corporatist-style partnership involving the TUC.

It is indeed a sign of how much the intellectual, ideological and political climate had changed by the end of the twentieth century that whereas the few texts previously written about incomes policy invariably concluded with a chapter discussing the future of such policies in Britain, and delineating the main features which such a policy might include (Jones, 1973: 188–206; Jones, 1987: 143–5; Towers, 1978: 30–2), we are now obliged to conclude that incomes policies have been consigned to the realms of history. The world has moved on, leaving incomes policies behind.

Bibliography

Aaronovitch, Sam (1981) *The Road from Thatcherism*, Lawrence and Wishart.

Abbott, Stephen (1966) *Industrial Relations*, Conservative Political Centre.

Abel-Smith, Brian and Townsend, Peter (1965) *The Poor and the Poorest*, G. Bell & Sons.

Abromeit, Heidrun (1988) "British privatisation policy", *Parliamentary Affairs*, Vol. 41, No. 1.

ACAS (1980) *Industrial Relations Handbook*, HMSO.

Addison, Paul (1977) *The Road to 1945*, Quartet.

Alderman, Keith, and Carter, Neil (1995) "The Labour party leadership and Deputy leadership elections of 1994", *Parliamentary Affairs*, Vol. 48, No. 3.

Allen, V. A. (1960) *Trade Unions and the Government*, Allen & Unwin.

Alport, Lord (Cuthbert) (1946) *About Conservative Principles*, Conservative Political Centre.

Amery, Leo (1946) *The Conservative Future*, Conservative Political Centre.

Anderson, Perry (1967) "The limits and possibilities of trade union action" in Robin Blackburn and Alexander Cockburn (eds) *The Incompatibles: Trade Union Militancy and the Consensus*, Penguin.

Ascher, Kate (1987) *The Politics of Privatisation: Contracting Out Public Services*, Macmillan.

Attlee, Clement (1954) *As It Happened*, William Heinemann.

Bacon, R., and Eltis, W. (1976) *Britain's Economic Problem: Too Few Producers*, Macmillan.

Baldry, Tony (1985) "Time to Talk", *Reformer* (Tory Reform Group), Summer.

Balogh, Thomas (1963) *Planning for Progress: A Strategy for Labour*, Fabian Tract 346, July.

—— (1970) *Labour and Inflation*, Fabian Society.

Barnes, Denis and Reid, Eileen (1982) "A new relationship: trade unions in the Second World War" in Ben Pimlott and Chris Cook (eds) *Trade Unions in British Politics*, Longman.

—— (1980) *Governments and Trade Unions: The British Experience 1964–1979*, Heinemann.

Barnett, Joel (1982) *Inside the Treasury*, André Deutsch.

Beer, Samuel (1965) *Modern British Politics*, Faber.

Benn, Tony (1980) *Arguments for Socialism*, Penguin.

—— (1987) *Out of the Wilderness: Diaries 1963–1967*, Hutchinson.

—— (1988) *Office Without Power: Diaries 1968–1972*, Hutchinson.

—— (1989) *Against the Tide: Diaries 1973–76*, Hutchinson.

—— (1990) *Conflicts of Interest: Diaries 1977–1980*, Hutchinson.

Bevan, Aneurin (1961) *In Place of Fear*, Macgibbon & Kee.

Beveridge, William (1944) *Full Employment in a Free Society*, Allen & Unwin.

Bevins, Reginald (1965) *The Greasy Pole*, Hodder & Stoughton.

Biffen, John (1965) "School for Tories", *The Guardian*, 27 August.

—— (1977) "The elephant trap", *Conservative Monthly News*, April.

Lord Birkenhead(1969) *Walter Monckton*, London: Weidenfeld & Nicolson.

Blackaby, F. T. (1978) "Incomes Policy" in F. T. Blackaby (ed.) *British Economic Policy 1960–1974*, Cambridge University Press.

Blackstone, Tessa and Plowden, William (1988) *Inside the Think Tank: Advising the Cabinet 1971–1983*, Heinemann.

Blair, Tony (1996) *New Britain: My Vision of a Young Country*, Fourth Estate.

Body, Richard (1972) "The road to freedom", *The Spectator*, 1 July.

Bosanquet, Nicholas (1970) "Do we need an incomes policy?" in Michael Ivens and Clive Bradley (eds) *Which Way?*, Michael Joseph.

Bourlet, James and Roots, Michael (1974) *Step by Step Against Inflation*, Selsdon Group.

Bow Group, The (1965) *The Confidence Trick*, Conservative Political Centre.

—— (1972) "Paying the price of reform", *Crossbow* July–September.

Boyle, Edward (1966) *Conservatives and Economic Planning*, Conservative Political Centre.

Boyson, Rhodes (1978) *Centre Forward*, Temple Smith.

Brittan, Samuel (1969) *Steering the Economy*, Secker & Warburg.

—— (1975) "Towards a corporate state", *Encounter* 44.

Brittan, Samuel and Lilley, Peter (1977) *The Delusion of Incomes Policy*, Temple Smith.

Brown, George (1971) *In My Way*, Book Club Associates.

Bruce-Gardyne, Jock (1969) "The pursuit of the unattainable", *The Spectator*, 23 May.

Bullock, Alan (1967) *The Life and Times of Ernest Bevin: Volume Two; Minister of Labour 1940–1945*, Heinemann.

Bulpitt, Jim (1986) "The discipline of the new democracy: Mrs Thatcher''s domestic statecraft", *Political Studies 34*.

Butler, Lord (Rab) (1971) *The Art of the Possible*, Hamish Hamilton.

Cairncross, Alex (1985) *Years of Recovery: British Economic Policy 1945–1951*, Methuen.

—— (1997) *The Wilson Years: A Treasury Diary 1964–1969*, Historians' Press.

Callaghan, James (1971) "The way forward for the trade unions", *AUEW Journal 38 (1)*.

—— (1987) *Time and Chance*, Collins/Fontana.

Campbell, John (1993) *Edward Heath : A Biography*, Jonathan Cape.

—— (2000) *Margaret Thatcher, Volume One: The Grocer's Daughter*, Jonathan Cape.

Carpenter, L. (1976) "Corporatism in Britain", *Journal of Contemporary History*, Vol. 1.

Carr, Robert (1975) "Incomes policy", *Political Quarterly*, Vol. 46.

Castle, Barbara (1970) "A Socialist incomes policy", *New Statesman*, 25 September.

—— (1980) *The Castle Diaries 1974–76*, Book Club Associates.

—— (1990) *The Castle Diaries 1964–1976*, Papermac.
—— (1993) *Fighting All The Way*, Pan.
Chapple, Frank (1984) *Sparks Fly!*, Michael Joseph.
Clarke, David (1947) *The Conservative Faith in the Modern Age*, Conservative Political Centre.
Clegg, Hugh (1971) *How to Run an Incomes Policy and Why We Made Such a Mess of the Last One*, Blackwell.
Coates, Ken (1979) "What Went Wrong?" in Ken Coates (ed.) *What Went Wrong?: Explaining the Fall of the Labour Government*, Spokesman.
Coates, Ken and Topham, Tony (1980) *Trade Unions and Politics*, Spokesman.
Cockett, Richard (1994) *Thinking the Unthinkable: Think Tanks and the Economic Counter-Revolution, 1931–1983*, HarperCollins.
Commission on Social Justice/Institute for Public Policy Research (1994) *Social Justice: Strategies for National Renewal*, Vintage.
Conservative Central Office (1947) *The Industrial Charter: A Statement of Conservative Industrial Policy*.
—— (1949) *The Right Road for Britain*.
—— (1968) *Fair Deal at Work*.
—— (1976) *The Right Approach*.
Conservative Industrial Department (1963) *Trade Unions and the Government*.
Conservative Political Centre (1963) *Industrial Change: The Human Aspect*.
—— (circa 1966) *Masterbrief 32: Strikes*.
—— (1968) *Notes on Current Politics*, April.
—— (1971) *Monthly Notes No. 68*, February.
Conservative Trade Unionists National Advisory Committee (1966) *Industrial Advance*.
Cox, Andrew (1989) "The Failure of Corporatist State Forms and Policies in Post-War Britain" in Andrew Cox and Noel O'Sullivan (eds) *The Corporate State: Corporatism and the State Tradition in Western Europe*, Edward Elgar.
Cripps, Francis and Ward, Terry (1982) "Road to recovery", *New Socialist*, No. 6, July/August.
Crossman, Richard (1975) *The Diaries of a Cabinet Minister: Volume One, Minister of Housing 1964–66*, Hamish Hamilton/Jonathan Cape.
—— (1976) *The Diaries of a Cabinet Minister: Volume Two, Lord President of the Council and Leader of the House of Commons 1966–68*, Hamish Hamilton/Jonathan Cape.
—— (1977) *The Diaries of a Cabinet Minister: Volume Three, Secretary of State for Social Services, 1968–70*, Hamish Hamilton/Jonathan Cape.
Crosland, Anthony (1956) *The Future of Socialism*, Jonathan Cape.
—— (1971) "Time to review Labour policy", *GMWU Journal*, June.
Crouch, Colin (1982) *The Politics of Industrial Relations*, second edition, Fontana.
Dean, A. H. (1978) *Incomes Policies and Differentials*, National Institute Economic Review.
Dell, Edmund (1991) *A Hard Pounding*, Oxford University Press.
Denham, Andrew and Garnett, Mark (1998) *British Think-Tanks and the Climate of Opinion*, UCL Press.
Department of Economic Affairs (1964) *Joint Statement of Intent on Productivity, Prices and Incomes*, HMSO.

—— (1967) *Prices and Incomes Policy after 30 June 1967*, HMSO.

Department of Employment (1988) *Employment for the 1990s*, HMSO.

—— (1992) *People, Jobs and Opportunity*, HMSO.

Dewdney, Kim (1992) "Who runs Labour?", *Fabian Review*, Vol. 104, No. 4, July.

Donaldson, Peter (1965) *Guide to the British Economy*, Penguin.

Donoughue, Bernard (1987) *Prime Minister*, Jonathan Cape.

Dorey, Peter (1991) "Corporatism in the UK", *Politics Review*, Vol. 1, No. 2.

—— (1995a) "Between principle, pragmatism and practicability: The development of Conservative Party policy towards the trade unions in Opposition 1974–79" in David Broughton *et al.* (eds) *British Elections and Parties Yearbook 1994*, Frank Cass.

—— (1995b) *The Conservative Party and the Trade Unions*, Routledge.

—— (1996) "Exhaustion of a tradition: the death of 'one nation' Toryism", *Contemporary Politics*, Vol. 2, No. 4.

—— (1999a) "No return to beer and sandwiches: Industrial relations and employment policies under John Major" in Peter Dorey (ed.) *The Major Premiership: Politics and Policies under John Major, 1990–1997*, Macmillan.

—— (1999b) "The Blairite betrayal: New Labour and the trade unions" in Gerald Taylor (ed.) *The Impact of New Labour*, Macmillan.

—— (2001a) "Margaret Thatcher's taming of the trade unions" in Stanislao Pugliese (ed.) *The Thatcher Years: The Rebirth of Liberty?*, Greenwood Press, USA.

—— (2001b) "Privatisation" in Barry Clarke and Joe Foweraker (eds) *Encylopedia of Democratic Thought*, Routledge.

—— (2001c) "Britain in the 1980s and 1990s: the redundancy of social partnership" in Stefan Berger and Hugh Compston (eds) *Social Partnership in the 1990s*, Berghahn.

—— (forthcoming) "Industrial relations as "human relations': Conservatism and trade unionism, 1945–64" in Stuart Ball and Ian Holliday (eds) *Mass Conservatism: The Conservatives and the People, 1867–1997*, Frank Cass.

Dorfman, Gerald (1973) *Wage Politics in Britain 1945–1967*, Charles Knight.

—— (1979) *Governments Versus Trade Unions in British Politics since 1968*, Macmillan.

Driscoll, James (1965) "National wages policy", *Crossbow* The Bow Group.

Dykes, Hugh (1968) "Trade unions: Have we really got the answer?", *Crossbow* The Bow Group.

Eden, Anthony (1947) *Freedom and Order*, Faber.

—— (1960) *Full Circle: Memoirs*, Cassell.

Elliott, Larry (1999) "A balanced account", *The Guardian*, 30 August.

Farnham, David and John Pimlott (1986) *Understanding Industrial Relations*, Cassell.

Fellner, W. *et al.* (1961) *The Problem of Rising Prices*, OECD.

Fels, Allan (1972) *The British Prices and Incomes Board*, Cambridge University Press.

Field, Frank (1975) "What is poverty?", *New Society*, 25 September.

Fielding, Steven (1995) *Labour: Decline and Renewal*, Baseline.

Fishbein, Warren (1984) *Wage Restraint by Consensus*, Routledge & Kegan Paul.

Fisher, Nigel (1973) *Iain Macleod*, André Deutsch.

Flanders, Allan (1974) "The tradition of voluntarism", *British Journal of Industrial Relations*, Vol. 12.

—— (1975) *Management and Unions: The Theory and Reform of Industrial Relations*, Faber.

Fox, Alan (1974) *Beyond Contract: Power, Work and Trust Relations*, Faber.

Fraser, Michael *et al.* (1973) *The Strategic/Tactical Situation in 1973*, Conservative Party Archives, Advisory Committee on Policy (Steering Committee) 73/17, 14 February.

Gamble, Andrew (1988) *The Free Economy and The Strong State*, Macmillan.

George, Stephen and Rosamond, Ben (1992) "The European Community" in Martin J. Smith (eds) *The Changing Labour Party*, Routledge.

Gilmour, Ian (1983) *Britain Can Work*, Martin Robertson.

—— (1992) *Dancing With Dogma*, Simon & Schuster.

Glyn, Andrew and Morrison, John (1980) *The British Economic Disaster*, London: Pluto Press.

Glyn, Andrew and Wood, Stewart (2001) "Economic Policy under New Labour: How Social Democratic is the Blair Government?", *Political Quarterly*, Vol. 72, No. 1.

Godber, Joseph (1964) *Conservative Campaign Guide 1964.*

Goodman. Geoffrey (1979) *The Awkward Warrior*, Davis-Poynter.

Gormley, Joe (1982) *Battered Cherub*, Hamish Hamilton.

Gould, Philip (1998) *The Unfinished Revolution: How the Modernisers Saved the Labour Party*, Little, Brown.

Haines, Joe (1977) *The Politics of Power*, Jonathan Cape.

Halcrow, Morrison (1989) *Keith Joseph: A Single Mind*, Macmillan.

Hall, Robert (1961) "Britain's economic problems", *The Economist*, 16 September 1961.

Hanson, Charles (1991) *Taming the Trade Unions*, Macmillan.

Harris, Nigel (1972) *Competition and the Corporate Society*, Methuen.

Hattersley, Roy, *et al.* (1983) *Labour's Choices*, Fabian Society.

Hattersley, Roy (1987) *Choose Freedom*, Penguin.

Hawkins, Kevin (1981) *Trade Unions*, Hutchinson.

Hay, Colin (1999) *The Political Economy of New Labour*, Manchester University Press.

Hay, Colin, and Watson, Matthew (1999) "Labour's economic policy: Studiously courting competence" in Gerald Taylor (ed.) *The Impact of New Labour*, Macmillan.

Heald, David (1989) "The United Kingdom: Privatisation and its political context" in John Vickers and Vincent Wright (eds) *The Politics of Privatisation in Western Europe*, Frank Cass.

Healey, Dennis (1989) *The Time of My Life*, Michael Joseph.

Heath, Edward (1998) *The Course of My Life*, Hodder & Stoughton.

Heffernan, Richard (1996) "'Blueprint for a Revolution'?: The Politics of the Adam Smith Institute" in Michael Kandiah and Anthony Seldon (eds) *Ideas and Think Tanks in Contemporary Britain, Volume 1*, Frank Cass.

—— (2001) *New Labour and Thatcherism: Political Change in Britain*, Palgrave.

Heffernan, Richard and Marqusee, Mike (1992) *Defeat From the Jaws of Victory: Inside Kinnock's Labour Party*, Verso.

Heald, David (1983) *Public Expenditure: Its Defence and Reform*, Martin Robertson.

Hillman, Judy and Clarke, Peter (1988) *Geoffrey Howe: A Quiet Revolutionary*, Weidenfeld & Nicolson.

Hinchingbrooke, Lord (Victor Montagu) (1944) *Full Speed Ahead: Essays in Tory Reform*, Simpkin.

—— (1946) "The course of Conservative politics", *Quarterly Review*, January.

Hindmoor, Andrew (2000) "Public Policy 1998–99: A Honeymoon Ending?", *Parliamentary Affairs*, Vol. 53, No. 2.

HMSO (1944) *Employment Policy*, Cmnd 6527, HMSO.

—— (1956) *The Economic Implications of Full Employment*, Cmnd 9725.

—— (1962) *Incomes Policy; the Next Step*, Cmnd 1626.

Hodgson, Geoffrey (1981) *Labour at the Crossroads*, Martin Robertson.

Hodgson, Patricia (1975) "The moral appeal", *The Spectator*, 19 May.

Hogg, Quintin (1945) "Too many Micawbers in the Tory Party", *Daily Mail*, 11 September.

Howe, Geoffrey (1976) *A Policy for Incomes*, Conservative Research Department.

—— (1995) *Conflict of Loyalty*, Pan.

Howell, Chris (1995/6) "Turning to the State: Thatcherism and the crisis of British trade unionism", *New Political Science*, Vol. 33, No. 4.

Howell, David (1972) "Putting the boot into liberal society", *The Times*, 25 April.

Howell, Ralph (1974) "Up to date sense about unemployment", *The Spectator*, 24 August 1974.

Hughes, Colin and Wintour, Patrick (1990) *Labour Rebuilt: The New Model Party*, Fourth Estate.

Hurd, Douglas (1979) *An End To Promises*, Collins.

Hutton, Will (1996) *The State We're In*, Vintage.

—— (1999) *The Stakeholding Society: Writings on Politics and Economics*, Polity.

Hyman, Richard (1993) "Praetorians and Proletarians: Unions and Industrial Relations" in Jim Fryth (ed.) *Labour's High Noon: The Government and the Economy 1945–51*, Lawrence & Wishart.

Hyman, Richard and Brough, I. (1975) *Social Values and Industrial Relations*, Blackwell.

Inns of Court Conservative & Unionist Society (1958) *A Giant's Strength*.

Jenkins, Peter (1970) *The Battle of Downing Street*, Charles Knight.

Jenkins, Roy (1991) *A Life at the Centre*, Macmillan.

Jones, Aubrey (1973) *The New Inflation*, André Deutsch.

Jones. Jack (1986) *Union Man*, Collins.

Jones, Russell (1987) *Wages and Employment Policy 1936–1985*, Allen & Unwin.

Kavanagh, Dennis (1987) *Thatcherism and British Politics*, Oxford University Press.

Kavanagh, Dennis and Morris, Peter (1989) *Consensus Politics: From Attlee to Thatcher*, Blackwell.

Kay, John, Mayer, Colin and Thompson, David (1986) (eds) *Privatisation and Regulation: The UK Experience*, Clarendon.

Kellner, Peter (1992) "Time for Labour to bid goodbye to the unions", *The Independent*, 12 June.

Labour Co-ordinating Committee (1980) *There is an Alternative*, LCC.

Labour Party (1958) *Plan for Progress; Labour's Policy for Britain's Economic Expansion*.

—— (1981) *Statements to Conference by the National Executive Committee*.

—— (1986) *People at Work: New Rights and Responsibilities.*
—— (1988) *Social Justice and Economic Efficiency.*
—— (1989) *Meet the Challenge, Make the Change.*
—— (1990) *Looking to the Future.*
—— (1996) *New Labour: New Life for Britain.*
Labour Party/NEC (1982) *Labour's Programme 1982.*
Lawson, Nigel (1992) *The View From No.11*, Bantam Press.
Lever, Harold (1971) "Co-operation – the fairer way to fight inflation", *The Times*, 27 January.
Lewis, Russell (1970) "Do we need an incomes policy?" in Michael Ivens and Clive Bradley (eds) *Which Way?*, Michael Joseph.
Lloyd, John (1987) "Unions and economic management" in Ben Pimlott (ed.) *Labour's First Hundred Days*, Fabian Society.
Lovell, John and Roberts, B. C. (1968) *A Short History of the TUC*, Macmillan.
Ludlam, Steve (2001) "New Labour and the Unions: The End of the Contentious Alliance?" in Steve Ludlam and Martin J. Smith (eds) *New Labour in Government*, Macmillan.
Luxemburg, Rosa (1900) *Reform or Revolution* (reprinted in Mary Alice-Walters, *Rosa Luxemburg Speaks*, Pathfinder Press, 1970).
MacDonald, D. F. (1960) *The State and the Trade Unions*, Macmillan.
Macmillan, Harold (1927) *Industry and the State*, Macmillan.
—— (1938) *The Middle Way*, Macmillan.
—— (1946) "Strength through – what?", *Oxford Mail*, 26 January.
—— (1971) *Riding the Storm 1956–1959*, Macmillan.
—— (1972) *Pointing the Way 1959–1961*, Macmillan.
—— (1973) *At the End of the Day 1961–1963*, Macmillan.
MacShane, Dennis (1993) "State of the unions", *New Statesman and Society*, May.
Mandelson, Peter and Liddle, Roger (1996) *The Blair Revolution*, Faber.
Marsh, David (1992) *The New Politics of British Trade Unionism*, Basingstoke: Macmillan.
Marsh, Richard (1978) *Off The Rails*, Weidenfeld & Nicolson.
Maudling, Reginald (1978) *Memoirs*, Sidgwick & Jackson.
McIlroy, John (1991) *The Permanent Revolution: Conservative Law and the Trade Unions*, Spokesman.
—— (1995) *Trade Unions Today*, second edition, Manchester University Press.
Middlemas, Keith (1979) *Politics in Industrial Society*, André Deutsch.
Mikardo, Ian (1988) *Backencher*, Weidenfeld & Nicolson.
Millward, Neil, *et al.* (1992) *Workplace Industrial Relations in Transition*, Dartmouth.
Ministry of Labour & National Service (1942) *Post-War Wages Policy*, HMSO.
—— (1943) *Draft Proposals for Legislation on Wag Agreements*, HMSO
Minkin, Lewis (1991) *The Contentious Alliance: Trade Unions and the Labour Party*, Edinburgh University Press.
Mitchell, Austin (1983) *Four Years in the Death of the Labour Party*, Methuen.
Monday Club, The (1963) *Strike Out of Strike Bound*, Conservative Political Centre.
Monks, John (1998) "Government and trade unions", *British Journal of Industrial Relations*, Vol. 36, No. 1, March.
Moran, Michael (1977) *The Politics of Industrial Relations*, Macmillan.

Morgan, Kenneth (1985) *Labour in Power 1945–1951*, Oxford University Press.
—— (1997) *Callaghan: A Life*, Oxford University Press.
Musson, A. E. (1972) *British Trade Unions 1900–1875*, Macmillan.
Muller, Christopher (1996) "The Institute of Economic Affairs: Undermining the Post-war Consensus" in Michale Kandiah and Anthony Seldon (eds) *Ideas and Think Tanks in Contemporary Britain; Volume*, Frank Cass.
National Board for Prices & Incomes (1968) *Third General Report*, Cmnd 3715, HMSO.
Nelson-Jones, John/The Bow Group (circa 1972) *The Wages of Fear: A Bow Group Memorandum on Pay, Inflation and Incomes Policy.*
Norton, Philip (1978) *Conservative Dissidents: Dissent Within the Parliamentary Conservative Party 1970–74*, Temple Smith.
Owen, David (1981) *Face the Future*, Oxford University Press.
Pahl, Ray and Winkler, Jack (1974) "The coming corporatism", *New Society*, 10 October.
Panitch, Leo ((1976) *Social Democracy and Industrial Militancy*, Cambridge University Press.
Patten, Chris (1983) *The Tory Case*, Longman.
Pelling, Henry (1963) *A History of British Trade Unionism*, Penguin.
Ponting, Clive (1990) *Breach of Promise*, Penguin.
Powell, Enoch (1968) *Conference on Economic Policy for the 1970s*, Monday Club.
—— (1969) *Freedom and Reality*, Elliot Right Way Books.
Price, David (1977) "Whither Labour's social contract?", *Tory Challenge* (Monday Club), June.
Price, John (1940) *Labour in the War*, Penguin.
Prior, James (1986) *A Balance of Power*, Hamish Hamilton.
Pym, Francis (1985) *The Politics of Consent*, Sphere.
Raison, Timothy (1977) "Where do the Tories go from here?" ,*The Spectator*, 25 April.
—— (1979) *Power and Parliament*, Basil Blackwell.
Reading, Brian (1967) *A New Incomes Policy – Comments*, Conservative Research Department.
Richardson, Jeremy (1994) "The politics annd practice of privatisation in Britain" in Vincent Wright (ed.) *Privatization in Western Europe*, Pinter.
Ridley, Nicholas (1974) "Why the Tories must break out of a make-believe world", *The Times*, 30 December 1974.
—— (1976) "Against incomes policy", *The Spectator*, 27 March.
—— (1991) *My Style of Government*, Hutchinson.
Rodgers, William (1982) *The Politics of Change*, Secker & Warburg.
—— (1984) "Government under stress – Britain's Winter of Discontent", *Political Quarterly.*
Rogin, Michael (1962) "Voluntarism: The political foundation of an anti-political doctrine", *Industrial and Labour Relations Review*, July.
Rowthorn, Bob (1981) "The Politics of the AES", *Marxism Today*, January.
Royal Commission on Trade Unions and Employers' Associations 1965–1968 (1968) *Report* Cmnd 36234, HMSO.
Sapper, Alan (1981) "Industry on the scrapheap", *New Socialist*, No. 1, September/October.
Seldon, Anthony (1981) *Churchill's Indian Summer*, Hodder & Stoughton.

Sewill, Brendon (1967) *A New Incomes Policy* Conservative Research Department.

—— (1975) "A view from the inside: In place of strikes" in Ralph Harris and Brendon Sewill *British Economic Policy 1970–74; Two Views*, Institute of Economic Affairs.

Shaw, Eric (1994) *The Labour Party Since 1979: Crisis and Transformation*, Blackwell.

Shenfield, Arthur (1975) "What about the trade unions?" in Rhodes Boyson (ed.) *An Escape from Orwell's 1984*, Churchill Press.

Shepherd, Robert (1994) *Iain Macleod*, Hutchinson.

Shore, Peter (1983) "The Purpose of Labour's Economic Programme" in Gerald Kaufman (ed.) *Renewal: Labour's Britain in the 1980s*, Penguin.

Short, Edward (1989) *Whip to Wilson*, Macdonald.

Sirs, Bill: (1985) *Hard Labour*, Sidgwick & Jackson

Steel, David (1980) *A House Divided: The Lib–Lab Pact and the Future of British Politics*, Weidenfeld & Nicolson.

Stevenson, John (1982) "Early trade unionism: radicalism and respectability1750–1870" in Ben Pimlott and Chris Cook (eds) *Trade Unions and British Politics*, Longman.

Stewart, Michael (1972) *Keynes and After*, second edition, Penguin Books.

—— (1977) *The Jekyll & Hyde Years*, J M Dent.

—— (1980) *Life and Labour*, Sidgwick & Jackson.

Taylor, Robert (1982) "The trade union 'problem' since 1960" in Ben Pimlott and Chris Cook (eds) *Trade Unions and British Politics*, Longman.

—— (1993) *The Trade Union Question in British Politics*, Blackwell.

—— (1996) "The Heath government and industrial relations: myth and reality" in Stuart Ball and Anthony Seldon (eds) *The Heath Government 1970–74*, Longman.

—— (2000) *The TUC: From the General Strike to New Unionism*, Palgrave.

Taylor, Teddy (1972) "The struggle against inflation", *Monday News*, July, The Monday Club.

Tebbit, Norman (1975) "Unions must abide by the law", *Industrial Outlook*, January, Conservative Central Office.

—— (1988) *Upwardly Mobile*, Weidenfeld & Nicolson

Thatcher, Margaret (1993) *The Downing Street Years*, HarperCollins.

—— (1995) *The Path to Power*, HarperCollins.

Thompson, Noel (1996) "Supply side socialism: The political conomy of New Labour", *New Left Review*, Vol. 216.

Titmuss, Richard (1962) *Income Distribution and Social Change*, Unwin.

Towers, Brian (1978) *British Incomes Policy*, University of Leeds/University of Nottingham.

Treasury (1956) *The Economic Implications of Full Employment*, Cmnd 1417, HMSO.

—— (1962) *Incomes Policy: The Next Step*, Cmnd 1626, HMSO.

—— (1972) *A Programme for Controlling Inflation: The First Stage*, Cmnd 5125, HMSO.

—— (1976) *The Attack on Inflation: The Second Year*, Cmnd 6507, HMSO.

—— (1977) *The Attack on Inflation after 31st July 1977*, Cmnd 6882, HMSO.

—— (1978) *Winning the Battle Against Inflation*, Command 7393, HMSO.
TUC (1948) *Report to Special Conference of Trade Union Executive Committees.*
—— (1966) *Written Evidence to Royal Comission on Trade Unions and Employers' Associations.*
—— (1974) *The TUC's Initiative.*
—— (1975) *The Development of the Social Contract.*
—— (1978) *Pay Policy After July 31.*
TUC–Labour Party Liaison Committee (1973) *Economic Policy and the Cost of Living.*
—— (1981) *Economic Issues Facing the Next Labour Government.*
Varley, Eric (1983) "Trade Unions: What Are they For?" in Gerald Kaufman (ed.) *Renewal: Labour's Britain in the 1980s*, Penguin.
Waldergrave, William (1978) *The Binding of Leviathan* , Hamish Hamilton.
Walker, Peter (1977) *The Ascent of Britain*, Sidgwick & Jackson.
—— (1991) *Staying Power*, Bloomsbury.
Walsh, T. and Tindale, S. (1992) "Time for divorce", *Fabian Review*, Vol. 104, No. 4, July.
Webb, Sidney and Webb, Beatrice (1894) *The History of Trade Unionism*, Longman.
Weighell, Sidney (1983) *On the Rails*, Orbis.
Whitehead, Phillip (1985) *The Writing on the Wall*, Michael Joseph.
Whitelaw, William (1989) *The Whitelaw Memoirs*, Aurum.
Whiteley, Paul (1983) *The Labour Party in Crisis*, Methuen.
Wickham-Jones, Mark (1995) Anticipating social democracy, pre-empting anticipations: Economic policy-making in the British Labor Party, 1987–1992", *Politics and Society*, Vol. 23, No. 4, December.
Wilberforce, Lord (1972) *Inquiry Report*, Cmnd 4903, HMSO.
Williams, Marcia (1972) *Inside Number 10*, Coward, McCann & Geoghegan.
Williams, Shirley (1981) *Politics is for People*, Penguin.
Wilson, Harold (1957) *Remedies for Inflation*, Labour Party.
—— (1971) *The Labour Government 1964–1970*, Weidenfeld & Nicolson/Michael Joseph.
—— (1979) *Final Term: The Labour Government 1974–1976*, Weidenfeld & Nicolson/Michael Joseph.
Woolton, Earl of (1959) *Memoirs*, Cassell.
Wootton, Barbara (1954) *Social Foundations of Wages Policy*, Allen & Unwin.

Index

Page numbers in bold type indicate main or detailed references.